D0925150

RECEIVED
JUL — 2010
By_____

NO LONGER PROPERTY OF
SEATTLE PUBLIC LIBRARY

RECEIVED
FEB 0 1 2018
By

Movies That Mattered

More Reviews from a Transformative Decade

DAVE KEHR

Foreword by
JONATHAN ROSENBAUM

The University of Chicago Press
CHICAGO AND LONDON

The University of Chicago Press, Chicago 60637
The University of Chicago Press, Ltd., London
© 2017 by The University of Chicago
All rights reserved. No part of this book may be used or reproduced in any manner whatsoever without written permission, except in the case of brief quotations in critical articles and reviews. For more information, contact the University of Chicago Press, 1427 E. 60th St., Chicago, IL 60637.
Published 2017
Printed in the United States of America

26 25 24 23 22 21 20 19 18 17   1 2 3 4 5

ISBN-13: 978-0-226-49554-5   (cloth)
ISBN-13: 978-0-226-49568-2   (paper)
ISBN-13: 978-0-226-49571-2   (e-book)
DOI: 10.7208/chicago/9780226495712.001.0001

Material originally published in the *Chicago Reader* is reprinted with permission, 1975–1986 by STM Reader, LLC.
Material originally published in *Chicago* magazine (1979–1986) is reprinted with thanks to *Chicago* magazine and tronc, Inc. (formerly Tribune Publishing).

Library of Congress Cataloging-in-Publication Data

Names: Kehr, Dave, author.
Title: Movies that mattered : more reviews from a transformative decade / Dave Kehr ; foreword by Jonathan Rosenbaum.
Description: Chicago ; London : The University of Chicago Press, 2017. | Includes index.
Identifiers: LCCN 2017009036 | ISBN 9780226495545 (cloth : alk. paper) | ISBN 9780226495682 (pbk. : alk. paper) | ISBN 9780226495712 (e-book)
Subjects: LCSH: Motion pictures—Reviews.
Classification: LCC PN1995 .K394 2017 | DDC 791.43/75—dc23
LC record available at https://lccn.loc.gov/2017009036

♾ This paper meets the requirements of ANSI/NISO Z39.48-1992 (Permanence of Paper).

CONTENTS

Part 3: Favorites (*Reader*)

Part 4: Autopsies/Minority Reports

FOREWORD

BY JONATHAN ROSENBAUM

For all the differences between the history of cinema and the history of the Internet, one disturbing point they have in common is the degree to which our canons in both film and film criticism are determined by historical accidents. Thus we've canonized F. W. Murnau's third American film, *City Girl* (1930), ever since a copy was belatedly discovered in the 1970s, but not his second, *The Four Devils* (1928), because no known print of that film survives. Similarly, we canonize Josef von Sternberg's remarkable *The Docks of New York* (1928), but not the lost Sternberg films that preceded and followed it, *The Dragnet* (1928) and *The Case of Lena Smith* (1929). And it's no less a matter of luck that all of my long reviews for the *Chicago Reader*, published between 1987 and 2008, are available online, but none of Dave Kehr's long reviews for the same publication, published between 1974 and 1986—a body of work that, together with Kehr's columns for *Chicago* magazine in the 1980s, strikes me as being the most remarkable extended stretch of auteurist criticism in American journalism.

I hasten to add that, unlike the missing films of Murnau and Sternberg, Kehr's writing for the *Reader* and *Chicago* has never been lost. Yet it's one of the crueler aspects of Internet culture that items that aren't online are effectively treated as nonexistent—which is what gives this collection and its predecessor, *When Movies Mattered* (2011), the force of revelation, especially to younger readers encountering Kehr's pieces for the first time. For the range of films and filmmakers treated, the analytical tools employed, and the intellectual confidence and lucidity of the arguments, Kehr's prose really has no parallels, which is why so much of it reads as freshly as if it were written yesterday.

The range of films being dealt with is especially impressive: children's films and Westerns, international art films and American blockbusters, porn and horror, literary adaptations and remakes, comedies and melodramas—all get treated with equal amounts of unpatronizing scrutiny. And because Kehr is also a public intellectual as well as a passionate cinephile, his analyses invariably go beyond issues of style, form, and genre, which are examined with rigorous care, to broader social and cultural matters. The epigrammatic brilliance that often shines in Kehr's capsule reviews for the *Reader* is developed into arguments that illuminate entire careers. ("For [Werner] Herzog, plot is mainly a support structure: it holds the images, it doesn't generate or advance them.") And sometimes aesthetic points merge seamlessly into social critique: *Kramer vs. Kramer*'s "chief failing as art—its wavering point of view—becomes its most potent commercial guarantor."

Furthermore, in the course of describing what makes *Used Cars* "the first post-OPEC comedy, the first film to perceive how treacherously our symbols have turned on us in the past few recessionary, deflationary years," Kehr carves out an elegant, poetic prose summary of a national zeitgeist:

> The affordable family car once represented the fruit of American life: unchecked personal mobility, the unlimited flow of material goods, the triumph of free enterprise—the chrome-plated proof that every American could live like a king. But when those symbols won't start, when their tanks run dry, they mock us. Rusting in the driveway, they're like the skull—the memento mori—that Renaissance gentlemen kept on their writing desks: they stare back with intimations of mortality. When the dream car loses its patina, its promise of health, wealth, and happiness, every car becomes a used car—a ton of metal twisting in the sun.

Writing about adaptations of Joseph Conrad, F. Scott Fitzgerald, E. M. Forster, Thomas Hardy, Ernest Hemingway, and William Shakespeare, Kehr demonstrates that he's also a first-rate literary critic, but not one who ever loses sight of the cinematic, historical, and cultural issues at stake in these adaptations. And despite his decision to subdivide these essays between appreciations of favorites and "autopsies/minority reports," these examinations rarely qualify as "thumbs up" or "thumbs down" reviews. His exemplary consideration of Bernardo Bertolucci's much-reviled *Luna*—probably the best critical treatment that film has received anywhere, and one that drove me immediately to take a second look—turns out to be every bit as conflicted as the object of its focus, even though it's grouped with Kehr's favorites:

> The usual line on films as radical as this is that you'll either love 'em or hate 'em. I found myself loving and hating *Luna* indiscriminately, and sometimes simultaneously. I hated its hermeticism, its inconsistency, and its lack of discipline, but I loved its size, its audacity, and its complete unpredictability. The film may turn out to be more valuable for its outrages than for its accomplishments: if it doesn't satisfy, it still gives a damn good shake. Meanwhile, it's worth bearing in mind that one of the more pertinent derivatives of the Latin *luna* is "loony."

In short, even though Kehr remains one of the most responsible of film critics, he also proves that one reason why he deserves this distinction is that he knows the value of irresponsibility—as his treatment of Russ Meyer's *Supervixens* also demonstrates.

In order to appreciate fully the historical importance of these essays, one should distinguish between the relative homogeneity of academic and journalistic criticism in continental Europe and the United Kingdom and

the relative estrangement between those realms in the United States—
an estrangement that becomes especially pertinent during the 1970s and
1980s, the same period when Kehr was publishing these essays.

In his introduction to *When Movies Mattered*, aptly subtitled *Reviews
from a Transformative Decade*, Kehr focuses on the parallel developments
of the alternative press and auteurist criticism as sparked by Andrew Sarris's seminal *The American Cinema* (1968), which was inspired in turn
by writing about Hollywood that appeared in *Cahiers du Cinéma* during
the 1950s and 1960s, before more theoretical and ideological persuasions
overtook that magazine for a spell in the 1970s in response to the upris-
ings in May 1968. Although Kehr discusses these developments chiefly in
order to clarify his distance from them, it's important to acknowledge that
while Roland Barthes and Umberto Eco were able to air their positions in
mainstream newspapers, and Peter Wollen, writing under the pseudonym
of Lee Russell in *New Left Review* in the United Kingdom, was able to
combine a certain amount of academic film theory with auteurist journalism, Kehr was operating from a different set of platforms in the pages
of the *Reader* and *Chicago*, where no such accommodations would have
been tolerated. Yet, despite these distinctions, the differences between
Lee Russell's "structural" analyses of Samuel Fuller, Budd Boetticher,
and Anthony Mann and Kehr's treatments of Boetticher, Clint Eastwood,
Stanley Donen, and Elaine May is arguably more a matter of terminology
and prose than one of critical and analytical substance. Stated differently,
Kehr's acquaintance with theory, ideology, and critical methodology arguably often runs deeper than his writing is ready to acknowledge, given the
orientation of his audience.

*

When the *Reader* started to post its movie reviews online in March 1996, I
had already been their staff critic for nearly a decade, thanks to Kehr having named me as his successor—a gift that afforded me not only the best
job in my career but a unique one in terms of space and freedom because
of Dave's own initiatives during his stint at that alternative weekly. The
posting of the *Reader*'s extended film reviews gradually proceeded back-
ward, from present to past, eventually encompassing all my long reviews
but lamentably stopping short of including any of Dave's. This had the
untoward effect of creating an unfortunate cleavage between our online
profiles that has persisted ever since, despite the posting of all of Dave's
capsule reviews on the *Reader*'s website and all his *New York Times* writing
(including his superb weekly DVD column, which lasted from 1999 through
2013) on their own site, not to mention the excellent film blog open to
group discussions ("Reports from the Lost Continent of Cinephilia") that
he maintained for many years at davekehr.com—no longer active but still
available online the last time I looked.

That Kehr considers cinephilia a "lost" continent and that the titles of his collections are in the past tense are what mainly separate his current position from mine—a position that I'm sure has also been inflected by the urgency of his exciting and vigorous second career, which he began in late 2013, as an adjunct curator and archivist at the Museum of Modern Art's Film Department, which is dedicated to resurrecting and preserving treasures that otherwise might be lost. I'm sure his pessimism is well founded (and grounded), even if I can't entirely share it. I also wonder if the banishment of his best prose from the Internet may have played some role in his viewing of cinephilia as largely a thing of the past. As I read this prose now and coordinate some of my own viewing in relation to it, cinephilia feels very much alive to me.

INTRODUCTORY NOTE

Unlike the previous collection of my work published by the University of Chicago Press (*When Movies Mattered*, 2011), this anthology includes pieces that appeared in *Chicago* magazine as well as the *Chicago Reader*.

The *Reader* was one of the best of the many "alternative weeklies" that appeared in the early 1970s—publications that blended the iconoclastic youth appeal of the fading underground press of the '60s with the business model of the free weekly shoppers familiar in many communities. Because these publications were distributed without charge, depending on advertising revenue rather than newsstand sales, they could offer both the controlled circulation that advertisers craved and the editorial freedom that writers loved. The theory was that readers would pick up the free papers anyway—if only for the music listings and the classified ads—so it didn't much matter if the cover story was a 50,000-word piece on beekeeping or if the movie critic took a dim view of the latest Hollywood blockbuster. (For more on the experience of working at the *Reader*, let me refer you to the introduction in that earlier volume, which can be found at http://press.uchicago.edu/sites/kehr/index.html.)

Another burgeoning journalistic format of the period was the city magazine—local monthlies that looked like the slick national publications coming out of New York City but were able to deliver upscale readers to national advertisers at rates considerably lower than *Esquire* or *Sports Illustrated*. The model for many of these publications was *New York*, a glossy weekly that publisher Clay Felker had spun out of the Sunday magazine supplement of the dying *New York Herald Tribune*. Aimed at a more affluent, suburban audience than the alternative weeklies, the city magazines mixed service articles and dining guides with full-color ads for cars, watches, and other high-ticket items. Though much more consumer-oriented than the alternative weeklies, the city magazines could also offer an editorial freedom almost unthinkable in the click-driven marketplace of today. If readers bought the magazine to learn about the latest tapas restaurant or get the list of the city's top ten podiatrists, they were not averse to accepting some thoughtful personal essays or sophisticated arts coverage as part of the package.

Chicago magazine's cultural credentials were particularly strong. Beginning as a program guide for the city's leading classical-music station, WFMT, it became a monthly publication in 1976. Among the new magazine's first hires was Christine Newman, a brainy University of Chicago graduate who became *Chicago* magazine's literary editor. Among Chris's more inspired ideas was instituting an annual literary prize, the Nelson Algren Award, whose first winner was the then-unknown Louise Erdrich. Less explicable was her decision to bring me on to write a monthly movie column, which I did from August 1979 through September 1986 while continuing my weekly duties at the *Reader*.

Chicago wasn't quite as indulgent as the *Reader* when it came to according acres of space to unknown movies, but I don't recall changing much else about my approach. Chris was a kind and patient editor, and when it became clear that the magazine's three-month lead time would make it difficult to cover new releases every month (then, as now, most movies were screened for the press shortly before their theatrical release), Chris allowed me to branch out into less topical think pieces (like the "Westerns" and "Sequels" columns reprinted here) and deeper dives into older films, such as the Powell and Pressburger piece (it's hard to realize, but in 1986 Michael Powell was still an unknown quantity to most American cinephiles).

After 32 years at *Chicago* magazine, Christine Newman was let go in 2009. In its current incarnation, the magazine features neither film coverage nor fiction. Times change.

On the Selections

The selections in this volume are evenly divided between pieces originally published in these two sources—25 from the *Reader* and 25 from *Chicago* magazine.

Part 1, "From *Chicago* Magazine," includes 20 *Chicago* columns— reviews of individual films (including three that were number one in my top ten lists: *L'argent*, *Ran*, and *Shoah*), think pieces, and discussions of retrospectives.

Part 2, "From the Top Ten (*Reader*)," includes ten *Reader* reviews of movies from my top ten lists.

Part 3, "Favorites (*Reader*)," contains another ten pieces from the *Reader*, these concerning films that didn't make it into my top ten lists but were particularly interesting and rewarding to me.

Part 4, "Autopsies/Minority Reports," requires a little more explanation. The ten selections here, five from the *Reader* and five from *Chicago*, contain some of my more or less negative assessments of films that were critically lauded at the time. I begged to differ, so these reviews are more polemical than the favorable ones that make up the bulk of both this volume and *When Movies Mattered*. I hope they shed some light (and don't just generate heat) concerning what I found troubling in these works (and in their reception).

The appendix contains my top ten lists from each year of my *Reader* tenure; the list for 1986 was prepared for the *Chicago Tribune*, but I included it since I was still at both the *Reader* and *Chicago* for much of the year.

As noted above, the introduction to *When Movies Mattered* contains a detailed discussion of my critical orientation when I wrote these pieces. The afterword to this volume concerns my current views.

Acknowledgments

I'd like to express my eternal gratitude to the editors and proofreaders at the *Chicago Reader* and *Chicago* magazine who kept me from looking excessively foolish—in particular Michael Lenehan, Patrick Clinton, and Christine Newman. And I owe a huge debt of gratitude to Rodney Powell of the University of Chicago Press, who had the audacity to conceive this collection and the patience to see it through.

PART 1

From Chicago Magazine

The Black Stallion

Directed by CARROLL BALLARD {April 1980}

The first movie ever made, an 1877 experiment by Eadweard Muybridge, was about horses. And when the movies reached maturity, around the turn of the century, the genre that quickly established itself as the most popular and durable was the Western—a genre that many critics would describe (and not without some truth) as still primarily about horses. There seems to be a fundamental affinity between the movie mechanism and the speed, grace, and force of equine movement. The spectacle of a horse in flight seems to tap the essence of film: the ability to apprehend and poeticize movement on a scale much larger and grander than that available to the proscenium-bound arts of dance and theater.

There is a moment in Carroll Ballard's *The Black Stallion* when the camera goes underwater to capture the title creature in the uncharacteristic act of swimming. As the horse's hooves pierce and divide the water, as the legs jut down and drift slowly back for the next thrust, one has the sensation of seeing the animal function truly—and beautifully—for the first time. It must be the same sensation that Muybridge's primitive film produced: in the slowed motion of cinema, an everyday occurrence is transformed and aestheticized; the movement we take for granted becomes something rich and strange.

Ballard's film (it is his first feature) is about just such transformations— the transformations of film worked not only on horses but on people and places, and even on mud puddles and cigarette smoke. Ballard has selected a subject that cuts to the primal appeal of movies, and he has selected a style that draws on only the most elemental components of film: sound, image, rhythm. His story, taken from a children's novel by Walter Farley, has been barely dramatized. His characters, deliberately, are generalized and vague, and he seems to have enforced a quiet, hesitant style on his players that is barely perceptible as "acting." Instead, he concentrates on the physicality of the filmed moment, on the shades of light, the touch of objects and animals, the sound of wind and rain and fire. Ballard has chosen the most dangerous and contradictory of artistic approaches, that of the self-conscious primitive. He must convince us of the utter simplicity and freshness of everything he does, and he does everything through the most sophisticated technology of New Hollywood filmmaking. That Ballard largely succeeds in making us forget the batteries of lights, the recording equipment, and the long hours of editing needed to produce the impression of spontaneity, of seeing things for the first time, is the surest testament to his talent. At its best, *The Black Stallion* manages one of the most difficult artistic feats—it rediscovers reality, finding a world apart within our world.

The film begins in a burst of exoticism, placing the audience in the middle of the Mediterranean circa 1947, on board a steamship populated by character types—gamblers, traders, inscrutable Orientals—who could have stepped out of a Warner Bros. spy thriller. A group of men play poker in a smoky, darkened lounge; a middle-aged American in a loud Hawaiian shirt is winning. Meanwhile, his son (Kelly Reno) explores the corridors of the ship. A muffled whinny, the stirrings of some large body, comes from one compartment. The boy approaches cautiously; his offer of a lump of sugar is accepted by a black snout that pushes through a porthole and then disappears.

The black stallion's presence never becomes much more concrete— Ballard's visual style allows it to remain an ideal, a principle of force and speed beyond complete comprehension. By shooting the horse in sections—a head, a back, or a leg will fill the screen—Ballard gives us the pieces of a mythic puzzle, to be assembled, in our own imaginations, into something larger than life. Ballard suggests the whole by its parts: parts that can be photographed, and a whole—because it exists beyond the grasp of the literal image—that can't. When the horse is seen full figure, the shots are carefully backlighted, turning the animal into a jet-black figure against a bright color field. He seems to tear a hole in the screen: stripped of detail and dimension by the backlight, the horse is both there and not there.

As a rule, animal pictures try to humanize their subjects, giving the Lassies and Flickas and Rin Tin Tins a range of emotions—love and loyalty, courage and compassion—that would challenge Sir Laurence Olivier. Ballard, instead, has chosen to abstract his stallion. The horse emerges with the pure form of a Brancusi sculpture, above sentiment and cuddlesomeness. There's something threatening, almost supernatural in its figure, as if the horse were an emissary from another level of existence where primal forces run free. The element of danger gives a keen, exhilarating edge to what might have been the most conventionally cute sequence in the film, in which the boy and the horse find each other on a deserted island after their ship has sunk in a storm. It's an Edenic setting, dripping with greenery and ribboned by white sand. But although Ballard is sometimes guilty of arranging his shots for pure pictorial effect, the sequence never degenerates into mere prettiness. The boy and the horse approach each other with a degree of suspicion; some testing and thinking has to go on before they become friends. And when the tension between them is finally resolved—the boy mounts the horse for a wild ride along the surf—there is no sense of the horse's having been conquered or domesticated. Instead, they seem to reach an understanding based on mutual regard. The horse has condescended to meet the boy; their relationship is privileged, unique.

And then Ballard does an amazing thing. With a quick cut, the action moves back to America—to the medium-sized Midwestern town that is the boy's home. (These scenes were actually filmed in Toronto.) The boy has been rescued; the stallion has come back with him. Yet, even in the abrupt shift from desert-island exoticism to gray urban reality, the aura of privileged feeling continues to glow. It's one thing to whip up a sense of lyrical intensity in the middle of the Mediterranean; it's something else— and much more difficult—to find the same feelings in familiar, prosaic surroundings. But Ballard does, and brilliantly, again using the horse as an agent of magical transformation. Pent up in the backyard of a modest tract house, the stallion dominates and redeems his environment. When the horse takes off, galloping down a tree-lined street, he seems to carry his power with him: the rows of houses and the factories and waste lots and fields all seem newly beautiful as he dashes by them.

The horse leads the boy to a small farm owned by an aging trainer (Mickey Rooney, whose role is a resonant expansion of his part in *National Velvet*). There, a secret society forms around the stallion—Rooney and the boy are joined by a black junkman (Clarence Muse) and the night watch-man of the local racetrack (Ed McNamara) as they prepare the horse for competition. There are a few missteps here: clichés of action and character that haven't been sufficiently reworked, some fake newsreel footage that borders on the cornball. But even the film's most artificial character—a racetrack reporter with a campy delivery and an absurdly large retinue—is redeemed when he provides the premise for one of the film's most elegantly wrought visual effects: a midnight test run in the rain, with horse and rider illuminated by a ring of limousine headlights.

The Black Stallion is, above all, a sensory experience. Ballard doesn't deal in ideas, and he seldom stops long enough to examine the emotions that he's conjured. He doesn't analyze or offer perspectives: instead, his involve-ment with his material seems almost epicurean; he takes a voluptuous pleasure in textures and colors, gestures and rhythms. Caleb Deschanel, his cinematographer, offers the perfect complement to Ballard's sensibility, drawing warm, burnished tones and delicate shades of light while keeping his images in prickly sharp focus. It's a movie that makes you want to reach out and touch.

The Black Stallion is a perfect movie for families. Its elemental appeal cuts across age lines—anyone can honestly enjoy its layered sounds and rich, seductive images. There's no better film around right now to introduce young children to the imaginative power of movies: for a child who knows only the flat talking-heads style of television, the depth and expansiveness of *The Black Stallion* could open up a whole new world. And it may well do the same for many adults.

Used Cars

Directed by ROBERT ZEMECKIS {September 1980}

Used Cars is a compilation of dirty jokes, car stunts, strip shows, racial stereotypes, obscene Sunbelt architecture, hammering violence, and the psychic residue of too many nights spent in front of the television set plowing straight from *The Late Show* through *Sea Hunt* all the way down to *Farm Report*. It's the most bumptious, crass, and distasteful comedy of the summer, and it is easily the best.

Used Cars is the work of Robert Zemeckis and Bob Gale, two young writer-directors who got their start when Steven Spielberg backed their *I Wanna Hold Your Hand* in 1978. A high-pitched, pounding invocation of Beatlemania—watching it was a lot like listening to WLS through headphones with the volume turned all the way up—*I Wanna* died an inappropriately quiet death at the box office. (If ever a film deserved to go out kicking and screaming, that was it.) Since then, Zemeckis and Gale have gained some notoriety as the screenwriters of Spielberg's *1941*, otherwise known as the Black Plague of comedy—a picture distinguished by what is certainly the lowest ratio of laughs obtained per dollar spent in film history. The big news of *Used Cars* is that *1941* wasn't the fault of Zemeckis and Gale—it was Spielberg's, for trying to make a classy, glossy, pretty film from material that was resolutely, passionately vulgar. It's a mistake that Zemeckis and Gale don't repeat in *Used Cars*.

Everything here, from the casting to the cinematography, has an ineffable air of the cheap, the ersatz. The lighting is overbright, glaring—all the better to emphasize the nauseous colors of the film's palette: throbbing purples, bilious yellows, polluted sea-greens, pasty pink skin tones. Even the release prints have the dulled, smeary tones redolent of rushed, discount film processing. Nothing could be further from the delicate pastels and shimmering, filtered lighting of *1941*. Zemeckis and Gale have mastered the first rule of filmmaking: match the style to the substance.

And the substance of *Used Cars* is the lowest possible filtrate of American popular culture. Filmed in and around Phoenix, Arizona, the film seems to take place in the final junkyard of Western civilization: Ribbons of smoldering asphalt stretch for miles through arid scrubland, an aching emptiness broken only by occasional clusters of franchise restaurants. Studded throughout the vast, blasted landscape are the rotting hulks of America's highest icons of freedom, democracy, and industry: cars. In a sense, *Used Cars* is the first post-OPEC comedy, the first film to perceive how treacherously our symbols have turned on us in the past few recessionary, deflationary years. The affordable family car once represented the fruit of American life: unchecked personal mobility, the unlimited flow of material goods, the triumph of free enterprise—the chrome-plated proof that every American could live like a king. But when those symbols won't start, when their tanks run dry, they mock us. Rusting in the driveway, they're like the skull—the memento mori—that Renaissance gentlemen kept on their writing desks: they stare back with intimations of mortality. When the dream car loses its patina, its promise of health, wealth, and happiness, every car becomes a used car—a ton of metal twisting in the sun.

It is an image that's at the center of American life, and Zemeckis and Gale have put that image at the center of *Used Cars*. Their hero is Rudy Russo (Kurt Russell), chief salesman and driving force of New Deal Used Cars. It's Rudy's job to spin the dream, to turn the two dozen dilapidated vehicles on his lot into chariots, spaceships, dashing stallions. Rudy is cheerfully venal, unctuously dishonest, but his boss, Luke Fuchs (Jack Warden)—a gentle, befuddled old man who takes his pleasure in rebuilding engines—puts a limit on Rudy's hustle; he still has delusions of integrity. Since Luke is the only likable character in the film, we know he isn't long for its world. Sure enough, his end comes when his brother Roy (also played by Warden), the owner of the bigger, slicker lot across the street, decides to eliminate his competition by having one of his drivers take the frail, infirm Luke on a heart-stopping test drive. (The sequence is appallingly, wrenchingly tasteless—it goes beyond black humor into something cruel and macabre, with the ferocity of Joe Orton.) Rudy can't report the murder—with Luke dead, he'd be out of a job—so he and his coworkers bury the body in a grease pit, propped at the wheel of an Edsel, and explain that Luke has driven off to Florida for vacation. The lid is off now, and Rudy can get down to business—just in the nick of time, since he has decided to enter politics and needs $60,000, fast, to buy himself a seat in the state senate.

The bluntness of that gag, with its casual link between con man and politician, is symptomatic of *Used Cars*: we're not dealing with anything as subtle as satire here. Thorough, ongoing corruption is an assumed fact in the film, and Zemeckis and Gale don't offer the bribe with any observational flourish—it's not there to score a satirical point, but simply to impel the action. The brutality of the wit in *Used Cars* suggests something of Evelyn Waugh—there's no mincing of points, only a relentless, pounding drive—but *Used Cars* has none of Waugh's moral distance. While satirists traditionally put themselves at a safe remove, peering down at their characters as if they were bugs on a microscope slide, Zemeckis and Gale gleefully bind themselves up in the action. There's no ironic perspective in their approach and so no judgment or outrage; it's satire without contempt, without anger. *Used Cars* celebrates venality, vulgarity, and banality: in the end, the authors are inseparable from their characters, and it's this lack of a moral center, of any sense of judgment, that gives *Used Cars* its most original aspect—as well as its queasy, dangerous charm.

An illustration might help to define the film's comic sensibilities (insensibilities?). In the past few years, American cartoons of the thirties, forties, and fifties have taken a tremendous upswing in critical repute: dozens of writers now praise their free-form inventiveness and anarchic wit as root elements of a unique native art. Hence, it is intellectually respectable for Stanley Kubrick to quote from Chuck Jones's *Road Runner* series in *The Shining*, and for Spielberg to quote from Disney's *Dumbo* in *1941*. But when Zemeckis and Gale want to quote a cartoon, they allude neither to Jones's elegant fantasies of spatial-temporal displacement nor to Disney's nuanced, naturalistic style. Instead, they pop in a sequence from what must be the last remaining cartoon series that no one has ever made any artistic claims for, Paul Terry's hopelessly lowbrow *Heckle and Jeckle*. Terry's two crows, pounding each other with mallets, represent the null point in comic timing, imagination, and élan. *Used Cars* scores its greatest outrage by seizing that level of brute, physical humor—crude, uninflected—and turning it into an ideal. The gags in *Used Cars* are as tattered, crass, and intentionally second-rate as its subject matter, and they're funny because they are so depressingly familiar. The humor taps into a collective unconscious of half-remembered kiddie shows, situation comedies, and B movies—the dregs of popular culture. There is no other humor to apply to this debased milieu: banality comments on banality, and the whole enterprise is swept up in a giddy, escalating infantilism. At first you don't laugh at all, then you laugh with embarrassment, and finally, after the barriers have been broken down by the film's pure brute force, you laugh at everything. The film tramples on your taste, but the effect is weirdly cathartic, exhilarating.

Once that recuperative move has been made, retrieving and enshrining the lowest kind of humor, no joke seems too obvious, too violent, or too stupid. Even a device as hoary as the two brothers/one actor ploy fits seamlessly into the spirit of the thing: clichés are part of the film's cultural pedigree. And when the sitcom actors start showing up—Lenny and Squiggy (David L. Lander and Michael McKean) of *Laverne and Shirley* and, astonishingly, Al Lewis, the vampire grandpa of *The Munsters*—their presence is perfectly, horribly natural: they're the rightful inhabitants of this moldering environment. *Used Cars* revels in its trashiness, but it never lets us forget whose trashiness it is—it's yours, mine, and ours, the slag heap of American life. Zemeckis and Gale have made an offensive, appalling film, but in some strange way, they have also made a profoundly patriotic one.

Tess

Directed by ROMAN POLANSKI {March 1981}

Thomas Hardy wrote his novels at the moment when literature was turning from a social vision to an interior, subjective point of view. Roman Polanski began to make movies at the moment when absurdism merged with naturalism—when the interior, subjective vision of a meaningless, disordered world became, for many artists, the objective one. These two transitional figures, the social psychologist and the matter-of-fact surrealist, have come together in *Tess*, Polanski's sumptuously mounted, three-hour adaptation of Hardy's *Tess of the d'Urbervilles*. The slippery, pivot-point sensibilities of the two artists reinforce each other, and the result is a flashingly ambiguous film, a movie that changes its sense from moment to moment. On one level, it looks like a wide-screen, stereo-sound expansion of *Masterpiece Theatre*, a serene, complacent portrait of English country life, laced with discreet emotions and ravishing sunsets. On another, it's a cold, ironic tale of innocence beset by arbitrary evil, a vision of chaos, entrapment, and empty destruction sealed off by blank acceptance. The special, quiet power of *Tess* comes from its delicate balance: it is both social and personal, sanguine and unsettling, handsome and wrenchingly ugly. In walking the line, Polanski has made his best film in a decade.

Hardy's novel hangs on a firm idea of order, though it is an order inverted. Tess is the daughter of a scrabbling, drunken peasant who one day discovers that he belongs to the line of an ancient, aristocratic family—the Durbeyfields are really the d'Urbervilles, high and mighty after all. The discovery seems to account for Tess's extraordinary beauty and sensitivity; the most appropriate messenger, she is sent off to the d'Urberville estate to claim the rights of her family as poor relations. But the wealthy d'Urbervilles turn out to be frauds, a family of parvenu merchants, born Stoke, who purchased the name as an easy route to social respectability. Eric, the scion of the Stoke/d'Urbervilles, is amused by the irony and intrigued by Tess. He agrees to take her on as a servant—the fallen aristocrat will reign over the poultry shed.

False aristocrats at the top, false peasants at the bottom: Hardy posits a class system inverted, a world turned upside down. The agent of that inversion is the middle class, the new money that supplants the old. Eric will play out his role as a decadent aristocrat, seducing Tess and leaving her pregnant. Tess will adhere to her assignment as a peasant girl, returning home to bear her unhealthy child and watch its slow death in silence. But these roles now carry a sense of entrapment: the characters play out the fates that have been settled on them, but they are not free to choose. Their destinies are no longer natural; they belong to an old order, not this new industrial age of upheaval and apparent freedom. Tess is rescued from her misery by Angel, the freethinking son of a provincial pastor, whose radical ideas (he reads Marx in bed) embody the best hopes of the new era—a promise of genuine liberation. But Angel, too, is a victim of his class: when Tess tells him of her dead child, he is unable to forgive her; his father's strict moral precepts are still his own. He leaves her, and Tess sinks lower.

Polanski's adaptation is faithful to Hardy's structure. The screenplay, by Polanski, Gérard Brach, and John Brownjohn, is a graceful job of compression, reducing the novel's richness of incident to manageable movie length while still respecting Hardy's richness of detail. The film has the density of a novelistic narration, with well-developed motifs, a gradual revelation of character, and the enveloping Victorian sense of a world captured whole, every segment of society brought together in perfect, living proportion. So faithful is Polanski to Hardy's vision that it's difficult, at first, to discern his contributions; he seems hardly to have recast the material at all.

But on closer inspection *Tess* turns out to be one of those rare beasts of the movies, an adaptation made personal not by a shifting of physical details but by a transformation of spirit: Polanski's point of view, expressed through his visual style, makes the material inescapably his. The photography—begun by Geoffrey Unsworth and completed, after Unsworth's death, by Ghislain Cloquet—is carefully, elaborately lighted, with deeply saturated, softly glowing colors and a high, textured definition of surfaces. It is ravishingly beautiful, too beautiful, in fact, for my usual taste. Cinematography of this assertive, painterly sort often has a way of swamping the narrative; it turns the film into a distant, precious objet d'art. It's the style of David Lean—*Lawrence of Arabia, Doctor Zhivago*— obsessed with quality over directness, prettiness over purpose. If *Tess* makes money (and it has been successful in its first engagements), it will probably be because it can be mistaken for a polite, classy epic in the Lean manner. But it seems to me that Polanski is using the prettiness with a point; its function is ironic much more than decorative. Polanski doesn't want a simple identification between the audience and the characters: if we sympathize too much, the film turns into melodrama. He's using the aesthetic distance of the Lean style—the constant reminder that what we're watching is calculated, studied; is, in short, art—to take us out of the action, to give it an artificial shine. The too-pretty photography is an integral part of Polanski's emotional fine-tuning. He suspends us between identification and distance, between a sense of outrage over the harsh fate of his heroine and a subtler, somehow more disturbing acceptance of that fate—a sense of impotence, removal, resignation.

Hardy once said that he felt closer to Tess than any of his other characters, that her presence somehow stayed with him. There's no sense of that intense involvement in Polanski's film; the director stands back from the character, compassionate but not committed, just as his wide-screen compositions hold Tess firmly in the context of a setting and a social group, seldom granting her the privileged emotional space of a close-up. As Tess, he has cast Nastassia Kinski (the daughter of *Nosferatu*'s Klaus Kinski), an actress with an all but immobile face and a stiff, adolescent gait. In long shot, she bears an astonishing resemblance to Ingrid Bergman, but she has none of Bergman's emotional clarity; her feelings remain hidden behind her elegantly sculpted face. Tess becomes a preternaturally passive presence. Silent, timid, she adapts herself to the rhythms of whatever group she is in. Her few moments of self-assertion end in confusion, retreat. She is clearly superior—more delicate, more spiritual—to the people around her; yet she is unable to act on that superiority. In the harsh world of Roman Polanski, such a combination makes her, ineluctably, a victim.

Hardy's plotting, with its radical reversals of fortune, is forthrightly melodramatic. Polanski's distance transforms the melodramatic into the absurd: the ups and downs, coolly perceived, become the unfathomable fluctuations of an irrational world. Good fortune (Tess's marriage to Angel) can be just as devastating as bad; it is all, ultimately, meaningless. Polanski has been elaborating this theme—the innocent caught up in a malign, chaotic environment—since his earliest films. It informs *Repulsion*, *The Fearless Vampire Killers*, *Rosemary's Baby*, *Macbeth*, *What?*, *Chinatown*, and *The Tenant*, films that cover a tonal range from mocking to black humor to high tragedy. It's not hard to find the biographical root of Polanski's preoccupation—he grew up alone in the Warsaw ghetto, orphaned by the Nazis—and his art has been a continuing process of coming to terms with that experience, of trying to find a meaningful perspective on meaningless pain. When Polanski projects himself as a male hero (he himself plays the part in *The Fearless Vampire Killers* and *The Tenant*), the films become cruel, sadistic, overtly surreal. When his central figure is a woman (*Repulsion*, *Rosemary's Baby*), the films are more naturalistic, softer in their attitudes, though no less brutal in their action. With *Tess*, Polanski has broken through to a new response: its horror is masked by surface serenity, its anger by philosophical distance. It is neither comedy nor tragedy, absurdist nor realist, but something sublimely in between. *Tess* is dedicated to Polanski's wife, Sharon Tate, who was murdered by Charles Manson.

Westerns

{June 1981}

The long-delayed *Legend of the Lone Ranger* is finally coming out this month, an event that represents the first release of a proud self-proclaimed Western in quite a while. I haven't seen it, but, good or bad, I hope it's a huge success; any money that it makes will be a contribution to the Neediest Genre Fund. We've had crypto-Westerns (such as *Star Wars*, with its transference of Western themes to outer space), art Westerns (such as *Heaven's Gate*), post-Westerns (Clint Eastwood's *Bronco Billy*), and more parody Westerns (from *Blazing Saddles* to Jack Nicholson's *Goin' South*) than I care to remember. But straight, solid, traditional Westerns are all but extinct. Don Siegel's 1976 film, *The Shootist*, delivered an explicit eulogy for the genre, with its study of an aging gunfighter (John Wayne) who hopes to retire in peace but is forced into one last confrontation. *The Shootist*, grave and contemplative, turned out to be John Wayne's last film. With his death, the Western, for all practical purposes, died too.

The last genuinely great film to be made in the genre was *Once Upon a Time in the West*, which was released to indifferent audiences in 1969 and promptly cut to ribbons by its distributor. It was made not by an American but by the Italian Sergio Leone, whose three earlier films, with Clint Eastwood (*A Fistful of Dollars*, *For a Few Dollars More*, and *The Good, the Bad, and the Ugly*), had given the Western a much-needed infusion of energy and intelligence in the mid-sixties. *Once Upon a Time* continued the cynicism and brutality of the Eastwood films, but on a much grander, more resonant scale. With its fresh moral vision, its simultaneous criticism and celebration of the traditional Western form, its tremendous visual dynamism, and its overarching emotional rhythms of exuberance and regret, *Once Upon a Time* was a film that reinvented its genre. The possibilities that it suggested seemed rich enough to sustain the form for another decade; instead, the form collapsed. That a film like *Once Upon a Time in the West* could be made proves that the Western didn't die from artistic starvation. The creative energy was there in 1969, and it is probably there today. What happened, I think, has more to do with filmgoers than filmmakers: the Western died of culture shift, of a massive change in audience attitudes that made the kind of moral drama that the Western represented insupportable.

Two years ago, I did an interview with Bernardo Bertolucci, who, some time before his success with *Last Tango in Paris*, had been an assistant to Leone and had written the original story for *Once Upon a Time in the West*. Bertolucci had one question about American movies: Did I think the Western would ever come back? Two years ago, I didn't find it hard to answer. Sure, it seemed to me, Westerns were too much a part of American life to stay dormant for long. Two years later, I'm not so confident. The average age of today's moviegoer is said to be about 14. It that's true, we could be facing the first generation of filmgoers who have grown up without Westerns, who may never even have encountered one in a theater. Like most genres, Westerns depend on a pact of familiarity with the audience: themes are laid out symbolically, through the accepted shorthand of plot conventions and visual iconography. When audiences can no longer read that shorthand, when they can't recognize the conventions, it may be too late to revive the genre. Sooner or later, Westerns will become a dead language—they might as well be written in Latin.

When language dies, it's because there's nothing left to communicate; the words don't stand for anything anymore. The pundits tell us that we're living in an age inimical to heroes—that we're too sophisticated, too attuned to human failure and defeat, to believe in good guys any more. If that's true, the death of the Western would seem to follow automatically, but a look around our culture—at newsstands, at television, and at movies—suggests otherwise. The "people" magazines offer a steady stream of identification figures, mixing sitcom stars with pop psychologists who promise cures for every form of human suffering; television still carries a full line of standard action heroes (cops and private eyes), as well as the new breed of journalist-heroes, the gallant fighters-against-corruption such as Mike Wallace and Geraldo Rivera; the movies give us *Superman*, *Star Wars*, and *Flash Gordon*, while James Bond remains as popular as ever. A white-knight image got Jimmy Carter elected and then ensured his defeat when he couldn't live up to it. It was the myth that people voted for, not the man—and if today we are more sensitive to human weaknesses, more disposed toward disappointment, the myth remains as strong as it ever was.

Still, even if we grant that the hero myth has become hard to accept in its purest, most naïve form, we can account only for the disappearance of the B Western, the white hats/black hats "oaters" made for the kiddie trade. The finest achievements in the genre—the films of Hawks, Ford, Boetticher, Mann, and Walsh—were all composed in shades of gray; among all the richest Westerns, there is hardly an unambiguous hero to be found. The shift in audience attitudes must have taken place at a deeper level, somewhere beyond the presentation of individual characters and closer to the heart of the genre itself.

It has been said that Westerns, at their most profound, deal with the intersection of the individual and society, with what is gained and what is lost by belonging to a community. In the wilderness, the individual exists in perfect personal freedom; with the arrival of civilization—ranchers, farms, villages—some of that freedom must be sacrificed. The classical Western is concerned with the coming of law, the network of rights and obligations, freedoms and limitations that establishes a free and functioning society. The central irony of the classical Western is that the law must always be established through the kind of personal force and violence that the law is meant to eliminate. And so we have the hero standing as the perennial outsider (be he marshal or hired gun), using the methods of the outlaw to fight the outlaw, remaining himself too much of an outlaw to ever be fully accepted by the townspeople. The hero sacrifices himself for the sake of the law, willing his own extinction in the name of civilization.

If one thing killed the Western, it was the growing apprehension that the hero's sacrifice wasn't worth it. Through the dawning dissatisfaction of the early and middle sixties (and mainly through the films of Sergio Leone) the motives of the hero turned inward, toward personal vengeance and personal gain. After the explosion of '68, even personal motives no longer seemed strong enough. For an entire generation, law ceased to be seen as common property; for those who had flirted with radicalism, it could be understood only as a protective mechanism for the privileged few. For a brief, chaotic time, law and order became a synonym for repression, exploitation, injustice.

The late sixties produced a generation that could no longer conceive of "fighting for the law"; more disturbing, perhaps, they also produced a generation that could no longer conceive of fighting against it—against the social evils that "the law" had come to represent. The one lasting legacy of the sixties, of the toy revolution that failed, is defeatism, the sense that nothing can be done. In the handful of anti-Westerns that have appeared in the past decade—from *Little Big Man* and *McCabe & Mrs. Miller* to *Heaven's Gate*—the established powers are seen as omnipotent, unshakable, the social structure as incurably corrupt. Fighting the system is futile, these films say; it simply can't be changed. Our response is to withdraw further into ourselves, into goals ever narrower and ever more personal. The notions of community and civilization that the Western once celebrated no longer seem relevant.

The Western, I think, is an inherently optimistic genre, not because it always draws comforting conclusions about the basis of American life (very often, it does not), but because it is almost always concerned with beginnings—with the birth of civilization, with the establishment of new laws, new orders, new values. Perhaps we live in a culture that has lost sight of beginnings—we seem much more comfortable with the notion of *Apocalypse Now*—and perhaps that is why the Western feels archaic. I, for one, would find the return of the Western a much more hopeful sign than any gyration of the Dow Jones; it would mean that something essential had healed in the body politic. Good luck, *Lone Ranger*—you'll need it.

Disney Films

{January 1982}

Of the dozens of Hollywood movies that opened in Chicago this Christmas, only one could be fairly called a children's film—and that one, the Walt Disney *Cinderella*, is 31 years old. Where have the kids' movies gone? The market, certainly, is not what it once was. With dating teenagers now making up the majority of the moviegoing public, the social basis of movies has shifted profoundly. Where movies once were something that families could see together, most people now go to movies to get away from their families. Movies are a place of freedom for teenagers, unlike the rec room dominated by parental authority and the tyranny of the television set. A movie that appeals to the family audience doesn't really appeal to anyone; it gives neither parents nor children a reason to leave the television set, while children's movies are alive and well and are known as network programming. A family movie means a bland movie. When we go out, we want something different—something different in what we see and something different in whom we see it with.

Of course, family movies and children's movies can be two entirely different things. The former implies an element of parental supervision and approval; the latter, a private pleasure reserved for the young—a pleasure that may involve a touch of danger, the thrill of the illicit and the officially forbidden. Given a choice between *Frankenstein* and *Heidi*, most children will pick *Frankenstein*. There's more in it for them, more stimulation and more information. Children are rarely charmed by the childlike, though adults always assume that they are. The birdies and bunnies and fairies are there, I suspect, mainly to satisfy the adult ideal of childhood innocence—to evoke nostalgic (and usually false) recollections of our own childhood, which we now have an investment in seeing as irrevocably happy and gay, the paradise from which we have fallen. The child knows better: his existence is anxious as much as it is Edenic, frightening as much as it is free. As more than one critic has pointed out, *Frankenstein* is, at heart, a perfect childhood myth. It is a story of learning to cope with your body and the changes erupting within it, of learning how to control sudden strength and sudden anger, and what happens to you if you don't. The child who knocks over Mommy's favorite vase can identify like no one else with the monster who accidentally crushes a little girl—he didn't mean to do it; he didn't even know he could.

The Disney movies have far outlasted any other children's films ever made, and there's a good reason for their longevity. Only Disney knew how to make both a family film and a children's film at once—how to appeal to both parents and children, to distant nostalgia and to immediate anxiety. The Disney cartoons are full of sweetness and light—cuteness, sentimentality, pretty colors, and funny animals—but under that veneer of innocence exist some of the most profoundly disturbing childhood myths ever created. No one will ever convince me that the *Bambi* I saw as a kid was not a horror film; no one will convince me that *Pinocchio* is not a tale of primal terror, of how surpassingly awful it is to be a child.

There's a single narrative idea that runs through most of the Disney films, sometimes stated implicitly, sometimes (as in the two live-action *Witch Mountain* films) developed with brutal force and clarity. Children (be they animal or human) are separated from their parents by death (*Bambi*), kidnapping (*The Rescuers*), running away (*Pinocchio*), and even business trips (*Song of the South*). The abandoned child (sometimes there are two, brother and sister) acquires two distinct sets of substitute parents, one of them gentle, kind, childlike themselves, and predominantly male (the seven dwarfs, the Uncle Remus of *Song of the South*, the Merlin of *The Sword in the Stone*), the other evil, angry, vain, and invariably female (the witches of *Snow White* and *Sleeping Beauty*, the hags of 101 *Dalmatians* and *The Rescuers*). What's interesting here is how the fantasy inverts the traditional roles and values of American homelife. In the fantasy, the father becomes the emotional center, called back from his "real-life" role as breadwinner and disciplinarian to become a child himself—a bigger, stronger child, but still with a child's understanding. Meanwhile, the mother, who does the hands-on job of nurturing, protecting, and comforting the child, becomes wholly malign, Death incarnate (a skinny frame and straight, stringy hair are the hallmarks of Disney villainesses—there's nothing soft, rounded, or maternal about them). The fantasy is one partly of escape, partly of terror.

The Disney films, at their best, allow the child to enjoy an inversion of his life—an inversion that begins with the elimination of the everyday parents and proceeds to a radical reassignment of roles and personalities. The experience is sweetly terrifying, both a comfort and an assault. The films give the child a taste of anarchy, of a freedom from everyday rules and responsibilities—a freedom that is a child's fantasy of adulthood. But the child remains a child, and after a point the inversion becomes dangerous, potentially fatal. The evil mother is overwhelming, and the child must renounce the fantasy, which he can do in one of two ways: by renouncing his experiment with adulthood and returning to his real family (*Pinocchio, Song of the South*) as a child, or by accepting a genuine adulthood, with the limitations, responsibilities, and isolation that go with it (*Bambi, Lady and the Tramp*). One way or another, the traditional rules are ultimately reasserted, order is restored. While watching a Disney film, the child is allowed to unleash his forbidden feelings—his resentment, his frustration, his anger—and is then allowed what is perhaps a more sublime pleasure:

a return to the ordinary, a putting back in place, experienced now with gratitude and relief.

Disney protected his formula well. Only a handful of other films came close to penetrating his secret—*The 5,000 Fingers of Dr. T.*, based on a Dr. Seuss story; William Cameron Menzies's bizarre *Invaders from Mars*; the MGM production of *The Wizard of Oz*—and I have to dig hard for even those few. One film released last fall, Terry Gilliam's *Time Bandits*, came remarkably close with its story of a boy kidnapped by a band of other-worldly dwarfs and led on a tour of the time holes in the universe. All of the adults the boy encounters on his journey (including Napoleon, Robin Hood, and the Ultimate Being himself) are idiots or worse, save one—King Agamemnon, played by Sean Connery as one of the kindest, warmest, strongest father figures in film history. There is a climactic battle with Evil Incarnate, who, although he is played by a man (David Warner), dresses in black robes that any Disney witch would be proud to wear. (And of course, making Evil a man eliminates the unsettling sexism of the Disney concep-tion.) At the finish, returned to present time, the boy watches his parents destroy themselves and their home through a transcendental gesture of avarice and stupidity. Connery reappears among the firemen called to put out the parental blaze; he looks at the boy with recognition and a promise of protection.

The problem with *Time Bandits* is that it tips its hand. It doesn't have the Disney sweetness and light for camouflage, and no adult could pos-sibly miss what it's really up to. It's the perfect children's film in all but one respect—it isn't a family film as well. No self-respecting adult would take his child to a piece of propaganda as powerful as this; there aren't any birdies and bunnies and fairies to hide what's going on. The producers apparently realized that they had a problem, and the film was advertised everywhere as adult entertainment, with an unjustified emphasis placed on its science-fiction elements and its Monty Python connections. *Time Bandits* won't become a classic, because it's been blocked—censored, in a way—from the start. As the sad case of *Time Bandits* demonstrates, there is something paradoxical, self-contradictory, built into the very notion of children's films. They have to be made by adults and (at least partly) for adults. And yet, almost by definition, a good children's film is one that keeps adults away: grown-ups should never be allowed to understand it.

Budd Boetticher

{March 1982}

Witty, elegant, and frequently wise, the films of Budd Boetticher are among the major glories of American movies. Yet Boetticher is still barely known outside the small circle of film cognoscenti. Somehow, the cultural movement that elevated John Ford, Howard Hawks, and Alfred Hitchcock to the level of artistic respectability passed him by. Boetticher, who was born in Chicago, will be honored this month with an extensive retrospective at the Film Center of the School of the Art Institute (he will appear in person on March 12 and 13). It's an honor long overdue, as well as a rare chance to see and enjoy his remarkable work.

Boetticher's obscurity may be his own fault and, one suspects, his personal pride: he has never conducted his career along the approved professional lines, never asked for recognition, nor even made much of an effort to land the big-star, big-budget productions that confirm a director's reputation. Boetticher has preferred to work on small films of personal importance, away from the major studios and their interference—a tendency that reached its fatal apotheosis in 1960, when Boetticher left Hollywood at the height of his creativity to make a documentary on the Mexican bullfighter Carlos Arruza. Through a series of absurd complications, an eight-month shooting schedule turned into an eight-year nightmare. Boetticher stayed with the project, displaying a stubbornness that surpassed that of even his most obdurate screen heroes, but by the time he returned, Hollywood had forgotten him. *A Time for Dying*, a low-budget Western made for his friend Audie Murphy, followed *Arruza* in 1969; Boetticher has not made a feature film since. (As a further irony, neither of his last two films was widely released; both *Arruza* and *A Time for Dying* will be seen in Chicago for the first time in the Film Center series.)

Boetticher's best work was done in a disreputable genre, the Western, and was done, moreover, in the genre's most disreputable subclass—the low-budget B movie, short features designed to fill out the lower halves of double bills. But anyone who can stick with a documentary for eight years is clearly a person who thrives on adversity, and the budgetary constraints of the B's—together with their demands for formulaic, familiar plots—liberated something quite wonderful in Boetticher's art. The center of his achievement lies in a series of six B Westerns made in five years: *Seven Men from Now* (1956), *The Tall T* and *Decision at Sundown* (1957), *Buchanan Rides Alone* (1958), *Ride Lonesome* (1959), and *Comanche Station* (1960). All of them star Randolph Scott (the one actor in the world who could make Gary Cooper seem garrulous), and all of them have roughly the same plot: Scott is a lone figure (a former rancher, a former cavalry officer, always a former *something*) seeking revenge for the death of his wife. By coincidence, he is drawn into a dangerous situation (one that often runs parallel to the murder of his wife), which generally involves a woman alone (kidnapped or abandoned), a group of gunmen (led, inevitably, by figures much more charming and loquacious than Scott) who see some kind of profit in the woman's fate, and an external threat from Indians or the primitive landscape. At that point, the films become, in the words of Andrew Sarris, "floating poker games where every character [takes] turns at bluffing about his hand until the final showdown."

The pattern is incredibly tight, and Boetticher makes it even tighter by restricting his settings (civilization is generally represented by an abandoned way station in the middle of the wilderness), his characters (there are seldom more speaking parts than those outlined above), and his arrangement of scenes (daytime action sequences are followed by nighttime dialogue scenes, with nearly perfect regularity). Yet within these limits, which are self-consciously held to and made into formal, abstracting devices, Boetticher manages a rich range of effects, from the shocking black comedy of *Buchanan Rides Alone* and *The Tall T* to the subtle tragedy of *Comanche Station*. For Boetticher, the limitations of the B Western come to resemble the rules and regulations of the sonnet form; like a poet, he works minutely and meticulously, confronting the rules of the genre both as problems to be solved and potentialities to be realized, letting his art flow through the smallest channels for formal variation. As the British critic Jim Kitses suggests, the modification of a detail even as small as the dating of Scott's wife's death (recently in *Seven Men from Now*, ten years past in *Comanche Station*) can take on a powerful significance in this microchip context: the tone has been shifted philosophically, emotionally, and dramatically.

The West of John Ford's films is a social abstraction; in Anthony Mann's great Westerns, it is a psychological abstraction. But for Boetticher, the Western landscape is both abstract and concrete, an arena for stylized philosophical action and a place of pressing physical presence—a highly textured, tactile environment that must be attended to with the utmost sensitivity and intelligence in order to master its dangers. Perhaps Boetticher's dual vision of the West is the key to the unique temper of his work, which gives the sense of being at once immensely detailed and thematically generalized, dramatically alive and formally distant, consistently entertaining and deeply serious. Boetticher asks us to be highly aware, highly discriminating; at the same time he asks us to keep the broader issues constantly in mind. As in a good fable, we experience both levels simultaneously; they reinforce and invigorate each other.

Comanche Station, for example, opens with a long sequence without dialogue, without exposition: we have to deduce for ourselves what is going on, judging the signs and traces of the plot just as Scott judges the landscape he is riding through. Later, we will use the same skills on a psychological level, as Boetticher asks us to evaluate the personalities, motivations, and plans of his characters, heroes and villains alike, with a bare minimum of information. And finally, we are required to be infinitely discriminating on a moral scale as we compare Scott's crippling taciturnity and obsessiveness with the surface charm and apparent freedom of his opposite number (Claude Akins). Just as his style bridges naturalism and abstraction (while keeping both poles apart), so does Boetticher's moral sense depend on an absolute opposition of good and evil, filled by a fascinating gray area in between. In *Comanche Station*, the moral hairsplitting is impossibly fine: although Akins is clearly the "bad guy," he is not seen as genuinely evil until the very end, at which point Scott's purity is pulled into serious, simultaneous question.

The Scott films are a sealed, self-contained group (and they are even self-referential, with the last film, *Comanche Station*, rethinking the premises of the first, *Seven Men from Now*). Though they're perfectly coherent (and quite enjoyable) separately, they need to be seen together for the full range of their variations—their complements and contradictions—to be appreciated; all six will be shown, along with a number of other, unrelated Boetticher films, in the Film Center series. Similarly, Boetticher's last film, *A Time for Dying* (to be shown on March 27), is best seen in contrast to the Scott cycle; while preserving the basics of Boetticher's style, it inverts many of the premises of the Scott films, suggesting not so much a coda at the end of a career but a new beginning, taking off at an opposite angle. Where the Scott films are concerned with the traumatic past of an aging, hardened hero, *A Time for Dying* projects its issues into the future. Cass (Richard Lapp), the teenage protagonist, arrives in town fresh from the isolated farm where his father has taught him to shoot, determined to become a professional gunfighter; though he has the technical skills for the job, he hasn't yet acquired the practical intelligence and high sensitivity that define Scott. And instead of losing a wife, Cass gains one (when he is forced to marry a girl he has rescued from a gang of drunken townspeople). The Scott films are concerned with the exercise of knowledge and experience; *A Time for Dying*, with their acquisition.

With its naïve hero and episodic plot, the film has a comic, picaresque quality; it suggests a compressed, Western transposition of *Tom Jones*, and Boetticher is no less ironic toward his hero than Fielding was. All of Cass's certainties are undermined—the more he learns, the less he knows. At the beginning of the film, Cass shoots a rattler about to strike a wild rabbit; his moral sense amounts to little more than the simple conviction that the weak must be protected and the evil punished. But an overnight stay in the town of Vinegaroon, owned and operated by Judge Roy Bean (Victor Jory, in a broad, rousing theatrical performance), is enough to shatter his easy understandings. The sequence is beautifully sustained, with a larger-than-life, folktale quality and some of the blackest of Boetticher's black humor: Bean himself is a volatile mixture of childish innocence and calculating evil; in love with the law as an abstract ideal, yet given to pronouncing mad, draconian sentences, he embodies the injustice of justice, morality corrupting itself. A later, similar encounter with Jesse James (Audie Murphy) leaves Cass with a diminished faith in his gunfighting skills; being fast and accurate is only part of the game, and not the most important.

Boetticher's films often end with echoes of their beginnings: the characters separate, going back to their own lives, leaving a completed action but no fundamental changes behind them. The cycle will continue, will repeat, in the next film. In *A Time for Dying*, Boetticher takes the echo effect even further, first with a startling reversal that renders Cass's education (even in the negative form in which it has been presented) vain and absurd, and finally through a virtual restaging of the opening scene—all of which suggests not only that nothing of lasting importance has happened, but also that nothing ever can. The action will be repeated endlessly, meaninglessly; the film, in effect, begins again. For all of his lyrical evocations of the glories of the individual—his intelligence, his sensitivity, his moral discrimination—Boetticher can't escape the larger perspective, in which the individual seems hopelessly small, hopelessly ineffectual. But Boetticher will still celebrate the flashes of beauty that occasionally illuminate the void; his values, like his films, are modest, honest, solid. Though *A Time for Dying* suffers from the usual flaws of low-budget filmmaking (the performances, except for those of Jory and Murphy, are extremely poor), it's a work of deep perception and consummate formal control. It ought to be seen.

The Mystery of Oberwald

Directed by MICHELANGELO ANTONIONI {July 1982}

If video is the wave of the future, why does no one want to ride it? The technology is there, but so far it's been used only for routine TV shows, documentaries, and awkward video-to-film "instant movies" like *Harlow* and *Norman, Is That You?* No doubt there are dozens of avant-gardists working away in basement video labs, but none so far has produced a playable feature. Only the distant, withdrawn Jean-Luc Godard, in his film and video mix *Numéro deux* (as well as in, presumably, the two series he produced for French television, neither of which has been shown here), seems willing to confront the aesthetic problems and potentialities that the new medium poses. Even Francis Ford Coppola's much-ballyhooed *One from the Heart*, the production that was to initiate the video revolution, turned out to be a conventional piece of moviemaking in which video was used only as a support system (and not a particularly efficacious one) for standard technology.

It's strange, then, that no one has paid much attention to Michelangelo Antonioni's *The Mystery of Oberwald*. Made for Italian television in 1980, it's clearly a landmark—the first time an established director has tackled a full-length narrative feature on video. Though *Oberwald* has been transferred to film for export (it will be shown at the School of the Art Institute's Film Center on Friday, July 9, and Sunday, July 11), it is not simply a short-cut movie but a piece conceived for video—a work that goes looking for an aesthetic proper to the new medium and comes provocatively close to finding it. That Antonioni ultimately fails to reach his goal is not a damning fault; this is, first and foremost, an exploratory film, and getting lost is a valid kind of exploration, too.

Oberwald is an adaptation of Jean Cocteau's play *L'aigle à deux têtes* (*The Eagle Has Two Heads*), which Cocteau himself filmed in 1947. It's an arch, fablelike piece, suggestive in style and setting of Kleist's *Marquise von O . . .* , or, in its darker tones, of one of Isak Dinesen's *Gothic Tales*. Monica Vitti, Antonioni's discovery in *L'avventura* and his most potent icon ever since, plays the queen of a mythical Germanic country who has gone into seclusion after the assassination of her king on their wedding night. Her face hidden behind a black veil, she travels from château to château, leaving the state in the hands of Count Foehn (Paolo Bonacelli), the despotic chief of police. One night, while she is staying at the wooded Oberwald estate, an assassin slips through Foehn's guard and, wounded, breaks into her bedroom. The queen is not terrified, but fascinated. The assassin, Sebastian (Franco Branciaroli), bears an eerie resemblance to her dead husband; he is the author, she learns, of a satirical poem directed against her—a poem that she, in the self-hatred arising from her grief, has adopted as her personal anthem. She decides to protect the wounded man, though only for three days—at the end of which he must fulfill the role that fate seems to have thrust so firmly upon him, and kill her. But on the next day, they begin to fall in love: the queen is aroused by Sebastian's idealism and resolves to return to the throne; Sebastian is attracted by the warmth and vulnerability he finds in the queen and stands ready to leave his cause. Meanwhile, Count Foehn continues his plotting, hoping to lure Sebastian—whose identity the count has discovered—into his camp.

The first odd thing about this very modern experiment is Antonioni's choice of material. *L'aigle à deux têtes* must have seemed self-consciously quaint even when it was written, and with its brittleness, artificiality, and abstraction, it does not belong with Cocteau's most immediately commanding work. The piece seems a direct contradiction of the video aesthetic we know. While most video makers emphasize the medium's spontaneity and capacity for improvisation (a product of videotape's cheapness and erasability), Antonioni has chosen to suppress exactly these qualities, turning his cameras on an extremely calculated, highly literary subject. The 19th-century setting of *Oberwald* is, in a way, a denial of the very technology being used to record it. On video, period disparities seem more strongly marked than on film: the photographic image produces a soft, painterly light that can seem a legitimate part of a past world, while the shinier, harder surfaces of video seem unshakably modern. And by staying close to the original stage design of Cocteau's play, Antonioni has neutralized one of the medium's most striking properties—its open-air portability. Though *Oberwald* does occasionally venture outdoors (but then only for some radically stylized, unnatural effects), it is an overwhelmingly studio-bound work, with the action confined to three or four sets. Finally, there is the dislocating effect of Cocteau's erudite, high-flying dialogue and his broadly melodramatic plotting; rhetoric as rarefied as this simply does not belong in the electronic age, when stories must be told with speed and darkness.

By using video in an apparently inappropriate context, Antonioni carves off its cliché associations and too-pat meanings—its supposed realism, its modernity. He's hoping for a genuine dialectic, a collision between a new form and an old content that might produce something genuinely fresh, genuinely revolutionary. This oppositional stance is also reflected in the narrative (and is also, perhaps, embodied by the two-headed eagle of Cocteau's title), with its binary divisions of ruler and subject, politician and poet, individual and state, lover and assassin, life and death. Thematically, Cocteau achieves a synthesis with his double-twist, life-in-death ending, but Antonioni's stylistic synthesis is less clear, perhaps less successful. The collision of form and content exaggerates the artificiality of the work, which is for Antonioni a kind of meaning. But is its meaning enough to support a new art form?

Antonioni generates some of his most suggestive effects simply by applying the formal devices of film to video situations that seem to resist them. There is, for example, a montage sequence, set on the morning of Sebastian's first day at the castle, in which we see the servants getting up and going about their daily tasks. There's nothing extraordinary in it, except that it involves a quick cutting, vignette style of editing that we're not used to seeing in video, where long, handheld takes predominate. Simple montage, under these conditions, takes on a pointed freshness, an effable quality of surprise and renewal appropriate to Sebastian's new awakening. Antonioni's most direct manipulation of the medium comes in the form of bold color overlays and subtle color fades—he's manipulating the color saturation dial on his video console, giving, for example, a shot of peasants working in a field an overlay of shockingly effulgent yellow-orange, or dialing the color down to a drab gray-green whenever Count Foehn, the principle of death and repression, enters the frame. In a way, Antonioni is only continuing the color experiments of *Blow-up* and *The Red Desert*, and certainly his metaphors aren't very original; what gives the technique its power here is Antonioni's exquisite sensitivity to the particular palette that video offers. He exploits not only the brightness of video red and yellow, but also the tendency those colors have to break up and burn when they are too deeply saturated. The unhappy duke of Willenstein, whose love for the queen is not returned, is perfectly characterized in the first shot we see of him, stirring a fire in a furnace. The reds of the fire swell up and explode, as if the color itself had grown mad with passion.

In his search for the uniquely expressive properties of video, Antonioni finds, ironically, that those properties lie mainly in video's weaknesses—in the tension between the medium and subjects that it cannot treat naturally, in the brightness and instability of its color. But the weakness that seems to intrigue him the most is the video image's lack of depth, its tendency in bright light to crush all of the objects under its domain into a single, surface plane, and its equally strong tendency in low light to hold only a thin middle ground in focus, leaving the fore- and background in blurry indefinition. Antonioni uses the first weakness to collapse the space of certain scenes and create a sense of claustrophobia and entrapment, as when Foehn arrives to "warn" the queen of her assassin's presence. The second weakness is used more romantically, to create a limited, privileged space for the lovers, in which, while they are together in close two-shot, the world around them loses its sharp corporeality, fading into soft insignificance. Antonioni brings up a radiant blue-green during these sequences (interestingly, it's the same color that love has in the symbol scheme of Hitchcock's *Vertigo*), at one point superimposing an exotic mountain landscape on the wall behind the lovers, at another bringing the green up so intensely that the background is obliterated entirely, leaving the lovers in a wholly private, wholly abstract world of their own.

Hollywood's technocrats tell us that the day is coming when all movies will be made electronically—when video will supplant celluloid once and for all. Will the art be richer or poorer then? *The Mystery of Oberwald* gives a guarded, ambiguous answer. While Antonioni hasn't found a fully developed video aesthetic—something that would set it firmly apart from film—he has discovered a number of small distinctions, differences in the two mediums' presentations of color and space, that might make possible a new range of pinpointed emotional effects. What's dispiriting about Antonioni's discoveries is that they all depend on an implicit contrast with film—on points of tension, on points of weakness. Video depends on film to give its quirks meaning. It isn't something new, but—more narrowly—something different.

The French "Tradition of Quality"

{January 1983}

It's easy to get the impression that French cinema didn't begin until 1960, the year that Truffaut's *The 400 Blows*, Godard's *Breathless*, and Rivette's *Paris Belongs to Us* appeared and initiated the revolutionary movement known as the New Wave. The New Wave directors have dominated the art houses ever since; sometimes it seems that nothing existed before them. But a New Wave logically requires the existence of an Old—and what the crest of the New Wave obliterated was one of the oldest and richest filmmaking traditions in the world, second in depth and quality only to the American. For most American moviegoers, that tradition has disappeared: French films from the twenties, thirties, forties, and early fifties go unshown and unknown in this country. This sad neglect is largely the responsibility of François Truffaut, who, as a feisty, angry young critic before he became a filmmaker, spent much of the fifties attacking what he ironically labeled "the French Tradition of Quality"—the tendency toward stiff pictorialism, literary rhetoric, and empty, impersonal craftsmanship that did dominate many films of the period.

Truffaut was a good polemicist—probably too good, for he succeeded not only in establishing a critical atmosphere highly receptive to the films that he and his colleagues would make but also in completely destroying the international reputation of the older French cinema. Critics everywhere followed his lead, and soon "Tradition of Quality" became a withering, damning phrase. A lot of babies were thrown out with that bathwater.

The critical ban on the Tradition of Quality lasted some 20 years: now it is beginning to lift, and the welcome first sign of it is the 50-film series *Rediscovering French Film* that will run from January 12 through March 26 at the Film Center of the School of the Art Institute. The few Old Wave directors whose reputations survived Truffaut are represented, but not by their most famous films: Jean Renoir (*La Grande Illusion*, *Rules of the Game*) is present with the very rare *La vie est à nous* (February 5 and 9), Marcel Carné (*Children of Paradise*) with *Jenny* (February 4), René Clair (*Le million*) with *Quatorze Juillet* (January 19), Max Ophüls (*Lola Montès*) with *From Mayerling to Sarajevo* (February 19), and Robert Bresson (*Pickpocket*) with *Les dames du Boise de Boulogne* (February 25 and 27). But by and large, this is a collection of faces new to these shores, almost all of them worth knowing.

Jacques Feyder's reputation survives—though dimly—on the strength of *La kermesse héroïque* (*Carnival in Flanders*), an arch, rather overpretty antiwar comedy that is still occasionally revived. But the completely unknown *Pension Mimosas* (to be shown on January 30 and February 2), which Feyder made immediately before *Kermesse* in 1934, turns out to be a far superior film; it suggests that Feyder's strength lay not in pictorialism, but rather in an imposing psychological depth, built up through careful, leisurely exposition and a fine, pointed sense of environment. The environment in *Pension Mimosas*—a second-class hotel in Nice that caters to casino gamblers waiting for their luck to change (when it does, they move to a first-class establishment)—works as both concrete locale and abstract metaphor, each detail of Feyder's keen, patient observation adding at once to a portrait of a specialized society and an atmosphere of blind hope, repressed despair, and eternal instability. The story pits a character who has given his life up to chance (a petty grafter, played by the professionally effete Paul Bernard) against a character dedicated to control and stability (Bernard's godmother, the hotel keeper, played by Feyder's wife, Françoise Rosay). The drama—and considerable comedy—is developed along conflicts of rootedness and rootlessness, dutifulness and irresponsibility, middle-class balance and romantic self-destructiveness, as Rosay pursues Bernard to Paris, where he has taken up a life as a gigolo and a gambler, and induces him to return to her care. Feyder's great intuition is that the godmother isn't immune to the romantic extravagance that entraps her godson—that she is, in fact, in love with him, and all of her scolding, controlling, parental gestures serve only to draw her into a more dangerous, destructive passion than her godson has ever dreamed of.

Marcel L'Herbier was one of the leaders of the earliest avant-garde movement in film: between 1918 and 1924, he made a series of experimental features—*El Dorado*, *L'inhumaine*—that employed superimpositions, accelerated editing, and optically distorted images. He reached his critical peak in 1928 with the epic-scaled *L'argent*, but his kind of formal abstraction didn't play well after the coming of sound, and he was forced to tone down his style. The accepted line is that L'Herbier ceased to be a director of interest after the sound revolution, despite the fact that he continued to work until 1953; but if the 1935 *Le bonheur* (January 28) is any indication, we need to take another, closer look. *Le bonheur* is a remarkable blend of critical intelligence and emotional power—a film that works both as a deeply moving love story and as an indictment of the false commercial images that deeply moving love stories depend on. No film romance ever had a less likely premise: An anarchist (Charles Boyer, in a performance magnetic even by his standards) attempts to assassinate a famous romantic actress (Gaby Morlay); only by killing her, he believes, can he rid the world of the dangerous escapism that she represents. But his gunshot only wounds her in the shoulder—he, too, has been smitten by her allure, and the hint of truth and hope that her manufactured image contains. L'Herbier clearly sides with his hero's suspicions, but as Boyer falls under the spell of his intended victim, the mise-en-scène around him changes, becoming lighter, brighter, more radiant—as if Boyer were living the movies he despises. Ultimately, it is to the movies that Boyer must return—he knows the affair can't last—and the final sequence finds him in a theater, watching his lover on the screen for the one gesture, the one expression he will know is for him. The sequence is suffused with the romantic fatalism that French films once specialized in, yet it is also a sublime tribute to one of the true beauties of movies—the moments of personal feeling that dart suddenly from an impersonal spectacle.

The French consider Jean Grémillon one of their greatest directors; if he remains unknown in this country, it may be less the fault of the New Wave polemic than of Grémillon's own refusal to let himself be typed and classified. He made many different films in many different styles, ranging from the wartime allegory of heroic resistance *Le ciel est à vous* (to be shown on February 25 and 26) to the darkly poetic *Lumière d'été* (February 23); after the war, he turned almost exclusively to documentary. The discovery of the Film Center's program is the completely overlooked 1937 *Gueule d'amour* (February 9), a film originally intended as a follow-up to Julien Duvivier's internationally successful *Pépé le Moko*. *Gueule d'amour* (the title is the slang equivalent of "lover boy") reunites the stars of *Pépé*—Mireille Balin and the great Jean Gabin—for another drama of seduction and betrayal, though the setting this time isn't exotic Algiers but a small garrison town on the southern coast. Gabin, a dashing soldier, is fabled far and wide as a ladies' man (posters of him are sold in the local souvenir shop), but on leave in Cannes he meets his match—a mysterious brunette (Balin) who grandly risks all of his money on one turn of the roulette wheel and loses. Enthralled, he leaves the army and follows her to Paris, only to find that she is the mistress of a millionaire; with his fame and uniform left behind, Gabin is reduced to a job in a printing plant, but still he pursues the affair—on and on to its tragic finish. Grémillon's direction embraces a wide range of styles and tones, the directorial signature—from Sternbergian chiaroscuro to the flat, gray tones of neorealism—yet the emotional trajectory is clear, true, and forceful.

The Film Center's series comes full circle with its closing presentation on March 23 and 26: Jacques Becker's *Le trou* was released in 1960, alongside *Breathless* and *The 400 Blows*—a last masterpiece of the old school to welcome the new. Becker was best known for his satirically detailed social comedies (British critic Tom Milne calls him the French Preston Sturges), such as *Goupi mains rouges* (February 23): *Le Trou*, a prison drama, at first seems wildly uncharacteristic. But as Becker observes the five inmates of cell six, division II of Paris's Prison de la Santé going through their daily rituals of work, conversation, and cooperation, a social order emerges: the prison cell is a world entire, harmonious and strangely complete. The five men plot an escape, less, it seems, because they miss the outside than because of the opportunities given them by the hard physical labor of escape to further define and exercise their tiny community. While most escape dramas are allegories of emotional or spiritual liberation, Becker's film is resolutely concrete, not transcendent: its subject is in the here and now, in the hammering of lengths of steel against concrete floors, in the filing through of bars, in the careful surveying of the sewer system that lies beneath the prison. If the men hesitate for a moment before making their final break, it may be because they realize how rare their experience has been—never again will they find actions that so cleanly express what words cannot, or work that has such harmony and moral purpose inherent in it.

The Dark Side of Genius:
The Life of Alfred Hitchcock

By DONALD SPOTO {July 1983}

The big event in film circles this season hasn't been a new movie, but the publication of a new book—Donald Spoto's *The Dark Side of Genius: The Life of Alfred Hitchcock* (Little, Brown, $21.50). While most movie biographies consist of hastily assembled, barely rewritten newspaper clippings— or worse, the ghostwritten and unreliable recollections of aging stars— Spoto has managed to produce a meticulously researched, genuinely illuminating study of an important figure. In its approach and quality, it's the kind of biography generally reserved for "serious" subjects—novelists and politicians—and never before granted to someone as seemingly trivial as a Hollywood filmmaker. But Spoto regards Hitchcock as a major artist (it's an opinion I share), and he has given him the treatment due artists: the detailed portrait of personal and cultural background, the documentation of sources and influences, the careful charting of the periods of inspiration and the periods of frustration that invariably alternate in any creative life. Regrettably, the demands of the celebrity biography still make themselves felt. Hitchcock was a star as well as an artist, and stars require a certain amount of scandal mongering. Spoto appears to have ransacked Hitchcock's life for juicy tidbits, but in the end he has a hard time justifying his lurid title. The "dark side" turns out to be pretty punk—a taste for sadistic practical jokes and bathroom humor, a congenital inability to accept the friendship of colleagues, and, late in life, a series of romantic fixations on his leading ladies, all unrequited and unfulfilled. Hitchcock was a lonely, frightened man, and like all lonely, frightened men he could occasionally be cruel. In a genre dominated by the kiss-and-tell biography, the biggest scandal Spoto can unearth is that Hitchcock didn't kiss and didn't tell. It's a unique case for Hollywood biography: the scandal doesn't center on sexual excess, but on sexual parsimony.

Spoto's book is fundamentally a sober, scholarly one; the gossip is only a light sprinkling, highlighted for obvious commercial reasons. Yet, because the book is so strangely divided between the scholarly and the salacious, it has left itself open to interpretation—and some of those interpretations, notably by Walter Clemons in *Vanity Fair* and Richard Grenier in the *New York Times*, have been bizarre. In academic circles, Hitchcock's standing as a serious artist is as secure as anyone's could be. But in the popular press, where condescension to film as an art form has always been the rule, Hitchcock is generally considered no more than a good entertainer, his reputation mysteriously inflated by double-talking intellectuals and phantom conspiracies of French film critics. Movies, as we all know, are meant to be fun and nothing more. Both Clemons and Grenier seize on the peccadilloes outlined in Spoto's book as conclusive proof of Hitchcock's artistic limitations. Because Alfred Hitchcock played dirty tricks on his crew members, the argument goes, because he conceived pathetic crushes on his female stars, his work is necessarily worthless. All that remains are a few cold flashes of technical excellence, not enough to make up for his frigid themes and feeble characterizations. Grenier's piece, which appeared on the cover of the *Times Book Review*, rises to a fine, high hysteria with the ringing declaration that Grenier has never cared "whodunit" in any of Hitchcock's films, as if "whodunit" were ever an issue in his movies. (Hitchcock did make two murder mysteries among his 53 films, but in both of these—*Murder* and *Stage Fright*—the mystery element is marginal to the subject.)

With his smattering of sensationalism, Spoto has sown the seeds of his own destruction. His book is the first attempt (in English, at least) to elevate film biography to the standard of seriousness routinely applied to the other arts, yet Spoto's gossipy interspersions provide the perfect weapon for writers like Clemons and Grenier to pound movies back to where they think they belong—at the bottom of the pop-cultural heap. The standard is double: there's no real comparison between the pain Hitchcock caused in his life and, say, the genuine agony caused by a writer as deeply neurotic as Malcolm Lowry, yet no one would dismiss *Under the Volcano* because its author wasn't a nice guy. But Lowry, with his single masterpiece, is forgiven, while Hitchcock, with his six or seven, is condemned. (For that matter, it's hard to think of a single significant 20th-century artist who would pass the Grenier-Clemons morality test—Grandma Moses, maybe?) There's a strange sense of betrayal behind the reactions of Clemons and Grenier (and sometimes, perhaps, behind Spoto's too). This isn't the Alfred Hitchcock they expected, which is to say it isn't the dryly jovial fellow who used to appear on TV each week to introduce *Alfred Hitchcock Presents*. It is hard to shake that cozy, avuncular, carefully created, and infinitely reinforced image, but instead of being intrigued by the complex human being who existed behind the public-relations campaign, Clemons and Grenier seem disappointed. It's as if they'd never watched the films, and perhaps they never really have. It shouldn't be a surprise when an artist's life turns out to be consistent with the content of his work, but Grenier and Clemons aren't just surprised—they're astonished and angry.

It is much easier to imagine Spoto's Hitchcock—silent, isolated, fearful— as the author of *Rear Window*, *Vertigo*, *Psycho*, and *The Birds* than the genial TV host who lives on in popular memory: the life is indeed consistent with the work. But there is something in Spoto's approach (his model seems to be Leon Edel's psychobiography of Henry James) that insists not simply on consistency but on equivalence. Spoto's discoveries lead him to treat Hitchcock's films as symptoms of his inner turmoil—as the pure, unmediated products of his obsessions and neuroses. There is certainly plenty of evidence to support Spoto's contention: it is fascinating to learn, for example, that the first strongly marked appearance of Hitchcock's famous mother figure (in the 1943 *Shadow of a Doubt*) coincides with the death of Hitchcock's own mother, and that the character has been given his mother's name, Emma. But this kind of information is illuminating only up to a point; it helps to account for *Shadow of a Doubt* (which is, perhaps, Hitchcock's first masterwork), but it does not explain *Shadow of a Doubt*. And to continue to apply this explanation to the evolving complexity of the mother figure in Hitchcock's later work—where she is associated not simply with psychological trauma, but with much larger issues of corrupted affection, false order, and moral tyranny—is to reduce one of Hitchcock's richest metaphors to trivia. It isn't enough to say, as Spoto does, that Hitchcock's art lies in his ability to give his private fantasies and fears "universal appeal." The recurring images in Hitchcock's films—the mother, the handcuffs, the fall, the birds, the staircase, and many others—no doubt had their genesis in personal experience; they are not arbitrarily chosen symbols. But the art lies not in trotting them out and explicating their universal Freudian value, but in deploying and developing them—in the whole rich process of contextualizing, shading, shifting, and growing that turns static symbols into the expressive units of a personal discourse. Images (and sounds) were Hitchcock's language; if he was a prisoner of them, he was also able to speak through them—clearly, beautifully, searingly.

Perhaps the most interesting passages in Spoto's book are those that deal with the step-by-step creation of individual films, with a particular focus on Hitchcock's method of collaboration with his screenwriters. In almost every case, the film begins with a collection of snippets—images, fragmentary scenes, particular locations—in Hitchcock's mind, sometimes suggested by a novel or a short story, sometimes cut from whole cloth. It was the screenwriter's job, under Hitchcock's close guidance, to spin a narrative around these given elements—to create a plot to contain them and characters to live them. It is always the image that comes first; the dramatization is secondary, subsidiary. To see Hitchcock working this way lends substance to a suspicion I've had for a long time: namely, that Hitchcock, alone among the great Hollywood filmmakers, had very little interest in storytelling. Compared with the work of a Hawks or a Ford, his characters are thin and his narratives almost perversely misshapen (who else would stop a movie for ten minutes—as Hitchcock does with the crop-dusting sequence in *North by Northwest*—for a self-contained scene that in no way advances the plot?). Yet Hitchcock's films are among the most powerful, enveloping emotional experiences the cinema has to offer—and the source of that power isn't the prosaic drama, but the poetic image. Hitchcock's relegation of storytelling to a secondary role represents a firm break with the classical tradition; it is the source of the sharp sense of modernity that one feels in his films (behind their Gothic and Romantic trappings), the means by which Alfred Hitchcock enters and engages the rushing mainstream of 20th-century art.

Sequels

{September 1983}

A few days after this magazine appears, the summer movie season will officially come to an end with the release of *Smokey and the Bandit III*. It is only right that a season that began with a sequel (*Return of the Jedi*) should finish with one, too. In between, we have seen *Psycho II*, *Jaws 3-D*, *Porky's II*, *Staying Alive* (the sequel to *Saturday Night Fever*), and *Superman III*, not to mention *The Curse of the Pink Panther* and *Octopussy*, the latest installments of two series that originated back in the sixties.

If this has been a summer of sequels, it has also been a summer of Sunday newspaper think pieces on sequels. Most of the critics who have written on the sequel phenomenon have come to the same conclusion: that the proliferation of roman numerals means that Hollywood is in a deep crisis of creativity—that no one in Hollywood seems capable of an original thought. That may be true, but the audience must also accept some of the blame. In spite of its shuddering lack of originality, the summer of 1983 will set a new record for box-office receipts. Clearly, somebody out there likes sequels—they aren't being shoved down unwilling throats. Audiences now seem to be buying movies much the same way they buy toothpaste: on the basis of a familiar brand name.

There are some vague signs of a backlash: only one of the summer sequels was a runaway hit (*Jedi*, needless to say), and a few have been outright disasters. Yet the important consideration is that all of the sequels have been given a major national release, and in today's film business, just getting a movie into theaters is a guarantee of a certain success: if a film has been shown theatrically, its value to the videocassette and cable companies increases dramatically and a much higher price can be commanded for the subsidiary rights. Even if audiences were to boycott sequels entirely, they would probably still continue to be made. At a time when the star system is collapsing in Hollywood, sequels have come along to provide producers with a measure of the financial security that a Newman or a Redford would have guaranteed a decade ago. An investor is much more likely to put his money behind a known quantity than an untested original project. Because the title is already established in the audience's mind, it promises—no matter how bad the film—a certain amount of initial interest, enough to attract a distributor and justify the expense of an advertising campaign. Titles, not actors, are the stars of the eighties. There isn't a producer in the world who wouldn't rather have the rights to *Raiders of the Lost Ark II* than have Harrison Ford under lifetime contract.

Sequels, clearly, are here to stay for the foreseeable future, which means it's probably time to stop deploring them and find out what they really are. Where the star system produced one kind of movie, the sequel system will necessarily produce another, but what will its rules be? The need to foreground star personalities imposed a lot of limitations on the filmmakers of the studio era, yet it offered some creative possibilities, too—the opportunity to use stars as mythic figures or icons, to take the preestablished personality of a Bogart or a Cooper and find new context for it and new meanings in it. Sequels obviously impose their own strong limitations, but we shouldn't be too quick to assume that they don't offer some compensating opportunities, too.

Sequels murder originality: that's the sum total of the case against them. Yet I'm not sure that the death of creativity is necessarily swift and irreversible. A sequel means having to use preset characters in a preset situation, which is a powerful limitation. Yet American movies have always been slightly preset according to the requirements of stars and genres. A sequel simply tightens the vague limitations of "Humphrey Bogart" and "gangster movie" into specific demands. Originality of plot and character has never been a primary value in American films; in even the best of them, originality is much less likely to be found on the level of narrative than on the levels of form and theme. To see the amazing series of variations that Budd Boetticher worked out in his B Westerns of the fifties—all of them featuring the same star (Randolph Scott), the same setting, and, to an astonishing degree, the same plot—is to know that secondhand material doesn't automatically stifle the imagination. In Boetticher's case—as for many other American filmmakers—it seems to have stirred it. This kind of thing has happened in recent sequels: Richard Lester's *Superman II* accepts the cast and plot elements of Richard Donner's *Superman* and makes something entirely fresh of them. The characters are more full-bodied, the plot devices have more emotional resonance, and the world of the film has more density and shape. But the downside of this process is represented in Lester's *Superman III*; tired and dim, the film reeks of its defeated sense that all the possible moves have been made. It plainly is possible to make something original out of a sequel: the problem is a shortage of filmmakers with the desire to do it.

But the sequel system has other, subtler effects. Where sequels once were delayed afterthoughts to successful films, movies are now being made with the sequel possibilities in mind from the start. There's a pressure on writers to create the kind of open-ended stories that will produce a II, III, and IV somewhere down the road, and that pressure limits the kinds of stories that can be told. Tragedy goes out the window right away, but so do most other sorts of decisive, transforming action. The characters can't develop from sequel to sequel, but must remain exactly as the audience first found them—a limitation that effectively rules out most forms of human relationships as material. What remains, for the most part, is hero-villain stuff, context in which the characters can remain static and depthless while the action—thoroughly exteriorized as fights, chases, escapes—goes on around them. The only available models for this sort of structure are adventure serials and comic books, and the most successful sequel films have either imitated them (*Star Wars*) or purchased them outright (*Superman*).

The ways in which stories are told are affected, too. A sequel by definition has its beginning in another film; if it ever has a climax, it will be a movie years down the road. The classical three-act structure no longer applies: a sequel must be all second act, all middle. And middles, as every writer knows, are the most difficult sections to develop. Something new must happen or some new information must be revealed, but never so much that the climax is jeopardized. Middles are mainly for transitions, the rearrangement of the characters from their starting positions into their proper places for the finish. But when the finish isn't known to the writer—hasn't even been thought of—there's nothing to do but keep the characters moving, to form and reform patterns with no final configuration in sight. Movies thus come to resemble the form of weekly television, in which there is a great deal of movement but no genuine action, an eternal forward motion but no genuine progress.

We are much more likely to remember a spectacular special-effects image or an impressive, self-contained set piece (a dance, a fight, a joke) from a sequel than its overall rhythm or shape. The storytelling pleasures that old movies provide can't survive in the sequel context, and they've been replaced by a new kind of pleasure—a pleasure in the disassociated moment. We respond no longer to stories but to fragments, and if there is an aesthetic of the sequel film, it lies in the valorization of the fleeting moment—the striking image, the vivid but isolated emotion. What's surprising is how close all of this is to the things the modernist avant-garde was doing in the sixties and seventies: sequel movies, as much as any film by Jean-Luc Godard or Jacques Rivette, break apart the closed, balanced structure of classical narration, substituting an aesthetic of the random event, the unresolved plot, the arbitrary, enigmatic occurrence. The sense of universal instability that experimental filmmakers once struggled to express has been fully assimilated into today's entertainment. All that remains is for an American director to seize the aesthetic that commerce has conspired to lay before him and activate it artistically—to make conscious use of what has been unconscious. It hasn't happened yet, but I don't doubt that it will.

Jacques Rivette

{December 1983}

You think of a story, you write a script, you hire some actors, you shoot some film, you put your footage together at the editing table, and you're through. For 80 years, films have been made like this, but in France there is a filmmaker who has spent his career looking for another way. At 55, Jacques Rivette remains the least celebrated member of the original New Wave group, the band of critics-turned-filmmakers (Jean-Luc Godard, François Truffaut, Claude Chabrol, Éric Rohmer) who shocked the world in the late 1950s by taking their movies out of the studios and into the streets, abandoning the storytelling techniques of the classical Hollywood film in favor of a range of radical alternatives. If Rivette has never shared the fame of his colleagues, it's because his alternatives were the most radical of all. After making two films in the conventional way (*Paris nous appartient*, 1960, and *La religieuse*, 1965), Rivette launched *L'amour fou* (1968) with only a sketch outline of the action, determined to let the story take shape (or fail to) as it was being filmed. The 252-minute film that resulted baffled audiences everywhere, but Rivette continued his research with a series of increasingly difficult (and difficult to see) experiments: *Out 1: Spectre* (1973), *Céline and Julie Go Boating* (1974), *Duelle* (1976), *Noroît* (1977), *Merry-Go-Round* (1979), and *Le pont du Nord* (1981). On December 2, Rivette (with his producer Stéphane Tchalgadjieff), will visit the Film Center of the School of the Art Institute as part of a complete retrospective of his work (which will continue through the middle of the month); it's a perfect opportunity to get to know this fascinating filmmaker, whose work has been hidden for far too long.

What makes Rivette's obscurity difficult to justify is the fact that his films, once accepted, are fun. His films are animated by a sense of play— of fantasy, freedom, and wonder—that in some ways is very like Steven Spielberg's. The difference is that Rivette lets the audience play along, while Spielberg only lets us watch and admire the end result; we're participants in Rivette's films, passive observers in Spielberg's. Both men begin from similar premises: their sensibilities are rooted in children's adventure films, particularly serials, though where Spielberg cites the Republic chapter plays of the forties, Rivette goes back to the silent serials of Louis Feuillade, with their greater emphasis on mystery and their subversive habit of placing the most outlandish action in a perfectly naturalistic context of everyday life. Both men enjoy the arbitrariness of the serial, the lack of psychology that makes every action plausible, and the lack of physical limits that makes every action possible. But while Spielberg tries to excuse his arbitrariness (disguising it with the mystical themes of *Close Encounters* or reducing it to the camp of *Raiders of the Lost Ark*), Rivette embraces it as an aesthetic principle—a value in itself. The missed connections, confused motivations, and unresolved plot strands that the early serial makers achieved through naïveté are self-consciously accepted by Rivette as ways of breaking through the oppressively efficient machinery—the overperfection—of classicism. These intentional "mistakes" open holes in the film, letting in elements that the film can't account for—elements that belong to other worlds (even the real one, perhaps) or to other fictions. It's left to the audience to make sense of these gaps or not; if we're willing, we can supply the story, or at least the emotional sense, that lies beyond Rivette's story. Spielberg's work ties everything up, giving a closed, logical form to fantasy. Rivette's work is open, erratic, irrational, and—much more profoundly than Spielberg's—inviting.

Spielberg gives us a complete serial, all 15 chapters, in the two-hour running time of *Raiders*. But Rivette films, though they may run from two hours to 12, seem like single chapters from serials that, mysteriously, have been lost; they're the surviving fragments of stories and cycles that no longer exist as wholes. (Many of Feuillade's early serials have come down to us only in bits and pieces.) The premises were explained in an opening chapter that no one has seen; the resolution of the plot was contained in a concluding episode that has long since crumbled into dust. The films themselves seem suspended, caught in the process of assuming a final form that never arrives. It's this idea of an intermediary state, of a process, that fascinates Rivette on the levels of both story and technique.

Rivette begins not with a plot but with what he calls a "generating principle"—a collection, more or less arbitrary, of written texts, story ideas, structuring principles, particular actors, or particular qualities of an image that, with luck, will develop over the course of the actual filmmaking—growing either through interaction or through the remote, indirect intervention of the filmmaker. *Céline and Julie Go Boating*, for example, is based on the friendship of two actresses, Juliet Berto and Dominique Labourier, crossed with two forgotten early works of Henry James, *The Other House* and "The Romance of Certain Old Clothes." *Out 1: Spectre* has a remote basis in a pulpy work of fiction by Balzac, *L'histoire des treize*, filtered through two rival theatrical groups rehearsing productions of Aeschylus. *Le pont du Nord* takes its structure from a game of Snakes and Ladders, and the course of the action is largely determined by the severe restrictions of Rivette's tiny budget (i.e., no interior scenes that would require expensive lighting, no locations outside Paris). Instead of dividing writing, shooting, and cutting into separate stages of production, Rivette lets them flow together: a plot point may be determined by the way that an actress walks across a room or, weeks later in the editing room, by the accidental juxtaposition of two unrelated sequences.

Duelle, the 1976 film with which Rivette will appear, is obscurely based on Celtic myth, with a three-part structure somehow tied to the cycle of the moon. Out of this arcana emerges a moon goddess (the dark-haired Juliet Berto) doing battle with a sun goddess (blond Bulle Ogier) for possession of a magic stone that will grant its owner the power to remain on Earth beyond the 40 days allowed per year. Rivette might as well have taken all this from a comic book, but enough of the mythic basis remains to grant the story, if not the "meaning," something perhaps rarer and more intriguing—a residue of meaning, a shadow of substance. The action takes place in contemporary Paris, and it is filmed as Feuillade might have filmed it: in deep-focus long shots that closely link the characters to the décor, rooting them in a definite physical world. The grubby everydayness of the settings—a dance hall, a racetrack, a hotel lobby—at first seems to contradict the magical qualities of the characters, but as the film continues a productive tension grows between them: the sets, littered with mirrors and sheets of reflecting glass, seem to take on some magical properties of their own; the characters, stranded in a semblance of reality, acquire a weight and authority they would never possess in a fairy tale. The sound is all live, direct, and realistic, including the musical score, which is improvised by a pianist who can be seen, quite plainly, sitting at his instrument in the background of the scene. By bringing the music into his movie, Rivette is making a joking reference to the pianists who accompanied silent films, but it also works on another level, introducing another tension, another "process." The pianist plays in response to the action, amplifying and commenting on it, but the action—still improvised—also plays in response to the music, catching its changing moods and rhythms, leading the actors into a stylized movement something like dance.

So what is *Duelle* about? I don't know for sure, and I'm not sure that it matters. The complicated intrigues may well have an allegorical dimension (I'm told that *Le pont du Nord*, for instance, translates into a fairly dense parable on Parisian politics), and the elements that recur from other films (themes of conspiracy, performance, and domination) clearly have some personal significance for Rivette. But Rivette's work is less a matter of content than of texture, the sensuality (a sensuality that does not exclude the intellect) of shifting form, contrasting rhythms, different dimensions of myth and fact coming together and enriching each other. Ultimately, of course, the subject of *Duelle*, a film about two fantastic beings fighting to become real, is *Duelle* itself. It's the story of a story taking shape, a fiction coming into the world.

Boat People

Directed by ANN HUI {March 1984}

When *Boat People* was shown at last May's Cannes Film Festival, it had to
be smuggled in, something like the Vietnamese refugees that it deals with.
The Socialist government of France, which has been trying to strengthen
its ties with the former French colony of Vietnam, apparently objected to
the film's depiction of the current Vietnamese government as corrupt and
brutally repressive and requested that *Boat People* not be shown in the
official competition. But eventually it did turn up on the schedule, listed
in tiny type as "a film surprise"—the kind of shrewdly minimal publicity
that, in Cannes, ensures a huge turnout. *Boat People* was screened twice,
once with English subtitles and once with French. But to judge from the
next day's chatter, it was as if two different movies had been shown: the
leftist critics of France's *Libération* and *Cahiers du Cinéma* were lost in
unreserved admiration for the film they saw, while the largely liberal US
press corps loathed and despised the movie that was shown to them. For
the French, the film was an extremely well-made melodrama without any
troubling political overtones, but for the Americans, *Boat People* was a
crude piece of right-wing propaganda—a film that employed the shoddiest
techniques of mass-market moviemaking to elicit a primitive emotional
response to a highly complex political reality. When the film opened in
New York this fall, a *Village Voice* writer characterized it as a "lopsided,
irresponsible, and reactionary picture of Vietnamese society."

It's hardly unusual for French and American critics to divide at Cannes,
but it's amazing to find the Americans taking the line of political purity. By
nature, it is the French who ferret out the ideological underpinnings, while
the Americans are content to sit back and enjoy Sandinista training films as
fun-filled adventures. The reversal was so striking, in fact, that it made me
think that the real point of contention wasn't the politics of *Boat People* but
the movie's style. *Boat People*, which will be at Facets Multimedia Center
(1517 West Fullerton Avenue, 281-4114) for an extended run this month, is
forthrightly and uncompromisingly a melodrama, an aesthetic choice that
has continued to be an honorable one in Europe, while in America it has
become a capital offense.

When Ann Hui, the 36-year-old Hong Kong director who made *Boat People*, tells her interviewers that it's not a political film, I tend to believe her,
at least as far as the film's execution is concerned (it is certainly political in
its effects). For Hui, who comes out of the popular tradition of the bustling
Hong Kong studios, film is basically an emotional medium; there's no room
in *Boat People* for theatrical denunciations of the Vietnamese regime—

everything must be shown, and everything must be felt. Political issues aren't presented as issues but are recast as dramatic facts: hard and clear incidents that serve to advance the story line. Hui, in this film at least (her other movies are more abstract), is almost exclusively a narrative artist. She is interested not in psychology or formal relationships, but solely in the arrangement and unfolding of events—in shaping the narrative so that it achieves its maximum velocity and emotional impact. Her closest stylistic reference is perhaps Cecil B. DeMille, Hollywood's greatest architect of purely functional story structures. Like DeMille, she uses the opening sequences of her film to plant a little garden of story seeds, quickly sketching in a range of characters, conflicts, and possible directions for the plot. In her development, she chains these conflicts together, setting them up in a row so that the resolution of one problem triggers the explosion of the next, leaving no time for reflection or loss of momentum. At the climax, all of the interrelated plot elements suddenly click into place around a single, cataclysmic event (here, the departure of a boat that will take the heroine to safety), and the suspense inherent in the event is doubled by a suspense inherent in the structure: How can all the loose ends be resolved before the film is over? Like DeMille, Hui depends on simple, strongly massed images to convey the complexities of her plotting. With all the baroque detail packed into the narration, the shots mustn't be overburdened; they should yield their information quickly and then make way for the next image. Throughout *Boat People*, Hui's camera moves straight to the strongest, most privileged point of view possible; she has a remarkable instinct for locating the spatial and emotional center of a scene, for training her camera on the exact location where the lines of force cross.

This is superb filmmaking, but because of its speed and clarity it's likely to strike many viewers as false: it runs right over the ambiguities, hesitations, and narrative gaps that we've learned to associate with realism. Mike Nichols's *Silkwood* is no less an ideological project than *Boat People*, but because Nichols has allowed his narrative to go slack, his characters to remain ambivalent, and his chain of events to appear murky and discontinuous, *Silkwood* somehow seems more authentic, more believable. Hui streamlines reality, revving it up to the level of melodrama. Nichols overstuffs reality, making life seem even more clotted than it is; he brings reality down a notch, into the shadowland of naturalism. The point is not that one approach is superior to the other, but that the two styles represent a choice that every filmmaker must make for himself, based on the effects he wishes to create and the natural temper of his material. But I do think *Silkwood* might have been a better film had Nichols been willing to risk a touch of Hui's melodramatic drive; without it, *Silkwood* seems at odds with itself, a film with an unambiguous political position (nuclear power is bad) that deliberately drowns itself in ambiguity. Hui's blatant partisanship is, ironically, easier to grapple with, easier to resist: we sense it as an argument, a position that could be countered, while Nichols's naturalism leaves no room for discussion—it simply states that this is the way things are. I don't think that propaganda—of the leftist or rightist variety—has any place in a work of art, but when a film does have a message to push, it's better that it be identified as such and not disguised as something real.

Boat People also bears comparison with another recent American political film, Roger Spottiswoode's Nicaraguan adventure *Under Fire*. Like Spottiswoode, Hui picks a photojournalist for her hero; hers is Akutagawa (played by a doe-eyed Hong Kong pop star named Lam), a Japanese newsman who covered the liberation of Da Nang in 1975 and has been invited back by the Vietnamese government three years later to document the tremendous progress that has been made since the end of the war. As in *Under Fire*, the photographer remains absolutely impartial until he meets a representative of the oppressed class: a bomb-throwing guerrilla who is a fan of American baseball in *Under Fire*, a 14-year-old girl whose father was killed fighting for the South Vietnamese Army in *Boat People*. In both films, the hero's sense of professional impartiality is gradually worn down by his emotional involvement with a victim, and both heroes end by betraying their trade: the protagonist of *Under Fire* by faking a news photograph, the hero of *Boat People* by trading his camera for an "easy exit" ticket for his teenage friend. It's interesting that both films settle on the photojournalist as our century's ultimate embodiment of cold objectivity; the reasoning, I suppose, is that reporters are disinterested to begin with, but if they're ever tempted to slant their reports the mechanical objectivity of the camera keeps them honest. (These are both, of course, highly debatable propositions.) But both films invoke this figure only to bring him low—to demonstrate the immorality of objectivity and to provide the audience with an identification figure we can follow along the path to political enlightenment. I can't see any essential difference in methodology between *Boat People* and *Under Fire*, but still, *Under Fire* was praised to the skies by many of the same critics who dismissed *Boat People* out of hand.

I think Hui, in a strange way, has been punished for being a good director—for selecting a style (melodrama) and riding it through with energy and skill, where Spottiswoode, a much less proficient filmmaker, gains points for "realism" by letting his melodramatic premises peter out into halftones and confusions. I can't vouch for the accuracy of *Boat People* any more than I can vouch for the accuracy of *Under Fire* (though, as a good liberal, I know which way my sympathies lie), but I can vouch for Ann Hui's talent. *Boat People* is a movie that ought to be seen and ought to be reckoned with.

L'argent

Directed by ROBERT BRESSON {June 1984}

Can you like Robert Bresson and not be a monk, a masochist, or a professional film theorist? I think so. The legendary French director will officially
turn 77 this year (though unofficial reports put him in his 80s): he has made
only 14 films since 1943, each of them such a model of precision, concentration, and intelligence that it is almost impossible to distinguish among
them—his is a career composed almost entirely of major works. (His only
real minor effort is the hastily assembled 1962 *Trial of Joan of Arc*.) He is
an intimidating, even forbidding figure (though in person he is surprisingly
casual and witty), and for many people one taste of Bresson is enough:
this kind of seriousness, of this intensity and rigor, isn't what they go to
movies for. Bresson is one of the few significant religious artists of our time;
his films are far from being tracts (and very far from Hollywood's brand
of piety), but there's no getting around the fact that Bresson's principal
subjects are sin and redemption, topics you may not want to encounter
on Saturday night. His style is austere, minimal, and elliptical; he doesn't
allow the audience to identify with his characters (at least not in the usual
way), and though his films are full of events, they are seldom full of action—
movement is miniscule and stylized. To achieve the intensity of his films,
Bresson has invented for himself a cinematic language like no one else's;
though his personal grammar of sequence construction has been imitated
(notably and disastrously by Paul Schrader), no other filmmaker has been
able to capture its full, pure force—the startling clarity that bursts from
its eccentricity. But the pleasure of Bresson's work is real and immediate;
his is a ravishing intelligence, so powerful in its regard, so complete in its
artistic realization, that it can leave you transported, breathless.

L'argent ("Money") is Bresson's newest film, and it will be opening
sometime this month at the Fine Arts Theatre on South Michigan. It
nowhere feels like the work of an octogenarian; if anything, it has a vigor
and drive—a straight-ahead energy—that's been absent from Bresson's
work since *A Man Escaped* and *Pickpocket* in the fifties. A lot of things
happen in *L'argent* that don't usually happen in Bresson films: there is a
bank robbery, a shoot-out, a car chase, a prison insurrection, and, finally, two knifings and five ax murders. It's almost the *Friday the 13th* of
art pictures. Bresson doesn't shy away from the horror of the killings—
they're shockingly physical events, not tidy metaphors—and if anything,
the elliptical style in which they are registered (a chilling shot of a few
flecks of blood striking gray wallpaper) doubles their impact by leaving so
much to our imagination. But the sensational material is so well integrat-

ed into Bresson's project—so necessary to his narration—that it loses its ordinary meaning. It seems suspended, remote; we experience it not in the usual way but as something hushed, almost sacred. Bresson's story is of a heating-oil delivery man, Yvon, who accepts a counterfeit 500-franc note from a client. When he innocently tries to spend it, he is arrested and, though not jailed, is fired from his job. Broke, and with a wife and baby daughter to support, he agrees to act as a getaway driver in a robbery attempt. The holdup fails, and Yvon is sent to prison for a three-year term, during which he learns of the death of his daughter and his abandonment by his wife. Finally released, he walks straight to a nearby hotel and murders the manager and his assistant for the slim contents of the cash drawer. Wandering the streets the next day, he exchanges glances with a middle-aged woman and follows her to the rundown country house where she lives with her family. He confesses to her and she takes him in, but when he finds an ax near his bed in the barn, he's drawn to repeat his crime. The events of *L'argent* are the steps of Yvon's journey, a journey that will end in a flash of grace; as such, they are sacred, ordained. Bresson sanctifies events by reducing them to their absolute essentials. The bank robbery is represented by a single long shot of a gunman holding a hostage behind a glass door, the car chase by a close-up of a foot pressing an accelerator. These fragmentary, closely focused images are accompanied by an unusually crisp and vivid sound-effects track; it's what we hear, rather than what we see, that gives the film its dimension and reality. Unlike the soft-focus "spirituality" of most religious films, Bresson's cinema insists on the materiality of everything it shows. There are no transcendent symbols in his work, only hard-edged, immediate objects. By reducing actions to a few small, representative gestures, Bresson is hoping to objectify events—to make them as hard and concrete as things, with no room left for attitudinizing or interpretation. His approach to acting follows the same principle: he uses only nonprofessionals for his "models," as he calls them (the "model" who plays Yvon makes his living as an architect), and he instructs them not to portray any emotion. (In rehearsal, he has them repeat their lines and repeat their gestures over and over, until they come to seem meaningless.) For Bresson, any note of theatricality—of emotions affected or grandly displayed—is a false note, one that detracts from the honesty and substantiality of the actor's body. Emotion comes from elsewhere in Bresson's work—from the flow of images, the positioning of sounds.

In *L'argent*, Bresson photographs his models' faces in medium or long shot, but he films their hands in close-up. Hands are the real expressive objects in the film—Yvon's grimy workingman's mitts; the soft pink paws of the middle-class schoolboy who puts the false money in circulation—and Bresson uses them to say everything he needs to say about his characters. The hands of *L'argent* do two things: they grasp (money, at first, but later the ax handle), and they release (Yvon collars and shoves the waiter who has discovered the counterfeit bill and insulted him; the shoving gesture is followed by an extraordinary close-up of Yvon's open hand, an image that crystallizes his shock and regret at what he's done and also communicates a sublime fragility and vulnerability). This rhythm of grasping and releasing is also the film's dramatic rhythm; it is a movement between the material and the spiritual, the immediate and the external. When Yvon drops the ax he has used to kill the family into a stream that runs by their house, the moment of relinquishing is his moment of salvation—at last and alone of all the characters in the film, he is able to let go.

The hands that grasp and release are related to the film's secondary motif, doors that open and shut. *L'argent* begins with a close-up of the metal door of an automatic banking machine sliding silently and firmly back into place—an image of absolute, inflexible denial. Soon after, a woman closes a door to avoid talking to her son (he asks for money, she refuses), a gesture that is echoed in the various prison doors that close on Yvon. The doors divide space, seal it off, much as Bresson's tightly focused close-ups do; this is a world without continuity, without completeness, without freedom. The same divisions rule the dialogue: one character asks, another refuses—there is never any room for discussion, no possibility of softening. Lucien, the young shop clerk whose false testimony convicts Yvon on the counterfeiting charge, later repents and tries to make amends by becoming a kind of Robin Hood, stealing from the rich and giving the proceeds to charity. He will make the doors open (a safe; the automatic teller) by force and by stealth, snatching at salvation like the protagonist of *Pickpocket*. But Lucien's thefts are not a real redemption, because they only perpetuate the corrupt system embodied in the circulation of money. True salvation lies only in leaving the system, in rising above it (as the woman who takes in Yvon does) or in falling below it, as Yvon does.

There are two kinds of movement at work in *L'argent*: the circular movement of the first part of the film, in which we follow the path of the counterfeit money (a circle that closes in on the schoolboy but also widens to include an entire economy), and the vertical movement of Yvon's story, a descent that is ultimately an ascent. There is something almost sculptural in the way that Bresson plays these movements against each other. They acquire shape and substance, like bodies frozen in space, pulling and straining but unable to separate. When the woman invites Yvon to sleep in her barn, she is inviting him to kill her. Her death is a suicide of the kind that haunts so many of Bresson's films (with her nightmarish life of family obligations, she could be an older sister to the farm girl who kills herself in *Mouchette*), but it is also a gift she gives to Yvon. Only in killing her can he touch bottom and begin the journey back. Immediately after the murders, Yvon confesses to two policemen standing at the bar of a country inn. As they lead him to the door, a crowd gathers to watch.

Bresson holds the shot—his final one—for a few seconds after Yvon and the policemen have passed; the crowd remains frozen in place outside the inn, staring, apparently at nothing at all. And then we realize what has transfixed them: the door is still open, letting a warm light out into the night. No one moves to close it.

A Sunday in the Country

Directed by BERTRAND TAVERNIER {December 1984}

This particular Sunday belongs to an early fall in an early year of the 20th century (1912), and the country is that of one of the small villages that lie beyond Paris, newly made accessible to city dwellers on their Sunday excursions by the burgeoning network of railway lines. The house and studio of M. Ladmiral (Louis Ducreux) lie exactly ten minutes by foot from the train station; 40 years ago, when he was at the height of his success and celebrity as a painter, he purchased the property for just that reason. These days, he no longer takes the train to the city; instead, his son's family takes the train from the city each Sunday to visit him. M. Ladmiral still walks down to the station to meet them, but he always arrives a little late. The walk, mysteriously, now takes 20 minutes, but M. Ladmiral prefers to think that the trains are arriving ten minutes early.

Betrand Tavernier's new film *A Sunday in the Country* spins its gentle, autumnal mood with such assurance and elegance that, at first, it's almost off-putting. Tavernier seems ready to plunge into a swamp of conventions: he lays out a sweetly nostalgic setting, bathes it in a beautifully sharp white light that trails off into rich black shadows, and brings out a lovable old man whose big brown eyes brim with sad wisdom. The stage is set for an all-too-familiar kind of art film. We wait for the children to arrive, so that kindly old M. Ladmiral can begin imparting his wry aphorisms, penetrating insights, and twinkling lessons in life.

But, amazingly, there are no lessons in *A Sunday in the Country*. Tavernier's aims are not didactic but descriptive, analytic, and at times choreographic. As the film evolves, it becomes clear that M. Ladmiral's family is a failure. His son, Gonzague (Michel Aumont), is a stiff, trussed-up figure; he wanted to be an artist, but fear of competing with his father has driven him to take refuge in an opposite kind of life—he married Marie-Thérèse (Geneviève Mnich), his secretary and a formidable organizer, and became a model petit bourgeois. M. Ladmiral dislikes his daughter-in-law ("She had all the virtues," says Tavernier's narration, "but well hidden") and takes his son's filial devotion for granted; because they are much rarer, he looks forward much more excitedly to the visits of his daughter, Irène (Sabine Azema). Irène is a spectacularly, almost manically free spirit: Young, attractive, and unmarried, she operates a boutique in the capital (and plunders her father's attic for resale goods). She doesn't take the train, but arrives behind the wheel of a massive, gleaming automobile, announcing her imminent departure even before she's said hello. M. Ladmiral lights up when he sees her (rushing into the garden, she startles him out of the cat nap that Gonzague has lured him into); when Gonzague sees Irène, his face darkens with the knowledge of his father's favoritism. But as much as Gonzague resents his father's neglect, he is unconsciously perpetuating his crime within his own family. Gonzague and Marie-Thérèse indulge their two boys; here it is the girl—tiny, sickly Mireille (Katia Wostrikoff)—who is always forgotten.

None of these tensions come to a head. The characters themselves don't seem to perceive them; they have become too much a part of their lives and personalities to be taken notice of, and it is only Tavernier's wandering, curious camera that brings them out. The camera moves independently of the characters, tracking in to inspect the furnishings of a room or pulling back from the dramatic center of a scene to examine the reactions of characters who may not seem directly involved. When the camera moves—in long, graceful floating arcs—it affects the transitions, comparisons, and climaxes that are absent from the largely plotless narrative. A camera movement will bring on a note of nostalgic reverie (M. Ladmiral conjuring a vision of his late wife) and end with a return to prosaic reality (the camera drifts slowly toward the door through which Gonzague will emerge to announce lunch), or glide from a moment of affectionate expression between two characters to a bristly exchange between two others. The movement of the camera provides a link, a sense of basic continuity and equivalence, between all of the film's disparate moods and emotions. Tavernier suggests that these feelings are too tightly bound, too interdependent, to be separated out into neat dramatic packages; he suggests also that as these feelings are bound, so is the family.

The first half of *A Sunday in the Country* consists almost exclusively of the leisurely gathering of these understated moments and of their placement in a nonjudgmental context. Strengths are allied with weaknesses, kindnesses with cruelties; no one character—and certainly not the "wise old man"—has a corner on virtue. For all of the underlying tension, the family presents a sense of equilibrium, of an emotional balance that has been achieved with the passing of time. When Irène arrives unexpectedly after lunch, the film's rhythm is irretrievably altered. Irène seems to intensify everything around her; though she is the most demonstrative, the most aggressively cheerful of the family members, she is also the most anguished and secretive—she makes anxious calls to Paris, trying to placate an angry lover whose existence she feels obliged to keep hidden from the family. Irène doesn't upset the equilibrium, but she strains it mightily. At one point in the late afternoon, she takes her father for a ride in her new car—a jaunt that is also an escape from the family. They pause at a riverbank café for a drink, and in this archetypically impressionist setting—working-class couples dance on the outdoor platform behind them, sheltered by the autumn trees—M. Ladmiral offers an apology for his art. Impressionism passed him by, he says—he was brought up in the academic tradition, and he stuck with it, though it now seems to him that he might have tried for something freer, more adventurous.

Prompted by Irène, M. Ladmiral's confession is as close to a conventional climax as *A Sunday in the Country* comes. It is the moment of self-consciousness, of self-questioning, that provides the turning point of every Tavernier film from *The Clockmaker* to *Coup de torchon*, but whereas in the past Tavernier has been concerned with the consequences of that moment, in *A Sunday in the Country* he is concerned with its antecedents. Accentuated by Irène's presence, the tensions of the morning have led to the discovery of the afternoon; Irène, herself a highly theatrical, even artificial figure, leads her father from the unacknowledged failures of his life to the more objective, quantifiable failures of his art. When M. Ladmiral speaks of his hesitancy to abandon the rules his masters taught him as timeless, he is also speaking of his reluctance to give up the idealized image of his family that he has nurtured over the years. He is a prisoner of ideals—of classicism, of symmetry, of beautiful surfaces—and his adherence to the rules prevents him from taking too hard a look at either his subjects or his life.

There are times in the film when the voice-over narration (spoken by Tavernier himself, it comes from the novel, Pierre Bost's *Monsieur Ladmiral va bientôt mourir*, on which the film is based) appears to be doing the work of characterization and development that, in the movies, is more properly the province of the image. There is, for example, a long scene in which Irène and her father look through a trunk of antique lace while the narrator describes the meaning of the slightly awkward looks they exchange—M. Ladmiral suspects his daughter has a lover, but does not want to be told; Irène knows that he knows, but would rather respect his wishes than break the silence. In the movies, it is always irritating to be told what you would prefer to discover for yourself. But the slight irritation here is more than compensated for by the delicate contrast in time frames that it allows Tavernier to create. The body of the film, with its relaxed rhythms, unfocused narrative, and subtly drawn-out, privileged moments, plays in the range of real time. The narration, distanced, reflective, and analytic, imposes a sense of literary time, of looking back. The conjunction of the two time schemes produces a powerfully poignant sense of moments that, as soon as they blossom in their full immediacy, abruptly fall back to a distant past—of the present becoming the past, second by second. In this film, set at the end of an old man's life and the end of the 19th-century world he embodies, time is the most precious commodity; Tavernier lets us feel it slipping between our fingers.

Irène drives back to Paris, and Gonzague's family boards the train, leaving M. Ladmiral alone for the film's coda, which becomes the emotional summation—the coming home—of all the themes the film has developed. The action is simple: M. Ladmiral walks back from the station, through his garden, and into his studio, where he takes out a fresh canvas and looks for a moment into its whiteness. But it is transformed by Tavernier's control of the pure plastic elements of filmmaking: the placement of the music (by Gabriel Fauré); the bluish, twilight tint that seeps into Bruno de Keyzer's muted cinematography; the harmony of the actor's stride with the gliding movement of the camera; and, above all, the meticulous timing of the rise and fall of emotional rhythms add up to a virtuoso passage of pure cinema of a kind that no more than four or five working directors are capable of creating. Tavernier isn't ashamed of the wave of feeling he brings to the surface; his sensitive, intelligent, masterly film has earned it.

Mikey and Nicky

Directed by ELAINE MAY {April 1985}

It's never easy to say why a film fails to find its public. After a long period in the editing room, Elaine May's *Mikey and Nicky* made its New York debut in 1976 and sank more quickly than a bowling ball in a vat of custard. Apparently it wasn't a matter of bad reviews so much as no reviews at all: for reasons that will forever remain mysterious, it was a film that no one wanted to see, despite the impressive track record of its maker (*The Heartbreak Kid*, *A New Leaf*). May hasn't signed a film since, although she has worked steadily as an anonymous script doctor (on such films as *Reds* and *Heaven Can Wait*).

Still, the film's occasional screenings over the years—notably at the 1981 Toronto Film Festival—have earned it an underground reputation, and now it has been reissued by an independent distributor (it's due at the Fine Arts Theatre sometime this month). It may be that *Mikey and Nicky* will find its audience after all. Funny, incisive, and finally haunting, it is one of the most striking American films of its decade; its courageous risk-taking and cutting intelligence make it seem more contemporary than any Hollywood film released this year.

Mikey and Nicky came out at the end of a cycle of "buddy movies"—films about rapturous male friendships that seemed to revel in an adolescent resentment of the opposite sex. But *Mikey and Nicky*, a buddy movie made by a woman, is to *Butch Cassidy and the Sundance Kid* what *Breathless* is to gangster movies or *The Searchers* to a Roy Rogers Western: it takes the deepest, unspoken assumptions of the form and holds them up for scrutiny; it takes the form's mechanics—its dramatic conventions and tricks of structure—and turns them upside down, exposing just those elements that the form was meant to hide. Instead of Newman and Redford, the buddies are John Cassavetes and Peter Falk—two of the American cinema's great outsiders, actors who have developed for themselves a style of playing (impulsive, improvisatory, extravagant) and a tonal range (hysteria, desperation, vulnerability) that contradict at every level the requirements of a conventional star performance. One of the loveliest things about *Mikey and Nicky* is the way in which May effaces herself before the singular acting team that Falk and Cassavetes represent. She puts her camera completely in the service of her actors, always leaving enough room in her framing to catch the spontaneous gesture, the sudden movement. And the dialogue, though tightly scripted, has been tailored so closely to the personalities of her performers that there isn't a moment in the film that doesn't feel as if it had been invented on the spot. If it were nothing more, *Mikey and Nicky* is the story of a small-time hood (Cassavetes) who has been caught stealing from a numbers bank; his partner in the scam has already been killed, and Nicky, convinced there is a contract out for him as well, has holed himself up in a fleabag hotel. He calls Mikey (Falk), a childhood friend who is also a member of the syndicate, for counsel and support—a call motivated more by habit than trust, for he isn't sure where Mikey's loyalties lie. Mikey arrives at the hotel and, after a long struggle, persuades his friend to go with him to a bar. Once he's lured his buddy into the open, Mikey marches straight to the phone and calls the portly hit man (Ned Beatty) who has been assigned to the job, telling him exactly where they can be found.

Betrayal isn't usually counted among the most hilarious of movie subjects, but that's how, in the early scenes of her film, May plays it—as an anxious, jumpy comedy of desperation. Wired up by the danger he sees all around him, Nicky isn't a cooperative target: from second to second he flips between swaggering self-confidence and craven terror, and Mikey can't get him to leave the hotel until he agrees to trade coats with him—there might be someone lying in wait in the lobby. (There's another trade, too: as a proof of trust, Mikey asks Nicky to give him his gun; Nicky won't give it up until Mikey offers him something in return, so he gives him his watch. This unstressed moment is typical of May's economical approach to characterization—Nicky lends Mikey the symbol of his bravado; Mikey returns the symbol of his reliability and dutifulness. In no more than two or three shots, May lays out the basis of their friendship—it's an exchange of strengths.) Once Mikey has gotten his buddy to the bar, he's got to keep him there, no simple matter given the contradictory impulses that whiz through Nicky's addled brain—he wants to visit his ex-wife; he wants to see his girlfriend; he wants to go to an all-night movie. Meanwhile, the hit man (May introduces him with a wonderful touch—he's seen flipping channels on a TV until he finds a soundtrack that suits his mood: the wailing, doom-laden score of a forties film noir) has managed to get lost in the crosstown traffic. The minutes tick by, and still the killer doesn't show—and we find our sympathy slowly turning to Mikey, as it always does to the modest, methodical man who's just trying to get a job done.

On the surface, *Mikey and Nicky* seems loose, casual, even disconnected. But the force of the film comes from the way in which May suspends this casual surface over a very tight structure. The film lives in the tension between the completely impulsive and the carefully planned, which is also the tension between its main characters. While Falk and Cassavetes play their dazzling behavioral games, May is careful to limit herself to the classical unities: unity of time (the film takes place in one night), of space (a few square blocks of the unnamed city—May even shows us the map), and, of course, of action (not for nothing did she spend her college years at the University of Chicago). The format is one of Attic tragedy, and there is something fateful about the unfolding of the action—in the way that it seems to escape the control of the characters—once it has been set in motion by the decision to betray. Yet May peppers it with a specifically cinematic, almost Griffith-like suspense. As she crosscuts between Mikey and Nicky passing the long night in forced camaraderie and the killer who is constantly coming closer, the film becomes a variation on a silent melodrama's race to the gallows: the question is not whether the governor's pardon will arrive in time to save the hero from an unjust execution, but whether Mikey will find his affection for his friend sufficiently rekindled to try to rescue him.

May passes this volatile relationship through three different frames of reference. Finally, on their way to the all-night movie (Mikey has arranged for the hit man to meet them there), Nicky suddenly decides that he must visit his mother's grave. Scaling the wall of the locked cemetery (the slapstick here is a reference to a Laurel and Hardy short), they find themselves back in their childhood, as if the presence of death has made them infants again. Childhood intimacies reemerge: Nicky tells the story of Mikey's younger brother who one day went suddenly bald. The boys made fun of him, and the next morning he was dead of scarlet fever. The memory is both funny and appalling, and it is here that May touches her most profound mix of emotions—the film moves into that rarefied, dangerous zone where comedy and tragedy merge, where a laugh is the same as a scream.

Too much death conjures a need for warmth, and the two friends, again grown close, decide to visit Nicky's girl (the hit man, still waiting at the theater, has been forgotten). Delicately played by Joyce Van Patten, she is a lonely, fading office worker of 40 or so with a too cheerfully decorated apartment: one of those cruelly sidelined, not-quite-attractive-enough women who seem to find their voice only in May's movies (May herself in *A New Leaf*; her daughter, Jeannie Berlin, in *The Heartbreak Kid*). Nicky makes perfunctory love to her while Mikey waits, mortified, in the kitchen. When Nicky is through, he suggests to his buddy that he take a crack too. The woman, humiliated, rejects him, and Mikey suddenly suspects that he's been set up—that Nicky is making fun of his sexual insecurities, just as he did in high school. The friendship shatters again (and Nicky smashes Mikey's watch against the pavement of the street), and the two men separate.

Their relationship has moved through childhood (the cemetery) and adolescence (the woman's apartment); now, as the sun begins to come up, it moves into the crueler light of adulthood. Mikey returns home (the hit man follows him, just in case Nicky decides to come back for help), and we see his house—a modern, comfortable upper-middle-class home situated in an exclusive neighborhood policed by private patrol cars. Whatever the roots of Mikey's betrayal—the resentment, the closeness, the needfulness, the envy, all simmered together over the years—in the cold light of day it comes down to this: Mikey must betray his friend in order to preserve the little place that he has made for himself in the world. Mikey's wife has waited up for him, his son is asleep in the next room, and in a moment Nicky's knock will sound at the front door. The film began with the image of a door barricaded against the dangers of the outside world—the door of Nicky's hotel room. It will end with a closed door, too.

The Coca-Cola Kid

Directed by DUŠAN MAKAVEJEV {July 1985}

Filmgoers who haunted the art houses in the sixties and early seventies will always remember Dušan Makavejev for the remarkable series of wise and funny collage films he made in his native Yugoslavia: *Man Is Not a Bird* (1966), *The Case of the Missing Switchboard Operator* (1967), *Innocence Unprotected* (1968), and, supremely, *WR: Mysteries of the Organism* (1971), a mixture of mock documentary (on the crackpot sexual theories of Wilhelm Reich), excerpts (from Stalinist propaganda films), and lurid fiction (about the fatally unhappy love life of a champion ice skater) that was one of the first films to explore the notion that political structures are the products of personal frustrations. But since he left Yugoslavia, Makavejev's career has been spotty: the much-censored scatological epic *Sweet Movie*, made in Canada in 1974 and barely released, made Makavejev unemployable for seven years; his comeback film, the Swedish-made *Montenegro*, found him pursuing a relatively conventional narrative structure and won him a modest commercial success. After four more years of silence, Makavejev is back with *The Coca-Cola Kid*, this time made in Australia. Though he hasn't lost any of his talent—this is a wonderfully fluid, bright film, filled with a hundred little pleasures of camera placement and dynamic editing—he does seem to have lost a little of his courage. Perhaps Makavejev has been contemplating the image of fellow Eastern European émigré Milos Forman, with his armload of Academy Awards (for *One Flew Over the Cuckoo's Nest* and *Amadeus*), and wondering whether he couldn't score a couple for himself. For all of its wit and anarchic eroticism, *The Coca-Cola Kid* has the air of a film made to order: it plays a bit too cozily into the themes and attitudes that have already proved their potency in the specialized film circuit. For the first time, Makavejev seems to be making a movie to please an audience rather than to please himself. It's as if the market pressures of the West had managed to do what the ideological apparatus of the Eastern bloc could not: with *The Coca-Cola Kid*, Makavejev has learned to toe the party line.

The story is going to remind a lot of people of *Local Hero*. Becker (no first name is given or implied) is a young, eager, frighteningly dedicated marketing whiz who bursts into the Sydney offices of the Coca-Cola Company, armed with orders from Atlanta to perk up the apparently sluggish Australian operation. Examining the demographic maps generated by the company computer, Becker is astonished to discover a tiny area in the country—a remote valley region—where not one single bottle of Coke has ever been sold. For Becker, the news that one spot remains in the world that has rejected the blessing of Coke comes as a personal affront, and he roars off in a Land Rover to find the reason why. The reason turns out to be a crusty, anachronistic individualist named T. George McDowell who has kept the valley supplied with his own soda pop, manufactured in a chugging, ramshackle 1920s bottling plant, for as long as anyone can remember. Like the protagonist of *Local Hero*, Becker is slowly seduced by the flinty, traditional values that live on in the valley, and rather than destroy McDowell, he offers him a franchise. But for the old man, signing up with a corporation means the loss of his personal freedom, and he is determined to preserve his freedom at any price.

Local Hero is, of course, only the most recent version of this gentle, day-dreamy legend of moral regeneration through contact with an alien culture; the movies have been pushing it ever since the aftermath of World War II, when the giant American corporations first emerged as dominant powers. Though the images of the alien culture have changed—from the cuddly communities of British eccentrics in the Ealing comedies of the fifties, to the noble tribes of American Indians in the anti-Westerns of the sixties, and finally to the aliens of a different kind in the science-fiction fantasies of the eighties—the enemy is always the same: the rigid, regimentalized world of corporate bureaucracy, where the employee must think only of the company, and the company must think only of profits. Each generation seems to discover this little parable for itself and claim it as its own. And yet it probably isn't the element of social criticism that has made the story so enduringly popular (the revolutionary fervor these films instill has a way of cooling down by the time you reach the parking lot) as much as the story's way of merging so smoothly with the basic, escapist ends of a night at the movies. The fantasy of flying to a foreign place, where life is simpler, work is more satisfying, and love is an ever-present possibility—this is the fantasy that has kept movie theaters full on Saturday nights since time immemorial, and it's the fantasy that these films deliver with an unusually literal force.

But Makavejev is a born subversive, too suspicious of culture myths—be they the omnipotence of Stalin or the existence of a Shangri-la—to let them stand unchallenged. He may never really confront the clichés embedded in *The Coca-Cola Kid*, but he does snipe at them, carrying on a kind of stylistic guerrilla warfare through unexpected inflections and unsettling asides. As played by Eric Roberts, Becker isn't sympathetic enough to serve as the transparent audience-identification figure the genre demands: he isn't a reluctant foot soldier of the corporation, as Peter Riegert was in *Local Hero*, but a true believer—a fanatic who sees his work for Coke as a continuation of his service in the marines. His mission is to bring the American way of life—as embodied by the brown, bubbly fluid—to all the unenlightened nations of the world. Roberts plays him from under a shock of highly artificial reddish-blond hair, and he again uses the straining, wheezy Kirk Douglas voice he had in *Star 80*, though this time he complicates it with a Southern drawl. The sounds that emerge from his throat are so strange, so dissonantly orchestrated, that the accents of the Australian actors immediately seem warm and familiar. More than a foreigner, Becker seems to be some sort of Martian, and there is a funny, haunting scene aboard the plane that takes him to Sydney, when the flight crew sprays the cabin with pesticides meant to prevent the introduction of foreign diseases into Australia. As the dense aerosol mist settles around Becker's head and shoulders, he coughs ferociously—he's the pest they're looking for.

Just as Makavejev diagnosed Stalinism as a nation's fear of sexuality in *WR*, so does he find a sexual root for Becker's obsessiveness in *The Coca-Cola Kid*. Becker is too involved in his flow charts to take notice of Terri, the secretary who has been assigned to him as an assistant and who, as played by Greta Scacchi, exudes a tawny, tigerish sensuality of a kind that hasn't been seen since the early Bardot. While the genre requires an airy, elusive, romantic figure (like the marine biologist and possible mermaid of *Local Hero*), Scacchi provides a creature of an almost frightening physicality: with her catlike movements and devouring eyes, she offers not an escape into fairy-tale fantasy but a kind of warm oblivion—an escape into animal instinct. Sexuality has always been the ultimate subversive force in Makavejev's universe. It isn't ideology that's going to overthrow oppressive governments (or even slow down the efforts of a Coca-Cola salesman), but the annihilating power of unbridled lust. For Makavejev, sex is revolutionary because it is so gloriously messy—no system of enforced order can withstand its call—and Terri is the most gloriously messy of Makavejev's heroines. When he introduces her, she is taking a slow, gooey bite from a bar of chocolate candy, goo that is quickly transferred to the telex announcing Becker's arrival, where it remains, symbolically at least, to the end of the film. Makavejev makes a bold and lovely move in deciding never to supply the slightest explanation for Terri's fixation on Becker. It is simply a fact of life, like a mountain or an ocean, and eventually even Becker must give in to it. When the moment comes, Terri is dressed in a Santa Claus suit for a Coca-Cola promotion; as Becker pulls it from her body, he rips into the pillow she's using for stomach padding, and suddenly the bedroom is full of a storm of white, prickly feathers, which continue to fall as they make love—gloriously and messily.

From the way that Makavejev skips over the unconvincing scenes of Becker's moral regeneration, it's clear that he doesn't really believe in them—he's just following out the formula as it's been handed down to him. And at the end of the film, there is a curious, cynical coda that's meant to suggest that Becker's salvation doesn't matter in the slightest—that the world will continue on its awful course without his help—but it comes too late (and is too much of a departure in style) to really undermine the basic sentimentality of the story line. Still, a Makavejev truly unbound seems too much to hope for in this timid era for the movies: in the meantime, *The Coca-Cola Kid* provides a welcome half-loaf.

Ran

Directed by AKIRA KUROSAWA {December 1985}

Japanese filmmaker Akira Kurosawa is one of the very few living legends of the movies. At the age of 75, and with a filmography that includes such titles as *Rashomon* (which, in 1951, became the film that introduced the Japanese cinema to Western audiences), *Ikiru*, *Throne of Blood*, and the towering *Seven Samurai*, he's reached that point in his career where each new film is acclaimed as a masterpiece from the moment it goes into production. *Ran*, his latest (the title translates as "chaos"), has been a masterpiece for nearly three years, from the moment in 1982 when French producer Serge Silberman agreed to take on the mammoth project that Kurosawa had conceived. There was never any doubt that *Ran* would represent the summit of Kurosawa's artistry, the themes he had explored over a lifetime, the technique honed by decades of experience, and the epic scale Kurosawa has always aspired to. Now that, $11.5 million later (the budget is modest by American standards but monstrous for a Japanese production), *Ran* has finally reached American screens, seeing it is almost anticlimactic.

Ran is an excellent film: for me, it's Kurosawa's most vigorous, most resonant work since *Seven Samurai*. But if it narrowly eludes greatness, it's perhaps because greatness has been built into the project from the beginning. It's an oddly predictable, familiar masterpiece, assembled according to the time-honored plan—a great director tackles a great subject (man's inhumanity to man) on a great scale. As good as the film is, it's haunted by the middlebrow ghosts of such movies as *Ben-Hur* and *The Ten Commandments*. The ideas that underpin it—*Ran* is against war, betrayal, and the breakdown of social order—are a little too homiletic, generalized, and bluntly put to sustain the sense of revelation that a great work must create, and the effects that they feed into (which are where, much more than in its themes, a great work must establish itself) lack detail, shading, texture. It's hard to avoid the feeling that Kurosawa has cut his sprawling narrative, with its stretches of redundant plotting and legions of superfluous characters, to the measure of his ambitions rather than the needs of his material. With *Ran*, Kurosawa clearly meant to create something big, final, definitive—a monument. But there's a reason why monuments are so often dull, undistinguished things, relegated to obscure corners of public parks and cemeteries; burdened with the impossible task of embodying a certain greatness, they almost always fall back on the same tired images and metaphors—of size, of weight, of occupied space. Using these old methods, *Ran* does present an image of greatness, one we all know how to recognize and read. But real greatness, of course, can't be planned for. It's something that comes on its own or doesn't come at all.

Ran's real qualities aren't in its size but in the details of its execution—in the quality of the light that inhabits its images, in the ritualized gestures of the actors, in Kurosawa's bold color design and his mastery of space. Set in the 16th century, during a time of national political instability that came to be known as "the Period of the Warring States," *Ran* is a free adaptation of *King Lear* (just as Kurosawa's 1957 *Throne of Blood* was spun from the plot elements of *Macbeth*). Having united all of the surrounding countryside under his rule, the aging warlord Hidetora Ichimonji (Tatsuya Nakadai) believes it is time to relinquish his leadership and spend his remaining years in peace. Actual power will be transferred to the eldest of his three sons, Taro (Akira Terao), but Hidetora is determined to preserve the signs of power—his title and his personal army—for himself. Bristling under this restriction of his authority, Taro plots with the second son, Jiro (Jinpachi Nezu), to wrest complete control from the old man. Only the third son, Saburo (Daisuke Ryû), remains loyal to Hidetora, although his father has banished him from court for his attempt to warn him of the threat against him.

Kurosawa began his artistic career as a painter, and he continues to plan his films by preparing hundreds of sketches and canvases. The images of his films reflect this formation: he uses the screen as a painter would, as a canvas to be filled. Instead of attempting an illusion of depth, Kurosawa often uses telephoto lenses that serve to flatten out perspectives, bringing all of the elements of the composition together on a single plane. Foreground and background are melded (there is seldom a middle ground in a Kurosawa composition—he is interested only in extreme spatial contrasts, never in intermediate distances) in a way that inescapably suggests a Japanese print; this is an extremely balanced, orderly, coherent world that contains no traps for the eye and can be comprehended in a single glance. The opening scenes of *Ran* are dominated by shots of characters grouped against mountain ranges, images that serenely convey a perfect continuity of line between the natural order and the human. The even, overhead lighting mimics the sun at high noon. There is no danger here, no shadow, just the fullness of the moment, an effect intensified by the rustling wind that threads between the human voices on the soundtrack.

But the visual plan shifts when Hidetora, seeking refuge in a remote castle, is suddenly set upon by the massed armies of his two eldest sons. The natural soundtrack is replaced by an orchestral dirge; the sun vanishes behind a curtain of clouds, and the serene flatness of the image is ripped by flying objects—flaming arrows, the bright red flash of rifle fire. The chaos of the title has been unleashed, yet what is most striking about this virtuoso sequence is the mysterious sense of distance and reserve that it maintains. Kurosawa's camera refuses to join in with the general shock and panic; it refuses, even, to evidence much surprise. Though the cutting is faster and more disorienting, Kurosawa's gaze remains steady and unperturbed. There are several chilly, cosmic moments, both here and in the battle sequence with which the film concludes, in which the camera peers down at a patch of ground just a fraction of a second before a dying soldier falls onto it, as if the exact time and place of every death had been preordained and the camera were merely checking whether or not the prophecy had been fulfilled. The camera's dispassionate stare suggests that for Kurosawa, the calm of the opening sequences and the chaos of the battle are both natural conditions; there is no reason to be astonished by the inevitable.

The aftermath of the massacre finds Hidetora mad, wandering the plains with the sole survivor from among his retinue, the court fool Kyoami (played by a Japanese performer who uses the stage name of Peter). But Taro, the eldest, has also been killed in battle, and leadership of the insurrection must pass to the weaker-willed second son, Jiro. Lady Kaede (Mieko Harada), Taro's ferocious, vengeful wife (her father was one of the lords Hidetora deposed), immediately throws herself on Jiro; he becomes a puppet in her plan to reduce Hidetora's domain to ruin. Lady Kaede seems to exist on pure hatred; like his frames, Kurosawa's characters are deliberately flat, stripped of psychology and reduced to one or two basic traits. To underline what he's done, Kurosawa has costumed each of the main characters in a different color—Taro in yellow, Jiro in red, Saburo in blue—emphasizing the elemental purity of their motivations. But both Hidetora and Lady Kaede are costumed in white, and both wear a heavy makeup meant to suggest the demon masks of the Noh plays. Though Hidetora and Kaede are enemies, they are linked by their immersion in violence and power: it is Hidetora's decision to step away from this bloody past that unleashes Kaede's fury, and as he grows weaker she grows stronger, as if she were feeding off the violent energies he has tried to abandon. This is Kurosawa's darkest intimation: the sense that violence has a life of its own, that it will always return. The order that Hidetora has imposed on his domain is not permanent; violently imposed, it will be violently overthrown at the first sign of weakness. For Kurosawa, human existence is little more than an endless cycle of repression and revenge. The serenity of the opening sequences is an illusion, a creation of Hidetora's hard-won power over his enemies. The chaos of the battle scenes is not its contradiction but its other face.

The actors in *Ran* move slowly, gracefully, deliberately: every gesture seems dictated by centuries of tradition. The only exception is Kyoami, who, as the court fool, is allowed a freedom of movement denied to the others. Kyoami mocks his masters, upsetting the imposed order (and he is the only character allowed to wear a multicolored costume, apparently assembled from scraps of material the others have cast off). Though *Ran* has been read as Kurosawa's reflection on old age, with the elderly Hidetora standing in for the director, I believe there's just as much of Kurosawa in the boyish Kyoami—he is the artist in his society, pointing out its flaws and undermining its repressive mechanisms. Though *Ran* seems designed as a roundly condemnatory antiwar film, it is Kyoami who brings a measure of complexity and paradox to its firmly stated themes. Kyoami is Kurosawa's admission that a bit of chaos can be a positive thing.

Shoah

Directed by CLAUDE LANZMANN {January 1986}

Claude Lanzmann's *Shoah* is a great film, but not only because, as a documentary on the Holocaust, it treats a great subject. Too many movies have used the Holocaust as a way of conferring importance on themselves, of borrowing an impact and stature that aren't really theirs. Some filmmakers, such as Stanley Kramer in *Judgment at Nuremberg*, have made use of the Holocaust for what presumably appeared to them as the highest of moral reasons—to educate the public, to help ensure that such a thing could never happen again. For other filmmakers, the Holocaust has simply been a way of eliciting a programmed response from an audience, of adding zap to otherwise routine, formulaic melodramas and thrillers. But the problem with all of these films is that once they've decided to incorporate these events into a fictional narration, the Holocaust ceases to be a fact and becomes a rhetorical device—just another cog in a storytelling machine designed to produce pity and terror, structurally interchangeable with such other arbitrary symbols of evil as the giant shark in *Jaws* or the high-rise fire in *The Towering Inferno*. No matter how noble the filmmaker's intentions, to "use" the Holocaust in a story is inevitably to reduce it, transform it, betray it.

Documentaries don't necessarily betray the fact of the Holocaust, but too often they betray its truth: the grainy footage of Nazi atrocities stimulates only nausea and revulsion (the choice is either to look away or to look and not see); the numbers totaled up by the narrators soon cease to have any meaning; the voices of the witnesses, floating free from any specified context of time and space, seem weirdly spectral, otherworldly. Lanzmann's *Shoah* contains no newsreel footage and no disembodied, voice-over narration. The witnesses are not ghostly figures but flesh-and-blood beings who are given the time to truly exist on the screen (they tell their stories at their own pace, and Lanzmann films them in continuous takes that can last ten minutes or more without a cut) and who are allowed, either through editing or through actual visits, to return to the scenes of their experiences as they exist today. *Shoah* is not a historical documentary—a film that seals its subject up in a hazy, distant past—but a movie made entirely in the present tense. For Lanzmann, the Holocaust isn't over: it persists in the traces it has left in the landscape, in the memories it has left in people's minds, and in the echoing absence—the absence of six million people—it has left in European life.

In rejecting the traditional approaches offered by both the documentary and the fiction film, Lanzmann has been led to create a new kind of narration. Though he doesn't come from a film background (before embarking on *Shoah* more than ten years ago, he worked with Jean-Paul Sartre on the French magazine *Les temps modernes*), Lanzmann has found his way independently to the extreme, avant-garde terrain occupied by such filmmakers as Jean-Luc Godard, Jean-Marie Straub, and Michael Snow. The miracle of *Shoah* is that it is able to make its radical formal strategies accessible and meaningful to mainstream audiences. The film is not only a work of high moral force but an aesthetic breakthrough as well—and these two qualities are ultimately inseparable.

Shoah (the word is Hebrew for "holocaust") is not so much a film about an event—which would imply that the event was ultimately comprehensible, digestible—as it is a film *around* an event. For nine and a half hours (the film is shown in two parts over two evenings), Lanzmann circles the fringes of an unimaginable horror, trying various paths of entry, following them for a while, and then moving on to others. The initial paths come around again, and Lanzmann explores them a little further. Slowly, this process of circling reveals the correspondences between the film's different sections as the images of one blend with the spoken words of another, as the same expression crosses the eyes of an Auschwitz survivor living in New York and a Treblinka survivor living in Israel, as Polish peasants from different villages repeat the same gesture—a finger drawn across the throat—as they speak of the vanished Jews. Lanzmann's circular narration accomplishes something that a standard, step-by-step linear narration could not: it gives a sense of the physical outlines of the thing, of its truly global vastness (the languages on the soundtrack include French, German, English, Polish, Hebrew, Greek, Yiddish, and Italian), and it gives a new kind of dimension, a sense of the sufferings buried within sufferings, of the countless individual crimes contained within the ungraspable whole. Where a linear narration would necessarily impose a certain logic and reasonableness on the unfolding events, Lanzmann's approach reveals the madness and chaos. Just as no search has yet turned up a single Nazi command to implement the "final solution," so does *Shoah* suggest that the Holocaust was an event without internal structure, that it proceeded in different ways at different places, largely improvised by the Nazi bureaucrats who found themselves in power.

In questioning survivors, Lanzmann avoids general, impressionistic questions—the "How do you feel?" of TV newsmen—focusing instead on the minutiae of everyday life. In the death camps, where did the members of the Jewish work details live? How were the transports unloaded, and by what route were the victims moved from the railroad sidings to the "undressing rooms" to the "showers"? Talking to a Jewish barber whose job it was to cut the women's hair before they entered the gas chamber, Lanzmann asks him to describe every individual snip: no, the women's heads were not shaved, because that would have made them suspicious; instead, they were given close but careful trims, yielding enough hair to suit the Nazis' obscure purposes while leaving enough to convince the victims that they would live beyond the next five minutes. As the barber recounts these tiny facts, he speaks carefully and forcefully, then suddenly breaks down. Lanzmann keeps the camera rolling as the barber struggles to collect himself, but this isn't the emotional exploitation of the six o'clock news: Lanzmann's refusal to cut away is itself an act of courage, as much as the barber's is in daring to remember. The decent thing to do would be to cut away, but decency counts for very little against the need to put these things on the record.

Lanzmann's working title for the film, according to an interview he gave to the French magazine *Cahiers du Cinéma*, was "The Place and the Word," and the whole impact and originality of *Shoah* are contained in the space between those two terms. The witnesses speak—not just survivors, but also Nazi officials and residents of the Polish villages that bordered on the death camps—and their words take root in the landscapes Lanzmann returns to again and again. The film is, indeed, as Lanzmann said in the same interview, "a film at ground level, of topography, of geography." Though Lanzmann takes his cameras to Auschwitz, where enough of the original structure remains to give an idea of the workings of the place, the most evocative landscapes are precisely those where there is nothing to see: Treblinka, where the buildings were plowed under by the Nazis themselves in an attempt to hide their crimes, and Chelmno, where the victims were gassed in trucks and their bodies burned in an open field. Lanzmann examines these empty places—little more than clearings in the midsts of forests—with a lacerating intensity, photographing them from every conceivable perspective, at every hour of the day, in every season of the year. The impression is one of perfect sylvan peacefulness and quiet; except for a cluster of stones raised as monuments, or the outlines of a foundation, the earth has swallowed up all the traces. Yet when we hear the words of a witness (Lanzmann mikes them very closely, with all background sound eliminated; they seem to be speaking right into our ears), the ground yields up its awful secrets: these are, and will remain, damned places.

Between the silence of the fields and the speech of the witnesses, only one sound intervenes—the steady, inexorable clatter of the trains that took the Jews of Europe to the obscure backcountry stations that were, and remain, Auschwitz, Treblinka, Belzec, and Birkenau. The trains have left the strongest traces on the landscape in the form of rusty, overgrown, but still-serviceable steel rails, and Lanzmann has unearthed one of the engineers of those trains, an elderly, grizzled Pole. Lanzmann films him at the controls of a rented locomotive pulling into the sleepy country depot that still bears the name, painted on a white signboard, TREBLINKA. As he stops his train, the engineer looks back to where the boxcars were and smilingly makes an instinctive gesture, drawing his finger across his throat. The end of the line.

The trains punctuate the words of the witnesses and violate the quiet landscapes as they steam through. They become the film's most vivid, demonic image of the Nazi death machine, of its mad efficiency and implacable hunger—lines of force that lead irresistibly, from every direction, to the black hole of the gas chamber. In the last shot of *Shoah*, the train is still running.

Michael Powell and Emeric Pressburger

{April 1986}

The gossip columnists have been patiently tracking the public appearances of Paul Newman and Tom Cruise, both in Chicago for the filming of Martin Scorsese's *The Color of Money*. But Scorsese's film (a Walt Disney production, it is a sequel to Robert Rossen's 1961 *The Hustler*) has also brought another visitor to the city, and if his name hasn't intrigued the columnists quite as much as Newman's, it is nevertheless a name with a distinguished place in film history: Michael Powell.

Between 1939 and 1956, working in close collaboration with screenwriter Emeric Pressburger, Powell created a series of 18 films that stands as the most stimulating, inventive, and expansive body of work in the British cinema. *The Red Shoes*, his 1948 musical drama of a ballet dancer whose life is consumed by her art, is perhaps his best-known film in America, but viewers of Channel 11, which owns a large number of Powell-Pressburger films, ought to be equally familiar with *49th Parallel* (released in the United States as *The Invaders*), *The Life and Death of Colonel Blimp*, *I Know Where I'm Going*, *A Matter of Life and Death* (retitled *Stairway to Heaven* in the States), and *Black Narcissus*.

But television, with all due respect, isn't the ideal place to see films as large and finely textured as these. By a stroke of luck, Ian Christie, a British film scholar and the author of two books on Powell and Pressburger, is in Chicago for one year as the visiting director of the Film Center of the School of the Art Institute; Christie has programmed an extensive retrospective, drawing on British sources for high-quality, newly restored prints (in some cases incorporating footage never before seen in the United States), to coincide with Powell's visit. It isn't unusual to have a filmmaker present for the opening of a retrospective, but I can't recall another time when the honoree has been around for the entirety of the presentation.

Powell has been a personal friend and professional adviser to Scorsese for many years (he counseled Scorsese on the black-and-white design of *Raging Bull* and more recently helped put the screenplay of *After Hours* into its final shape), though at first it's hard to see what a British gentleman of Powell's generation could possibly have in common with the urban, ethnic, volatile Scorsese. But, separated as they are by age and sensibility, both filmmakers share a passionate commitment to the medium's ability to restructure reality, to use color, texture, space, and tempo to break down the bland surfaces of the physical world and penetrate to that other dimension of energy, desire, and emotion. For Powell, as for Scorsese, the camera has never been a passive recording instrument; it is in the camera's inherent shortcomings, in its inability to fully reproduce the world that stands before it, that both directors find the possibility for personal expression—for transforming what is merely seen into a subjective vision. Not only can the camera be fooled—the camera must be fooled.

Here is one instance, from among many, of the creative use that Scorsese has made of Powell's example: in *The Life and Death of Colonel Blimp* (1943), Powell introduces a flashback by having the main character (an elderly, hidebound British officer, played in a mountain of old-age makeup by Roger Livesey) dive into one end of a swimming pool in a Turkish bath. The camera pans up, following his body as he swims underwater and emerges at the far end as the young man he was 40 years in the past. The shot is continuous, without a trace of the cut that would have allowed Powell to stop the camera, remove Livesey's makeup, and put him back in the pool. It wasn't until the third time I saw the film that I realized how it was done: the elderly man at the beginning of the shot isn't Livesey, but a double (we see him only from the rear); in the split second that the camera loses him as it begins its pan up to the far end of the pool, the young Livesey, out of camera range, pushes off and starts to swim. All of the beauty in this moment of magical rebirth (that it is a rebirth is reinforced by the water imagery) springs from the fact that no trick photography has been used: the shot is whole and complete; the unity of time and space has not been violated. What we see is impossible, yet, from the way it is shown to us, we know it is real.

At the end of *After Hours*, the hero (Griffin Dunne), trapped inside a plaster body cast much as Livesey was encased in his old-age makeup, bounces out of the rear of a moving van and crashes into the street in front of an office building. The cast shatters, and the camera pans up as he picks himself up, dusts himself off, and approaches the huge golden gates that bar the building's entrance—which then swing open, with a supernatural glide, and admit him as if he were entering a child's vision of the kingdom of heaven. Scorsese has repeated Powell's ingenious staging. Clearly, the violent fall from the van would have killed any actor, and Dunne has simply stepped in (again, in the split second that the camera loses sight of the body as it begins its upward tilt) and taken the place of the dummy thrown from the truck. Scorsese has adapted the effect to his own ends: what was, in *Blimp*, a very moving image of rebirth becomes, in *After Hours*, a highly ironic rendition of death and transfiguration (the paradise that Dunne ascends to turns out to be his own office, presided over by a benevolent, incorporeal computer-god). Yet the impact of the shot springs from the same paradoxical alignment of the incontrovertibly real (the seamless continuity of the shot) and the utterly fantastic (the camera shows us a man being killed—the impact is horribly vivid—and the same man walking away). Like Powell, Scorsese has taken advantage of the trust that we automatically put in the camera (it can show us only what's there, or so we believe) at the same time that he has capitalized on what he knows to be the camera's fundamental imperfection (in this case, a field of vision much narrower and less mobile than that of the human eye).

Powell's predilection for effects such as these made him very much an outsider in the British cinema of his time, which was (much as it continues to be) preoccupied with narrow notions of "realism"—drab dramas about drab people, as epitomized in the work of David Lean (*Brief Encounter*) and Carol Reed (*The Stars Look Down*). In his most recently published study of Powell and Pressburger, *Arrows of Desire*, Ian Christie links their films to a very different British tradition, "the proud, popular tradition that runs from Bunyan and Blake, through Dickens, Kipling, Chesterton, Wells, and Shaw" and incorporates a wide streak of the visionary, fantastic, and willfully eccentric. Occasionally, the work of Powell and Pressburger dealt with overtly supernatural themes (in *A Matter of Life and Death*, an RAF pilot accidentally survives a crash in which he was "meant" to die, and a celestial emissary is sent to pick him up); more often, the supernatural element is latent, expressed through structuring devices (in *Blimp*, the colonel is involved with three women during the 40 years we follow him, all of them played by Deborah Kerr), décor (the erotic allure that permeates the studio-created India of *Black Narcissus*), or the inflections of camera angles and composition (under the gaze of Powell's camera, the contemporary Scottish landscape of *I Know Where I'm Going* takes on the animistic coloration of the Gaelic myths that underlie the plotting).

These are the secret energies that Powell strives to express, yet, as *The Red Shoes* makes clear, their source is as much psychological as otherworldly: by counterpointing the Hans Christian Andersen fairy tale of a girl who is punished for accepting a pair of magic dancing shoes with the modern story of a young ballerina whose dedication to her art costs her her chance for human love, the film mingles the archetypal and the morbidly neurotic. The supernatural is as likely to be crushingly destructive (*Black Narcissus*, *The Red Shoes*) as it is to be liberating (*I Know Where I'm Going*, *A Matter of Life and Death*); the only certainty is that it arises to answer desires already present within the characters.

It's likely that Powell's work seems more meaningful and coherent to us now than it did at the time of its first release. The standards of realism are no longer so stringent, and the modern cinema that began with the French New Wave has accustomed us to accepting the kinds of radical breaks in tone (*Blimp* moves blithely from blunt wartime propaganda to acidic social satire to delirious romanticism) and sudden explosions of style (a sneezing-powder gag in *The Elusive Pimpernel* produces little flurries of animated sparks) that once earned Powell and Pressburger accusations of inconsistency and tastelessness. These films have found their echo not only in Scorsese's work but also in films as diverse as Neil Jordan's *The Company of Wolves*, Francis Ford Coppola's *The Cotton Club*, and Terry Gilliam's *Brazil*. Still, the real things are as good as they ever were, and perhaps better.

Home Video

{September 1986}

September is the time when Hollywood traditionally takes the month off. The summer blockbusters are winding up their runs, and the kids are too concerned with going back up to school to work up much interest in new releases. Nothing much comes out in September (and for the first two weeks, nothing at all), apart from a few low-budget exploitation pictures and action films that would have virtually no chance of seeing an actual theater screen during any of the busier months.

For the movie junkie, it's time to turn to alternative sources. Though VCRs have been around only for two years, I'm already finding it hard to remember how I used to survive September—surely not by going out into the fresh air and sunshine. When there's nothing to see on the big screen, it's a comfort to know that those little plastic boxes are waiting for me down at the video store. Here's the chance I've been waiting for to catch up with *Friday the 13th Part V*, *Revolution*, *Maxie*, and all the other pictures I took a pass on during flusher periods.

I'm glad the video store is there, yet in a way I wish it weren't. I'm cursed with an inbred Midwestern lassitude, so the last thing I need is another excuse not to rouse myself—why bother to drive five miles to see something such as *Out of Bounds* when the videocassettes will be begging from the shelves within a few months? But even the most hopeless movie is better in a theater. It's just simple human kindness to give every film its best shot and see it the way it was meant to be seen—in a big room, in the dark, and with other people.

I'll grant VCR one thing: my home system does give me better sound than the systems in a number of theaters I could name. And the image, though tiny, is generally in focus, which isn't always the practice at many of today's multiscreen complexes, where movies often run unattended while the projectionist dashes from booth to booth. Still, even a sloppy presentation can't alter the fundamental difference between movie theaters and living rooms. In a movie theater, the film *is* the environment: the image is huge, commanding, self-sufficient. In a living room, the film is only a part of another environment, one visual element among many, always susceptible to interruption or distraction. The phone doesn't ring when you're at the movies; there's no way the real world can get you.

As critic Fred Camper noted in an antivideo polemic in a recent issue of the avant-garde journal *Spiral*, even the rounded corners of the TV screen seem designed to undermine the impact and integrity of the image. The sharp, black borders that define the world of a movie give way to something soft and mushy, a lack of definition that deprives the filmmaker of one of his most powerful tools—the ability to leave things out, to focus his gaze with pinpoint specificity. At home, the cat lounging next to you on the sofa is as much a part of the world of the movie as the action on the screen; it all belongs to the same visual continuum. And it's a simple, sad, technological fact that, no matter how much TV receivers have improved in the past few years, video is incapable of capturing the same range of color, varying intensities of light, and accuracy of resolution as even the most primitive film stock. Even Super 8, the home-movie format, scores better than video on every applicable standard; compared with that of 35- or 70-millimeter film used in commercial theaters, the video image is just a smeary blur, an Edison cylinder next to a CD.

Jean-Luc Godard, the French filmmaker, recently proposed the term "reproduction" as a workable description of a film seen on videotape, as in "I saw the reproduction of *Casablanca* on TV last night" rather than "I saw *Casablanca*." It's a neat formulation, one that acknowledges the qualitative difference of the experience as well as providing a good alibi. Who has the time to trot down to the Art Institute every time you want to look at a Picasso, particularly when that big, fat retrospective book is sitting on the shelf? Granted, the Renoirs (Auguste) available on postcards come off better than the Renoirs (Jean) available on videotape (the public-domain copies of *The Rules of the Game* and *Boudu Saved from Drowning* currently in circulation are truly horrendous), but in both cases the simulations at least serve to remind you of the originals.

This is the truly redeeming facet of video: its value as a reference tool. I keep a small library of films I've taped off TV, and though I seldom watch them, it's good to know that when I need to check a shot or a line from *The Searchers* or *Citizen Kane*, it's not much harder than looking up a passage in a novel. Film studies was such a vague, undisciplined field for so many years precisely because the materials were so hard to come by: imagine being an English major if you could peek at *Macbeth* only two or three times a year. Video, for the first time, puts the texts in the students' hands; the field seems ready for a major flowering.

Not every film, of course, is available on video, and that's the catch: the range of what's out there seems downright bizarre. Even a video store that is extremely well stocked with esoteric films, such as Video Adventure in Evanston or Facets Multimedia on Fullerton, offers a much narrower choice of titles than a revival house such as the Music Box. Sure, you can check out virtually the entire oeuvre of Charles Bronson, but as far as I know not one single film by Josef von Sternberg is available, only one Preston Sturges movie is out (*Unfaithfully Yours*, probably in order to cash in on the recent remake), and once you get away from the two or three best-known films of such crucial directors as Orson Welles, Howard Hawks, John Ford, Fritz Lang, and Ernst Lubitsch, forget it. With foreign films, the situation is much worse: you can see a fair amount of Ingmar Bergman and François Truffaut, but usually the soundtracks have been dubbed into English; a number of foreign classics (such as the Renoir films mentioned above) have fallen out of copyright and are available from the discount houses, yet the print quality is generally so poor that you can't even read the subtitles. One video company, Media Home Entertainment, recently conducted a brave experiment by releasing Akira Kurosawa's *The Hidden Fortress* with the top and bottom of the frame masked down in order to preserve (approximately) the original dimensions of the film's wide-screen image. But this kind of respect is genuinely radical in an industry where no one thinks twice about releasing Cinerama film *How the West Was Won* on videocassette with no masking of any kind—a format that will allow exactly one-third of the original image to be seen. If a paperback house were to reissue *Gone with the Wind* with two-thirds of the pages randomly torn out, I don't think the public would take it lying down. And yet, every time you pop a Panavision or CinemaScope film into your VCR, you're witnessing exactly the same act of vandalism.

VCRs aren't going to go away: there were 30 million in use at last count, which represents one out of every three TV-owning households in America. But because VCR owners tend to be people (older, with kids) who have lost the moviegoing habit, the boom has had some positive economic effects. By opening what, in effect, is an entirely new audience for films, VCRs have reduced some of the risks of the movie marketplace: no longer is a film's moneymaking life limited to the four to six weeks of a theatrical engagement; it can continue to rack up profits (or, conversely, struggle to recoup its costs) for months and years thereafter on home screens. And because it's adults who rent cassettes (rather than the kids, who now dominate the theaters), Hollywood's need to pander to the adolescent market should, theoretically, be reduced. Suddenly, grown-up movies are commercially viable again. *Variety*, the show-business newspaper, has even cited surveys showing that VCRs are good for the theatrical box office: their interest in movies reawakened by what they've seen at home, people are rediscovering the pleasure of going out.

These are developments that ought to encourage more, better, and different movies, and no one could argue with that. Yet, at the same time that video is bringing new economic life to film, it may also be killing the medium aesthetically. The tiny images of network television have already had their influence on the visual vocabulary of film, forcing directors to rely more and more on close-ups that can be read on the small screen while shying away from the long shots and deep-focus compositions that give the movies their power to create genuine dramatic spaces. With the increasing need for films to play equally well in theaters and in homes, this tendency seems likely to increase. The reproductions are slowly supplanting the originals: within a few years, we'll have a whole generation that won't know the difference.

PART 2

From the Top Ten (Reader)

Supervixens

Directed by RUSS MEYER {May 9, 1975}

Russ Meyer's *Supervixens* ends fittingly with references to the Road Runner, Little Orphan Annie, and Porky Pig; for if we wanted to bless Meyer with a tradition, it would have to be that of the Hollywood cartoon. Along with Chuck Jones, Tex Avery, and the other animators at Warner Brothers and MGM in the forties and fifties, Russ Meyer belongs to the class of homegrown American surrealists.

Like the animators, Meyer exploits virtually complete control over the frame to push his films to the extremes of stylization. With *Supervixens*, Meyer bounds effortlessly over the lines of retrograde realism into utter abstraction, and for once the obligatory disclaimer, "Any resemblance between characters in this motion picture and any actual persons, living or dead, is purely coincidental," begins to make some literal sense.

Meyer chooses his actors not for their abilities to convey subtle psychological states, but for the (occasionally too real) plastic qualities of their bodies. Like cartoon characters, Meyer's creations tend to be principles of motion more than recognizable human beings, existing in a realm entirely outside the natural laws of physics, indestructible and indefatigable. One of the *Supervixens*, a young woman distinctively named SuperAngel, is knifed, strangled, drowned, stomped, and electrocuted at the beginning of the film, only to be reborn, phoenixlike on a smoking mountaintop, for the climax—just as a Tex Avery character, flattened by one of the omnipresent giant mallets that make life difficult in cartoons, immediately springs back into living 3-D. Pain is dismissed with the honking of a few bicycle horns on the soundtrack.

Meyer's plot lines are as formalized as his metaphysics. Where *Vixen!* was based on a mathematical permutation of all the possible couplings of its central characters, *Supervixens* tends toward planar geometry. At point A, we find our Apollonian hero going by the archly Meyeresque name of Clint Ramsey, pumping gas at Martin Bormann's Super Service (get it?) and living a less than idyllic life with SuperAngel, a woman best described physically in Meyer's words as "outrageously cantilevered." SuperAngel, sadly, suffers from a character flaw in the form of an all-consuming viciousness. Hot to freak out with the universe, she eventually dumps Clint, after a fistfight brought on by her unjust intimations of unfaithfulness, in favor of Harry Sledge (Meyer has a special genius with proper names), the cop who comes to break up the brawl. Harry, it turns out, is possessed of a few quirks of his own, and, prodded by SuperAngel's allegations of inadequacy, he rechannels his energy into the murder alluded to above. Clint immediately falls under suspicion and hits the road, encountering variously a man who doesn't take it kindly when Clint stoically spurns the advances of his female companion; a farmer with an Austrian mail-order bride who rapes Clint on a structurally unsound hayloft to the tune of "Rock of Ages"; and the six-foot, deaf and mute black daughter of a white motel owner. Now reaching point B on the edge of the Sonora desert, Clint discovers SuperAngel reincarnated as SuperVixen, her personality problems ironed out by the great psychiatrist in the sky, and presently operating a combination gas station and greasy spoon.

Things look good until Harry shows up, cunningly disguised as a fisherman in the middle of the desert, soon kidnapping SuperVixen and staking her out on the top of a mountain as bait to lure Clint to a final test of macho prowess. Decked out in a spiffy Green Beret uniform, Harry lets fly with guns, knives, and a compact bazooka as Clint tries to make it up the side of the mountain to extinguish the fuse of a stick of dynamite strategically placed on SuperVixen's person.

SuperVixen cannily points out to Harry that "All your schemes will fail, because you're evil and we're love." On one level, Meyer, of course, is kidding with dialogue like this, but on another, what she says is perfectly true. Only those two positions exist in *Supervixen*'s moral universe. Evil is characterized as any one of a number of varieties of sexual aberration, from SuperAngel's selfishness to Harry's sadism. Meyer is an underground moralist, but a moralist nevertheless. Harry's macho is caricatured in terms of the artificiality of the gear he adopts to substitute for his virility—his chosen weapons, uniforms, cigars, cars, and come-on lines (and particularly his archetypal mirrored sunglasses) serve to separate him from the sphere of nature and natural sex where Meyer deposits his values.

The settings of Meyer's films, cabins, gas stations, highways, and motels are always on the edges of vast forests or deserts, defining the close relationship his positive characters have with the primal forces of the natural world. Again and again, Meyer returns to the Edenic scene, the couple running naked through the woods or across the sand; a scene he parodies by using the shampoo commercial clichés of slow motion and low angles, but one that by virtue of its constant repetition seems to acquire a peculiar significance. The point is made comically but is not really compromised by the satiric presentation—youth, sex, nature, innocence, and monogamy remain valuable after the drive to sexual hysteria and mechanization has inevitably destroyed itself.

Meyer brings his thematic, narrative, and psychological stylization to focus on the level of his frames. The typical Meyer image is deliberate and formal—strongly composed, evenly lit, and brightly colored. The solid massing of the individual frame contrasts neatly with Meyer's fast-paced analytic montage, which breaks down or revises the apparent spatial simplicity of the compositions, insisting on a multiplication of points of view.

The technique produces a sense of continual vital movement, an energetic play of the filmmaker's imagination across the boundaries of time and space. Meyer's films are purely functions of his own imaginings, but the imaginings are given weight and dimension by the vivacity of their reflection on the screen.

This is turning into a pretty sober-minded discussion of what is, after all, a very funny film. But the fact that Meyer's work can stand up to these dabblings in structural analysis seems to me a large part of the reason why Russ Meyer is the best comedy director working in America today. Like Keaton and Chaplin (but not on the same scale), Meyer creates an internally consistent comic world, a fantasy life that overrides the commonplaces of psychology and corporeality. Meyer has a genuine comic vision, where Mel Brooks and Woody Allen have only a stock of one-liners.

Robin and Marian

Directed by RICHARD LESTER {April 23, 1976}

When Richard Lester made his unlikely comeback in 1973, emerging from five years of obscurity as the director of a costume epic called *The Three Musketeers*, who could tell that he'd decide to become the Cecil B. DeMille of the seventies? For a director of Lester's idiosyncratic tendencies, the swashbuckler might seem like an impossibly tight and limited genre. But it was just those tendencies—after the failures of *Petulia*, *How I Won the War*, and *The Bed Sitting Room*—that had swept him to the point of being virtually unemployable. *The Three Musketeers*, as good as it was, had the air of a commissioned project. If Lester was trying to reestablish his commercial viability, that was understandable. But then he followed with *Juggernaut*, *Royal Flash*, and (now) *Robin and Marian*—and it would be hard to imagine a group of films more unlike those with which he began his career.

Lester has continued to develop as an artist, but he's taken a strange course. From the informal New Wave structures of *A Hard Day's Night* and *The Knack*, he's gone to the traditional, tightly codified Hollywood narratives of *Juggernaut* and *Royal Flash*—a move exactly the opposite of most of his contemporaries. Robert Altman makes his formulaic *Countdown* in 1968 and his *Nashville* in 1975. Richard Lester makes his *How I Won the War* in 1967 and his *Robin and Marian* in 1976.

After four (or five, depending on how you want to count the two-part *Musketeers*) films in the same style, it's hard to accuse Lester of selling out. He's a solid commercial director again, and he wouldn't be making these pictures unless he wanted to. Lester's return to the old forms and formulas represents a deliberate artistic decision. Like Claude Chabrol, in his work with the melodrama, Lester uses the swashbuckler as a way of opening an immediate line of communication with the audience. The audience accepts the familiar ideas—the conventions of the genre—leaving Lester the freedom to then make those ideas unfamiliar, playing off our expectations, reformulating the formula.

The locus of Lester's transformation is the hero. Douglas Fairbanks and Errol Flynn stand behind his characterizations, ideal figures of nobility and courage against which Lester asks us to measure his own much reduced, painfully human protagonists. The weaknesses and failures that Lester ascribes to his heroes aren't the simple products of mechanical, Mel Brooks-ish parody. Lester profoundly respects the ideals of heroism, and so do most of his characters (Malcolm McDowell's Flashman in *Royal Flash* is the only exception, and even he becomes a hero in spite of himself). But Lester insists on a recognition of the hard physical and political limitations of heroism—there can only be ideal men in an ideal world, and the world of Lester's films is far from that. That crisis—of ideals subverted by actuality—is the focus of Lester's concern.

Near the beginning of *Robin and Marian*, Robin pleads with Richard the Lionhearted not to destroy a captured castle occupied only by women and children. Richard denies him; the massacre goes on. If Robin's heroism—in standing up to Richard, who promptly throws him in a dungeon—is necessary in a world where such atrocities can happen, it is also futile. No one man can change the world, but every man must *try*.

It's the sad truth of that contradiction that brings Robin, pushing fifty, back from twenty years of Richard's Crusades to Sherwood Forest, where he hopes to pick up the old pieces and resume his simple, unambiguous battle with the Sheriff of Nottingham—a return to the good old days of bad guys versus good guys. The Crusades were not clean; Sherwood—robbing from the rich and giving to the poor—will be, or so he hopes. But even Sherwood has diminished. Robin is old, Marian is old, and the Sheriff is stronger than ever.

Lester deftly changes the tone of his film—from comedy to tragedy—from scene to scene, and even, at times, within scenes. Robin and Little John struggle to scale a wall, trying to escape the Sheriff. The middle-aged men, heaving and panting as they claw their way to the top, are funny at first. But almost imperceptibly, the emphasis of the scene changes—they're in real danger, and suddenly we're afraid for these two old men who don't seem to know that things have changed, that they can't do what they used to do. The spirit wills, but the flesh can't respond.

Like Archie, the George C. Scott character in Lester's masterpiece *Petulia*, Robin enters middle age with a recognition of the gap between his ambitions and his accomplishments. He hasn't done what he thought he would be able to do—the world is in as much of a mess as it ever was. Only in his love for Marian can he escape the frustrations and petty absurdities of his life. Here, at least, is one plane of perfect and unfettered action. Lester draws the love scenes with an uncommon dignity and compassion. These key scenes, unfortunately, are also those marred most severely by James Goldman's atrocious dialogue. But if the words fumble, the sentiments are clear and graceful, expressed through the understatement of Connery's and Hepburn's performances, and the profound *tendresse* of Lester's framing.

When, in the end, Marian decides that she and Robin must leave the world that has no place for them, Lester fashions an image of their parting—an arrow that arcs into infinity—that crystallizes, for one heartbreaking moment, both the spirituality of the lovers and the transcendence of Robin's heroic quest. The arrow, you could object, is a cliché, but like so much in genre cinema, the image depends on how much truth the director can find in it. And Lester has found a good deal.

Islands in the Stream

Directed by FRANKLIN J. SCHAFFNER {April 29, 1977}

When the project was first announced, Franklin Schaffner seemed like the natural choice to direct *Islands in the Stream*, the film version of Ernest Hemingway's posthumously published novel—natural, but for all the wrong reasons. For the past ten years, Schaffner has been a specialist in prestige productions—serious-minded, ungainly epics based variously on biographies (*Patton*), history (*Nicholas and Alexandra*), and bloated best sellers (*Papillon*). With material like that, it's a wonder that Schaffner has survived at all: some of the big canvas boys, like David Lean and Carol Reed, slipped into obscurity as soon as the vogue for road shows passed; others, like Richard Fleischer, made an uneasy transition back to lower budgets; still others, like Francis Ford Coppola, have managed to convince themselves that the vogue still exists. But Schaffner, to his credit, tackled everything that came his way with the same restraint and dignity, no matter how strong the provocation (*Planet of the Apes*). While he seldom did anything of breathtaking originality, at least he never gave his material anything less than its due. All of his films display a far from contemptible talent for spending money: every dollar shows in a Schaffner film, and every extra counts in the crowd scenes. So given his record, and faced with an expensive property like *Islands*, the producers probably didn't hesitate for long in signing Schaffner—he'd guarantee, at least, a respectful, tasteful, and commercially safe film.

It seemed easy to anticipate what Schaffner would do with the novel: the film would run for about two and a half hours, contain some responsible performances mixed with a few inspiring shots of Caribbean seascapes, and spend most of its energy trying to make structural sense out of Hemingway's sprawling narrative and hopelessly overpopulated cast of characters.

But, thank God, I was wrong: *Islands in the Stream* is the film that finally brings Schaffner out of the shadow of his material and makes the self-effacing craftsman into an artist. It's the first of his films to consistently show the creative force of a director—a director, moreover, of an unusually refined and subtle sensibility. Schaffner has done more than make sense out of Hemingway's haphazard unfinished manuscript; he's reshaped and restructured it, condensing the story and shifting the thematic emphasis, giving life back to the ideas that Hemingway had grown tired of. It's a small, quiet film, running no more than 100 minutes, lacking any epic ambitions, and restricting its scope to a small group of characters—a film, in other words, unlike any that Schaffner has made since *The Stripper* in 1963. But it belongs, unmistakably, to its director, drawing its effects from a detailed and graceful mise-en-scène, achieving a fateful, elegiac tone with careful repetition of visual and dramatic motifs, and acquiring an overriding poignancy from its slow, deliberate rhythms and heartbreaking dissolves.

As a rule, novels shouldn't be compared to films: you don't compare sculptures to symphonies, or paintings to poems, so why should a book and a movie be lumped together? Logic aside, though, I have to admit that I've sometimes preferred the films that have been based on Hemingway novels to the novels themselves. I certainly do in the case of *Islands in the Stream*; and I'd add *A Farewell to Arms*, filmed by Frank Borzage in 1932, and Howard Hawks's masterful 1945 adaptation of *To Have and Have Not*. Borzage completely changed the emphasis of the novel, transforming Hemingway's story of love and war into a study in Christian mysticism, the triumph of love over death. Hawks, for his part, supplied what amounted to a new story. But in both cases the films drew something more than plot from Hemingway: Hawks and Borzage share his gift for compact images and simplicity of expression, a gift that could have made Hemingway into a first-class American film director. Hawks's visual style has sometimes been compared to Hemingway's prose; the clarity of Hawks's characteristic straight-ahead two-shot finds its literary equivalent in Hemingway's sinewy sentences. And if Hemingway expressed himself most effectively through action, he'd find no better cinematic collaborator than Hawks, whose films are conceived almost entirely in terms of physical movements and moral gestures. Hawks and Hemingway were friends sharing a mutual interest in hunting, and it was on one north woods excursion that Hawks made his famous bet: that he could take Hemingway's worst story (naming *To Have and Have Not*) and make a movie out of it. Hawks cheated and set his film in the time before the action of the novel begins, a maneuver that effectively inverted the theme of the book, remaking a story of moral disillusionment into a story of moral awakening. Harry Morgan (Humphrey Bogart), the captain of a charter fishing boat, comes to abandon his stance of cynical self-interest by adopting a woman (Lauren Bacall) and a drunk (Walter Brennan) and joining the Free French fight against the Nazis. Hawks's joy in the rituals of personal bonding replaces Hemingway's morbid fascination with the moral despair of his mercenary gunrunner.

Islands in the Stream shows signs of the influence Hawks's film must have had on Hemingway, a connection that Schaffner's restructuring of the material makes clear: the bewildering array of friends that Hemingway gave his protagonist, Tom Hudson, has been condensed into a single figure, a drunk (or rummy, in Hemingway's preferred phrase) named Eddie, who carries the name and, more or less, the persona of the Brennan character in *To Have and Have Not*. Much of the action has been moved from the shore (where Hudson, a painter and sculptor, maintains his studio) to Hudson's fishing boat, and the final movement of *Islands* has been reworked to fit the story line of Hawks's film: Hudson tries to smuggle a family of refugee

Jews into Cuba, just as Morgan had to land a French resistance officer in the Nazi-held port of Martinique.

Schaffner's use of *To Have and Have Not* isn't a question of idle *hommage* or (God forbid) plagiarism; the resemblance is there to point up the difference. Hawks's film is about the formation of a metaphorical family; Schaffner's is concerned with the forces that have drawn an actual family apart.

Schaffner's Tom Hudson is an older, more deeply flawed version of Hawks's Harry Morgan. Where Morgan remains a loner because he has never learned to trust his fellow creatures, Hudson has known love (through two wives and three children), but still chooses to live in isolation on a remote, thinly settled Gulf Stream island. The island is a place for people, like Tom (George C. Scott) and Eddie (David Hemmings), who couldn't survive anywhere else—a pressure-free playland, where drunkenness and irresponsibility are forgiven. But it's also a place in close contact with the elements, the life of the land and the sea, where an individual learns both self-reliance and a sense of humility. As emotionally incomplete men, Tom and Eddie share a bond, Hudson looking on his friend with a mix of love and pity, but also a vague revulsion, as if Eddie reminds him too much of his own failings. Eddie is no substitute for the family that Hudson has spurned, but this is the strongest relationship that he can maintain, and he is willing to settle for what he can safely have.

Schaffner has divided the narrative into three movements and a prologue, separated by titles. The first section, "The Boys," begins the dissolution of the self-contained world the prologue has portrayed, as Hudson's long-neglected three sons come to spend a summer on the island. At first, Hudson is frightened, sensing their hostility. But the summer wears on, in scenes bridged by Schaffner's lingering dissolves, and the boys learn Hudson's love and awe of the sea, sharing his self-willed loneliness when they see the dim fires of a freighter, torpedoed by a Nazi submarine, burning on the night horizon. The world moves on, without Hudson's knowledge or participation. By the end of the summer, the family bond has been reformed, but as Hudson sees his sons off in the mail plane that will take them back to the mainland, the eldest tells him of his plans to enter the war by joining the Canadian air force. The sequence ends with a montage reminiscent of one of Frank Borzage's finest effects: time and space are violated for the sake of a mystical emotional unity, as Schaffner intercuts shots of Tom writing a letter and his sons reading it, the two younger at a boarding school, the eldest at his squadron base in England, while Scott repeats the words of the letter in voice-over.

In the second section, "The Woman," Hudson is visited by his first wife (Claire Bloom), who tells him first of her plans to remarry and then of the death of their son. Bloom appears throughout as a romantic hallucination; we see her through Tom's eyes, an object of love lost forever. Shaken, Tom decides to return to the mainland, and the third passage, "The Journey," begins with his futile attempt to reject Eddie's friendship, and, thereby, the life of the island. But Eddie, reacting just as he does in *To Have and Have Not*, stows away on Tom's boat. At sea, Hudson finds the burning hulk of a friend's boat; as a sideline to his charter business, he's been running Jewish refugees to Cuba, but an attack by the Cuban coast guard has left him, his crew, and a refugee family stranded. Tom decides to take them in himself—if he can't save his own family, he can at least put his remaining self-respect and skill to work for someone else. By landing the refugees, risking the threat of the Cuban gunboats, Hudson finds a kind of salvation in performing an act of absolute selflessness, making a sacrifice for a group of strangers that he could never bring himself to make for his own wife and children.

Schaffner's visuals are expressive in a way that's becoming rare in American films. There are no stunning, virtuoso shots; instead, the director concentrates on finding smooth, unobtrusive ways of weaving action and image. The most sustained passage in the film, in "The Woman," begins with Hudson unexpectedly meeting his ex-wife in the barroom of the local hotel, develops as the man and woman walk back, along the beach, to the studio, and climaxes as Hudson realizes that his wife has come to tell him of the death of his son. The initial two shots could serve as a model of the use of offscreen space: we first see Tom, sitting at a table, turn and look past the camera. Schaffner then cuts to the reverse angle, finding Claire Bloom framed in the doorway of the hotel. She stands perfectly still, as if she had suddenly materialized there, out of the thin Caribbean air—which is, of course, exactly what she has done, from Tom's point of view. The hallucinatory quality is maintained as they walk up the beach; both are wearing tan and blue clothes that blend with the sand and sky, an image that links Tom, his wife, and the ocean in a mysterious emotional triangle. As they approach the studio, Tom tries to kiss her. She responds, then tells him of her plans to marry another man. The mise-en-scène now emphasizes the space between the two; the ocean, an emblem of Tom's artistic quest, now forces them apart. They pause on the veranda, Tom occupying the left foreground of the frame, partly in shadow, facing the woman who stands back, against the bright light of the sea. The line of the shore and the line of a railing converge on Bloom's figure, tying her, again from Tom's point of view, to a sculpture that stands behind her, near the water. Woman, water, art: the three elements combine to form an image of Tom's lifelong crisis, his inability to reconcile the abstract and eternal with the concrete and personal.

Once inside the studio, Bloom finds a portrait of herself that Tom had drawn during their time together—another of Tom's symbolic attempts to unite his life as an artist and his life as a husband. (Significantly, as an exile he now works only with abstract shapes.) As she takes a seat on the couch, Tom goes into the next room to fix a drink. Suddenly, the real reason for the visit dawns on him. Schaffner shows only the back of Tom's head as he slowly raises his left hand to touch the back of his neck—a delicate, movingly understated shot, making Tom's realization of his final loneliness almost visible.

Islands in the Stream comes so close to greatness at times that its faults seem all the more obvious. Schaffner's failings, for the most part, are banal ones: an entire sequence in which Tom teaches his son the art of deep-sea fishing is lost to mismatched footage (grainy stock shots of the fish, crystal clear shots of the fishermen) and overexplicit dialogue. The latter is at least partly Hemingway's responsibility; many of the film's most ponderous lines seem to have been lifted directly from the novel. But Schaffner's achievement is clear and undeniable; *Islands in the Stream* shows enough skill and sensibility to establish its director, at last, as a significant American filmmaker.

Moses and Aaron

Directed by JEAN-MARIE STRAUB [AND DANIÈLE HUILLET]
{May 13, 1977}

Jean-Marie Straub's *Moses and Aaron* is being offered as part of the "Operas, Opera Stories, and Opera Stars" series at the Art Institute's Film Center, although it hardly fits the mold of the stolid, overproduced, and underdirected filmed opera (inevitably Russian, and complete with smeary Sovcolor) painfully familiar to anyone who has ever taken a music appreciation course in college. *Moses and Aaron* is based on Arnold Schoenberg's 1932 opera, following Schoenberg's score apparently note for note and paying scrupulous attention to his original stage directions. But while Straub remains doggedly faithful to his text, it seems unfair to call *Moses and Aaron* an "opera film" at all. It's no bastard child of music and film, but an integrated, fully realized work in itself.

Straub is one of the most innovative and idiosyncratic filmmakers at work today, and he's earned that reputation, perversely enough, by working almost exclusively with strict adaptations of material from other media. His sources have included artists as diverse as Bertolt Brecht and Johann Sebastian Bach, Heinrich Böll and Pierre Corneille. As a Marxist, Straub is determined to undercut the traditional ideals of authorship and individual genius. There's no creativity in a vacuum for Straub and his fellow materialist filmmakers: art is produced by the interaction of historical and personal forces, and Straub emphasizes the point by selecting sources or subjects that seem purposefully irrelevant to his political concerns. Out of the collision of Straub and Bach, of Straub and Schoenberg, the artist looks for a fruitful synthesis.

It's hard to say where Schoenberg ends and Straub begins in *Moses and Aaron*. The music clearly belongs to its composer, but so, in some sense, do the images. Straub hasn't made a mere record of the opera, he's made a film out of the music. The tone of the score determines the tone of the sequence, the rhythms of the music become the rhythms of the cutting. Music and film blend, not in the facile sense of those coldly remembered rock documentaries of the late '60s, in which every beat was tied to a cut, but in a more profound way: the image is continuous when the score is continuous, fragmented when the score is dissonant. Image and sound anticipate or echo each other, playing a counterpoint.

Straub isn't the most immediately engaging filmmaker in the world, which is to say that *Moses and Aaron* is no *American in Paris*. Vincente Minnelli's 1951 Gershwin film also achieved a remarkable marriage of image and sound, but with Straub we're dealing with something very different. By discarding the traditional audience hooks of linear narrative and character identification, Straub has made his films as difficult to approach as they are to appreciate. Like his mentor Robert Bresson, Straub is less interested in an artistic reflection of reality than he is in the creation of an interior reality. There's little for the spectator to grab hold of on the first viewing. The films create their own, individual systems of meaning, and those systems sometimes become apparent only after the film is over. Straub's films are best seen once, thought about, and then seen again—the pleasure of his work is often an intellectual one, and often it is delayed.

Straub has been making films since 1963. During that time, he's realized only three features (*The Chronicle of Anna Magdalena Bach*, *Othon*, and *Moses and Aaron*) and a handful of shorts, a small output compared to most of his contemporaries. The paucity of Straub's oeuvre reflects not only the difficulty of finding funds for films as recondite as his, but also the extraordinary amount of planning that goes into his work. Every shot has its precise place in the overall design, every theme finds its echo in a subtheme or a rhyming image. The overriding impression I get of a Straub film is one of intensity, an almost frightening concentration. I remember being much relieved, when I met Straub in 1975, to find that he was an easygoing, open man, ready to consider almost any interpretation of his work that was offered. The mental image that we slaphappy Americans have of the archetypal European Marxist/structuralist filmmaker seems to be a horrifying blend of Leon Trotsky and Dr. Frankenstein, a stone-faced automaton who hasn't cracked a smile since May 1968. Straub is no Soupy Sales, mind you, but he is a gentle and reasonable man. You will find this thought a comfort if you chose to brave *Moses and Aaron* (and you should—please don't get me wrong).

Schoenberg's opera tells the story of Moses and the Israelites. Receiving his call from God, Moses despairs of convincing the people of the existence of an eternal, faceless, and nameless deity. God obliges by calling Moses's brother, Aaron, to act as his mouthpiece. Moses has a vision, Aaron will articulate it to the masses, using simple, solid images—the miracles of turning the staff into a serpent, of turning water into blood—to capture the belief of the people if not their understanding. After the 40 days in the desert (bridged in the gap between Act I and Act II), Moses repairs to Mount Sinai to await the word. The Israelites grow anxious in his absence, demanding of Aaron more concrete proof of his god's existence. Aaron gives in by creating the Golden Calf, a temporal, earthly image that immediately sets the Israelites off on a binge of temporal, earthly pleasures. Moses returns with the Law, but, finding everything in chaos, he smashes the tablets. Aaron argues that his image was the only way of keeping the people in the faith; Moses contends that their faith was bought at too great a price—the price of the truth. Act III (which Schoenberg never completed) continues the argument.

The material, of course, is so familiar that it hardly constitutes a story: *Moses and Aaron* is more of a ritual, with every step of the proceedings known and understood. As a ritual, it becomes open to a structural interpretation. It's tempting, although too facile, to assign the fundamental Moses/Aaron opposition to Marx and Lenin. Moses/Marx carries the word of communism, Aaron/Lenin gives it to the people in the form their corrupted minds can understand: state capitalism. So much for ideology. But the opposition is more fruitfully seen as an abstract confrontation of a truth and its symbol, of reality and the means we use to express it. The film becomes a study of how art is used to interpret the world, and opens up into a dizzying series of Chinese boxes: Straub's film is an interpretation of Schoenberg's music, Schoenberg's music is an interpretation of a Bible story, the Bible story is an interpretation of an eternal principle. With each link in the interpretive chain, the issues become more complicated, the "truth" further removed.

As a materialist filmmaker, Straub is dedicated to demystifying his art. In the traditional Hollywood film, technique was meant to be invisible. The audience, supposedly, never noticed the cutting or the framing, the means by which they were drawn into the film—the mise-en-scène worked surreptitiously, putting the spectator into a trancelike state in which he was to mistake everything he saw on the screen for "reality." (That, at least, is the current Marxist theory; for me, the value of American film lies in its subtlety—you can't appreciate the accomplishment of Hawks, Hitchcock, or Ford until you've developed a sensitivity to technique. American films are seen at their best when the viewer takes an active approach, not when he lapses into a coma.) Against this ideologically suspect "illusionism" (to use the Marxist term), Straub posits an obtrusive, unmistakable mise-en-scène meant to shatter the viewer's automatic identification with the drama. In the opening shot of *Moses and Aaron*, Moses is seen praying on sacred ground and receiving the guidance of God. But Straub, for the first few minutes of the shot, shows nothing more than the back of Moses's head, framed in a tight close-up from an unnatural downward angle. As the shot goes on, its artificiality becomes more apparent and more oppressive. We want to see more than the back of a head and a patch of dusty ground—we want to see the man and know him. But this is exactly what Straub wants to prevent. Moses is a character in a film, not a human being, and it can only cloud the issues to pretend otherwise. After some time, the camera moves away from Moses, panning up the side of a hill to the sky above it, and then continuing in a perfect 360-degree pan across the skyline and back to Moses, still standing in the same position. A Straub pan has none of the freedom of, say, a pan in a Renoir film. For Renoir, the character determines the movement of the camera; he moves, the camera moves to follow him. But Straub, again, insists on the artificiality of technique—his pan is a geometrical expression, not a human one. As such, it carries a strange, self-contained beauty. Camera movements and pans—and, in the case of *Moses and Aaron*, even the movements of the actors—take on a new significance in Straub's films because they occur so infrequently. After a lengthy static take, a sudden shift in the camera placement seems to open a whole new dimension on the action.

Like Jean-Luc Godard, Straub has been working to find a new aesthetic to replace traditional (and, to the Marxist, hopelessly reactionary) cinema. But Godard, at this point, seems to have found only a way of destroying the old aesthetic. His post-1968 films are cold and brutal, purposefully so, chopping away at the time-honored notions of art and pleasure. Straub, though, has made a step toward the creation of a new kind of film, one that offers the viewer a new kind of pleasure. Just as Arnold Schoenberg abandoned the standard elements of musical composition in order to create his twelve-tone system, so has Straub taken a new path in filmmaking. Straub's films, for many people, will be as forbidding as Schoenberg's music still is for me, but both men, I think, are worth some effort to understand.

Note: At the time of its release, this film was credited to Jean-Marie Straub. Subsequently it has been properly credited to Straub and his long-time collaborator, Danièle Huillet.

Blue Collar

Directed by PAUL SCHRADER {February 10, 1978}

There's an old school of auteur criticism that divides directors by the jobs they held before they moved behind the camera. Alfred Hitchcock, Vincente Minnelli, and Mitchell Leisen were art directors; their films, consequently, emphasize the expressive qualities of décor. Don Siegel and Hal Ashby were editors; ergo, their work depends on the dynamics of cutting. Billy Wilder, Preston Sturges, and Joseph L. Mankiewicz began as screenwriters; as directors, they tend to emphasize the clear, crisp presentation of dialogue and character.

Like most useful generalizations, this one begins to break down when you take a closer look. Directing is an amalgam of skills, and if one is too often allowed to dominate the others, a style soon goes flat—a problem that few of these filmmakers have had to face. I mention it here only because a new alternative to apprenticeship seems to have arisen in New Hollywood, an alternative that has nothing to do with the traditional route of learning by doing. It's a passive apprenticeship, spent not in the heat and glare of the studio but in the dust and darkness of libraries and screening rooms. It is, of course, Graduate Study—the route chosen by Francis Ford Coppola, Martin Scorsese, George Lucas, Brian De Palma, John Milius, and a number of other up-and-comers. If there's one skill that all of these directors specialize in, it has less to do with making movies than watching them: the ability to shuffle through a personal knowledge of cinema past and come up with evocative allusions (the reference to John Ford's *The Searchers* in *Star Wars*) or borrowed solutions to particular problems (the staging of the wild car ride in *New York, New York* lifted from Minnelli's *The Bad and the Beautiful*). A film school education has its drawbacks, too: there's a certain tendency on the part of some ex-students to make movies exclusively about movies, commenting on old forms and rehashing old genres, as if nothing existed apart from the silver screen—which, given the limits of campus life, might be a sadly accurate reflection of their experience. Still, film school seems to breed a basic respect for the integrity of the image, a respect that the TV graduates (Lumet, Frankenheimer, and so on) don't have. The lost art of mise-en-scène, the concept of the image as the prime vehicle for meaning, surfaces—when it surfaces at all in American films these days—almost exclusively in the work of the film school grads.

Paul Schrader took his graduate studies a little more seriously than most of his colleagues, actually finishing (and publishing) his thesis—a study of "Transcendental Style," as he defined it, in the work of Robert Bresson, Yasujirō Ozu, and Carl Dreyer. As a screenwriter, Schrader took an equally serious interest in pursuing big bucks—he reportedly gathered upwards of half a million dollars each for his scripts for *The Yakuza*, *Obsession*, *Taxi Driver*, and *Rolling Thunder*. Consequently, he has earned a strange reputation as part intellectual, part entrepreneur, a description that could be applied equally well to his first film as a full-fledged director, *Blue Collar*: it exists half as an exercise in the austere stylistics of Ozu, and half as yet another vehicle for the omnipresent Richard Pryor. Amazingly, it works very well on both counts. It's Pryor's best film, finally giving him a chance to exploit the neurotic, self-destructive streak of his screen persona, and it's also one of the most tightly controlled and technically accomplished first films I can remember.

Blue Collar is the story of three men—Pryor, Yaphet Kotto, and Harvey Keitel—who share the oppressive monotony of a Detroit automobile-assembly line; molding, bolting, and welding the cold metal that becomes, at the end of a long day of anonymous ministrations, a Checker cab. Schrader describes the milieu with remarkably little condescension: after a stifling day at the plant (short for "plantation," as Pryor observes), the men retire to a spare cinder-block bar to blow off steam, and then they slink home to their private lives—Keitel to a drab duplex with his wife's needlepoint portraits of John Kennedy on the walls; Kotto to a bachelor pad decorated in screaming crimson; and Pryor to his wife and three kids (six for tax purposes) permanently planted in front of the color television set. The TV is Pryor's private obsession; he busted his hump to buy it, and it's gonna stay on, goddamn it, even though it means watching the Sambo farce of *Good Times* and *The Jeffersons* (*Blue Collar*, not incidentally, was produced by Norman Lear's T.A.T. Communications). The television set is the prize the system gives Pryor for grinding away his life; this tinny materialism is all he knows, all he has been taught, and he will work his soul away to pay for it—and to pay off the loans he's taken from the company credit union to buy the things he can't afford. He doesn't make money, he only pays it back—the system has him hooked, and there's no way out.

No way, that is, until he joins Kotto and Keitel—both in similar financial straits—in a plot to plunder the safe of their thoroughly corrupt and ineffectual union. They make off with a disappointing $600, but Pryor finds a mysterious green ledger, filled with what seems to be records of illegal loans made from union funds. For what may be the first time in their lives, the three men are faced with a monumental moral decision: whether to turn the ledger in to the slightly sinister FBI agent who has been investigating the union's activities or sell the book back to the union bosses.

The decision—what to do with this sudden hint of power—lies at the center of Schrader's film. Pryor can be a hero or a pragmatist—both choices have their awards and punishments. But the important thing is that here, at last, is a taste of free will: the one thing the system will not tolerate.

Blue Collar proceeds like a theorem to its inevitable, despairing conclusion—it has the abstract, irresistible drive of pure, cold logic, a drive reflected in the sleek narrative and in the utter dispassion with which the camera fixes the characters. As in Ozu, the frame becomes an enclosure: the characters are free to move within it, but seldom can they leave it, walk offscreen, without the camera nailing them again from another, equally powerful position. The few camera movements are highly formal; in a curiously unsuspenseful chase sequence near the end of the film, they seem to be describing random arcs in the air rather than following the flight of an object. Schrader also uses Ozu's device of bridging scenes with shots of still, depopulated cityscapes—a resonant, almost mystical effect that, in Ozu's work, stirs a momentary realization of the fragility of human life as opposed to the permanence of nature and things. For Schrader, it is not nature that is permanent, but—in the colossal, impersonal factories—the system, which uses men only as fuel and seems perfectly capable, in these isolated, threatening shots, of getting along without them. There's a repeated shot of an electric billboard that tallies the number of cars rolling off Detroit's production lines; as it ticks away, coolly and steadily, it could well be registering the passage of souls.

Again, as in Ozu, the restricting, formal style clashes with the considerable warmth of the characters: Kotto is particularly appealing as a rough, bearish ex-con who operates on unbridled hedonism and utter selflessness (naturally, the system reserves its harshest fate for him). These are vital, engaging people, fighting forces they can see only dimly, and there is a subtle horror in the tension between their personal spark and the cold, unblinking gaze of the camera.

Blue Collar shares the ideological impetus of much recent French film. Although the Marxist hard core would probably resent the hopeless tone of the conclusion, this is one of the few politically self-aware films to come out of the commercial American cinema—a development even more remarkable considering that it comes from Universal, a studio with a longtime reputation as a sausage factory. Maybe they'll let Schrader do *Airport '79*—Robert Bresson meets Charlton Heston. But until then, Yasujirō Ozu meeting Richard Pryor will do just fine. Schrader was a good graduate student; he's an even better director.

Luna

Directed by BERNARDO BERTOLUCCI {October 26, 1979}

There may be better films this year, but there won't be any riskier ones than *Luna*, Bernardo Bertolucci's maddening, perverse, melodramatic, and uncomfortably personal examination of the ties that bind a mother and son. Perhaps that should be Mother and Son, for, despite the dramatic specificity of the characters, Bertolucci is less interested in personal psychology than in archetypal psychological forces—impulses that transcend personality and operate on the level of universal instinct, of primal myth.

The film begins with a moment of psychological displacement—a baby betrayed by his mother—and builds to a final moment of psychological integration. On one level, we see the birth of a neurosis followed by its eventual removal, played out in impeccably Freudian terms and completed with the castrating slap that silences the Oedipal impulse. In that sense, the film is perfectly linear, perfectly logical. But Bertolucci thwarts our easy reading of psychological cause and effect by perversely drawing us away from the characters. This broad, boisterous melodrama—full of emotions raging out of control—is shot almost entirely in alienating long shots and further abstracted by highly formal, self-conscious camera movements that often have little immediate bearing on the action.

The camera becomes a show in itself, distracting our attention from the drama. It's as if a third presence were in on this intimate struggle of mother and son, an invisible hand pulling invisible strings. That presence, of course, is Bertolucci, standing between the audience and the spectacle, making himself as conspicuous as possible. An authorial voice sounds throughout the film, sometimes drowning out the speech of the characters. The voice introduces digressions, offers asides, carries on its own discourse. It confronts the characters and shoves them away, puts them into conflict and then runs and hides when the conflict becomes too intense. Bertolucci created the characters; they belong to him, and there's no doubt whose feelings they represent. But when the characters merge with the actors, they acquire a life of their own, a dynamic independent of the director. Bertolucci's improvisational method encourages the separation of director and character, artist and creation. By depending so much on what the actor brings to the part—to appear in a Bertolucci film, as Brando discovered, is to some degree to write your autobiography—Bertolucci purposefully lets his people get away from him. They do things that surprise him, and, I think, sometimes shock him, too. His camerawork carries on a dialectic with the characters, constantly defining and redefining the director's attitude toward them. His camera moves in one direction, his actors wander off in another, interrupting his elegant pans with sudden bursts of emotion. In one particularly wrenching moment in *Luna*, mother and son strike out at each other. They fall to the floor, their fight hidden by the black body of an intervening piano. We can't see them, because the director can't bear to look at them.

I can't remember another film that displays such a deep degree of tension between the director and his actors. Bertolucci's camera criticizes his players, sometimes by refusing them close-ups, sometimes by settling down and passively recording their histrionic excesses. A painfully prolonged shot of Matthew Barry (the son) playing a drum solo with a table setting hardly seems calculated to endear him to us forever. Yet, Bertolucci gives him his head. He can't cut away, either because as a projection of his own ego, Bertolucci loves Barry so much that he can't deny him anything, or because as a projection of his own ego, Bertolucci resents the actor so deeply that he is more than willing to let him make a fool of himself. Both alternatives are probably true. Similarly, many of the close shots of Jill Clayburgh (the mother) are aggressively unflattering, emphasizing the cartoonish quality of her face through a subtle misuse of short lenses. Bertolucci gives her scenes that no actress, however talented, could play plausibly—flights of high melodrama that require either a complementary melodramatic style, or the affectation of a blank nonstyle that would surrender the actress to the action. Clayburgh's largely straightforward, naturalistic line readings strike neither extreme, and she is left as a strained principle of realism operating in a highly unrealistic mise-en-scène. Still, that discontinuity seems to be exactly what Bertolucci is looking for: *Luna* is a film that tears itself apart.

Luna is linear in the sense that it plants a Freudian puzzle in the first reel and resolves it in the last. But the body of the film is a pattern of endless digressions, drawing in characters and scenes that are only marginally supported by the plot. There are homosexual flirtations (one each for mother and son), disquisitions on the art of Giuseppe Verdi, snatches of Marilyn Monroe movies, comic interludes involving Fidel Castro, asides on life in Algeria, and incidental illustrations of the relation of life and art. None of it makes a lot of sense on a dramatic level (and the abrupt changes of tone, as Bertolucci doubtless intended, are extremely disconcerting), but the director's design, here as in *1900*, is less narrative than encyclopedic. Everything belongs in his film, simply because it happened in front of his camera. The digressions may illuminate the main action, or they may obscure it. Meanwhile, the titanic struggle of mother and son continues.

Clayburgh plays an American opera singer who flees to Italy, her teenage son in tow, after the death of her husband. (The death, itself, is presented as an act of will on the part of the director, as he conspicuously moves his camera to an open window to witness the husband's heart attack behind the wheel of a car—it's as if the camera movement caused the seizure.)

Young Joe, neglected by his mother, falls in with a bad crowd, and soon he's mainlining heroin at his birthday party. Joe's druggy, punk attitudes seem to belong to some '50s exploitation film—*High School Confidential*, for example—in which the main effect of drug abuse is talking out of turn in class. Joe's addiction has few physical complications—apart from a brief, almost lyrical bout of withdrawal pains—which demonstrates Bertolucci's almost complete lack of interest in the literal implications of his plot. For Bertolucci, the addiction isn't a problem—it's an image to be explored.

We know early on, of course, that the drug is a substitute for Mom, but which Mom is it? Loving, protective, mothering Mom, or sexual, threatening, smothering Mom? Joe himself doesn't seem quite sure, and Mom, for her part, isn't prepared for either role. As a performer, she has learned to project emotion to hundreds of people, but as a person, she seems incapable of one-to-one communication. Joe demonstrates his needfulness by going into withdrawal, and his mother responds (although with some reluctance) in a supremely protective, motherly way—she goes out and buys him another fix. Only when that doesn't quite work does Clayburgh turn to alternative two, gently masturbating her son as he lies like a baby against her breast. The gesture isn't as erotic as it is pitying, sad, and desperate. If these two people can't talk to each other, then sex is the only line open.

Mother and son achieve their intimacy in a dark, closed room—a private world much like Brando's apartment in *Last Tango in Paris*. There are other echoes of Bertolucci's past films in *Luna*: Joe dances with a homosexual man in an evocation of *The Conformist*, the Algerian boy provides a double for Joe out of *Partner*, and the farm used in *1900* makes an unbilled guest appearance. But Bertolucci's most important quotes are the theme of incest from *Before the Revolution* (the aunt and nephew of the earlier film become the mother and son of the more mature work) and the search for the father from *The Spider's Stratagem*—for, as Joe finds out, the man who died in America wasn't his natural parent. *Luna*, on top of everything else, thus becomes an anthology work: a collection and summation of Bertolucci's themes, and perhaps an attempt to resolve them.

The existence of the missing father is revealed on a trip through Parma, Bertolucci's childhood home. And when the phantom figure emerges from the mise-en-scène, there's little doubt who he is. The invisible presence from the first part of the film has materialized at last: the director becomes the father, stepping into the action that he has determined, unseen, all along. The missing father, of course, is revealed to have a mother complex of his own, and his scenes with Joe become a confrontation of man and child—a delirious collision of past and future that somehow produces, in its emotional shock, a unified vision of the present, obsessions lifted and emotional imbalances redressed. In the last sequence of *Luna*, all of its tensions relax: Mom sings, father and son embrace, the family heals, and the great silver moon of the title looks down to give its blessing.

The moon imagery that runs through the film seems coarse and obtrusive by ordinary standards, but it is here, I think, that Bertolucci effects his ultimate transformation of Freud's predeterminism into something grand, mystical, and eternal, turning a Freudian symbol into a Jungian archetype. The image doesn't "symbolize" the action as much as it guides it—as when, for example, Joe is interrupted in the midst of a tryst with a teenage girl by the sudden appearance of the moon, reminding him where his real priorities lie. The moon is a traditional image of female sexuality, but Bertolucci also allows it its full range of emotional connotations: it's something cold and remote, as well as warm and romantic. If it is sex with its divisiveness and destructiveness (*Last Tango*), it is also love with its promise of intimacy and fulfillment. All of these things are contained in the Mother, and Bertolucci has worked them out—more to his benefit and satisfaction than ours, perhaps, but with courage and candor nonetheless.

The usual line on films as radical as this is that you'll either love 'em or hate 'em. I found myself loving and hating *Luna* indiscriminately, and sometimes simultaneously. I hated its hermeticism, its inconsistency, and its lack of discipline, but I loved its size, its audacity, and its complete unpredictability. The film may turn out to be more valuable for its outrages than for its accomplishments: if it doesn't satisfy, it still gives a damn good shake. Meanwhile, it's worth bearing in mind that one of the more pertinent derivatives of the Latin *luna* is "loony."

Atlantic City

Directed by L O U I S   M A L L E {May 22, 1981}

When Burt Lancaster gets grabbed by the lapels in *Atlantic City*, he barks back, "Don't touch the suit"—and the line, as written by John Guare, seems to bounce back about 40 years, to the films noirs Lancaster starred in in his youth. What's remarkable is that it bounces forward again and makes an impact in the present tense. It's not hard to wring pathos from an aging movie star quoting from his glory days, nor is it hard to use a line like that for campy laughs: both effects depend on an easy displacement of the mythic past into the ironic present, with tears or snickers drawn from a sense of diminution. But there's something in Guare's placement of the line, and in Lancaster's unselfconscious reading, that cuts the quote marks from it—it's no longer a campy zinger but an honest expression of character, the character of a man who's constantly applying the past to the present, trying to prove to himself that he's still the man he used to be. *Atlantic City* is a film about endings and beginnings and how they blur together: how a dead city can give birth to a new one, how an old man can love a young woman, how the present fulfills the past by destroying it. The dialogue John Guare has written for *Atlantic City* embodies the same tension between old and new, and the same harmony: it is as terse and succinct as the dialogue of a '40s film, yet the curling, discursive rhythms of the conversations are those of the present. Guare is a superbly expressive writer: he puts his ideas in the shape of his speech.

Atlantic City was directed by Louis Malle, but Guare, I think, is its real auteur. It's his first solo work for film, following a coscreenplay credit on Milos Forman's 1971 *Taking Off*; he's best known, of course, for his stage plays—*Landscape of the Body*, *The House of Blue Leaves*, *Bosoms and Neglect*—which together make up what is probably the most substantial body of work of any contemporary American playwright. Stage talent doesn't always transfer to movies, as David Mamet recently proved with the plodding linearity of his screenplay for *The Postman Always Rings Twice*, but Guare seems a natural. He already has a firm grasp of movie rhythms, of how to launch a short scene and round it off, of how to play scenes against one another for contrasts in tone and texture. (Guare gets a dialogue going, not only between his characters, but also between his sequences.) Where Guare, in his stage work, embraces the conventions of the stage, restricting his action to a few long scenes played among a handful of characters on one or two sets, he moves easily to the more open conventions of film, spreading his script out over an entire city, drawing in a dozen or more characters, breaking his continuous, concentrated scenes into fluid units.

Movies give Guare the concept of simultaneity, the ability to launch separate but related actions. *Atlantic City* begins with two levels of action; as the film goes on they merge, and at the end they separate again. The picture opens on an expository passage that has a beauty beyond its function: we watch as an old man (Burt Lancaster's Lou) peeks out from behind the curtains of his darkened apartment, looking across an air shaft to where Sally (Susan Sarandon) stands at her kitchen window, stripped to the waist, rubbing fresh lemon juice over her arms and her chest. Malle doesn't really do justice to the perverse eroticism of the scene, though he and his cinematographer, Richard Ciupka, have devised a lighting scheme that turns Sally's gestures into a mysterious ritual, an ablution. A yellow highlight gives her a glow in the dark room, across the twilit air shaft; it picks her out like a spotlight on a stage or a candle on an altar. What's important for Guare's conception is Sally's separateness, the sense of self-containment communicated by her ritual (its meaning is known only to her) as well as the distance between her and Lou, conveyed by the spatial arrangement of the set. Guare is laying out the two levels of his screenplay—the contrasts of youth and age, beginning and end—but it will be several reels before the two levels connect. And yet the connection is already there, postulated at some deep level; here are two people alone together, separately sharing an intimacy.

A scene such as that might normally be shot from Lou's point of view, but Malle, in one of the shrewdest decisions he makes in the film, doesn't emphasize the subjective shots—it's a voyeuristic moment for Lou, but not, particularly, for the audience. The camera is already bridging the gap between the two characters, not by moving directly to Sally's room to her point of view, but by occupying the space between them. Though Lou, as the privileged spectator, gains the edge in audience identification (we watch him watch Sally), Malle doesn't throw us completely on his side; in his shots of Lou, he keeps the camera back far enough to let us see the emptiness of Lou's apartment, an image of his own loneliness, his own isolation. A beautiful balance is struck: the sequence gets us inside Lou enough to care about him, yet Sally remains a separate and distinct presence. She has an identity of her own, beyond Lou's fantasy projections.

Lou is a small-time numbers runner, picking up nickels and dimes in the slums of Atlantic City. The apartment building he and Sally live in is being torn down, apparently to make way for another new Atlantic City casino—an establishment that will drive Lou out of his job as well as his home. But for Sally, who is studying to be a blackjack dealer, the new casinos will mean a new beginning: with her dealer's license, she'll have a trade, an income, and independence for the first time in her drifter's life. Both characters have strong connections to the past. Lou's seems nostalgic, comforting; he likes to remember the days when he was a strong-arm man for Atlantic City's mob, and he remains attached to Grace (Kate

Reid), the widow of his old boss, serving her as a combination errand boy, bodyguard, and lover. Lou wraps himself in his past—it's his one source of esteem—but Sally is running from hers. Her husband (Robert Joy) ran off some years back with her sister (Hollis McLaren), but suddenly he's back on her doorstep, complete with sister (now pregnant) and a plastic bag stuffed with stolen cocaine. The return of Sally's husband threatens to cancel her future (she'll be thrown out of dealer's school if they discover she has criminal connections), but for Lou, he's a shot from a happy past. Meeting the husband in a bar, Lou is enlisted to help peddle the cocaine. As he makes his connections in shabby hotel rooms, Lou begins to live again: money flows with the impact of adrenaline.

Guare's plotting is an elegant system of checks and balances, arching out in intricate filigree. The film has a shiny classic symmetry, though it never seems artificial. Guare reveals the pattern gradually, drawing random events into his grand design, rather as if the social chaos of a Robert Altman film were evolving into the emotional orderliness of a Lubitsch. When Sally's husband is murdered by the mob, Lou, flush again and resplendent in a white leisure suit (the suit you shouldn't touch), sees his chance to approach her, first as a friend and then as a lover. During their short liaison, their respective pasts take care of themselves: the pregnant girl moves in with the gangster's moll, sharing confidences and foot massage techniques.

Relationships are constantly shifting in *Atlantic City*, rearranging and reversing themselves. Suspicion turns to affection and back again, protectors become the protected, and romance evolves into warm paternalism. In this interregnum Atlantic City, suspended between decay and rebirth, there are no set roles; people can be what they want to be, providing they know what they want. Lou's desires are all aligned with the past, Sally's are projected into the future: both characters reject the present, but it's the present, with its infinite opportunities for change, that offers the highest promise. If Sally's dream for the future eventually turns sour, so must Lou face the fact that his past wasn't as glorious as his memories of it. A final confrontation with the killers of Sally's husband brings Lou his fulfillment and Sally her freedom, both firmly placed in the here and now.

Lancaster's Lou has been hailed as a brilliant comeback, and brilliant it is—it's a consummate performance, based on Lancaster's still powerful body control. He acts with his stride, his stance, the way he holds his arms—precise, formal movements that would be perfectly expressive in a silent film. But to call his performance a comeback is to ignore the excellent work he's done in the last decade. Between *Ulzana's Raid*, *1900*, and *Twilight's Last Gleaming*, as well as a number of sterling contributions to lesser films, the '70s have shaped up as Lancaster's best period; he's gained depth and shading with age. The real surprise in *Atlantic City* is Susan Sarandon, who gives Sally a degree of inner definition that has never been hers before: the vague flakiness of *Loving Couples* and *King of the Gypsies* has coalesced into a real person.

If there's one central flaw with *Atlantic City*, it may be that Louis Malle respects John Guare's screenplay too much. The mise-en-scène is sturdy but oddly impoverished, as if Malle believed that too much detail in the visuals would detract from Guare's dialogue. There is a strange, antiseptic feel to many of Malle's compositions—the lines are too hard, the planes too clean—that suggests the compulsive overcontrol of a Stanley Kubrick film: the Overlook Hotel of *The Shining* wouldn't look out of place on Louis Malle's boardwalk. The dialogue seems almost to detach itself and float above the images; there's nothing in the visuals with enough heft and texture to hold it down. And the dialogue itself is directed in slow, deliberate rhythms; the careful phrasing makes some of the speeches come out like blank verse, and the artsiness of the effect squashes their spontaneity. Character moments become the writer's moments, as when Kate Reid's lovely disquisition on high-heeled shoes (if they were crystal, could you keep goldfish in them?) suddenly turns into a textbook exercise. Malle's circumspection may be misplaced, but it is nobly inspired: John Guare has constructed one of the finest screenplays in the history of American film, and a little awe seems appropriate.

Fanny and Alexander

Directed by INGMAR BERGMAN {July 8, 1983}

Next Tuesday, July 12, Ingmar Bergman will be 65 years old. Having reached the age of retirement, he has announced that *Fanny and Alexander* will be his last theatrical film, though he intends to go on working in television and on the stage. Bergman's announcement hasn't caused the outpourings of critical remorse that might have been expected, and it isn't only because he has hedged his retirement plans (*Scenes from a Marriage*, after all, was a TV movie). There's a general feeling, I think, shared by the art-house audience and all but a few diehard critics, that it probably is time for Bergman to step down; the only fan he seems to have left is Woody Allen. The last Bergman film to cause real excitement was probably the 1973 *Cries and Whispers*, which already had the feel of an autumnal, valedictory project. Since then, he has divided his time between minor, grace-note films (*The Magic Flute, Autumn Sonata, The Faro Document*), which have seen a moderate success, and ambitious, punishingly serious major films (*Face to Face, The Serpent's Egg, From the Life of the Marionettes*), which have been major disasters. The art-house audience no longer wants to hear from Bergman: the qualities of stylistic austerity, philosophical engagement, and literary construction that seemed so important in the '50s when film was fighting to be taken seriously as an art form seem superfluous now that the battle has been won and forgotten. Ingmar Bergman is no fun—a fact that made his reputation 30 years ago and now has broken it.

In *Fanny and Alexander*, Bergman makes a game attempt to *be* fun: the opening passages of this 197-minute film return to the turn-of-the-century gaiety and bawdiness of *Smiles of a Summer Night*, his most lighthearted and most frequently revived movie; there is even a fart joke that could be an homage to Mel Brooks. But as the film continues—drawing the silent figure of ten-year-old Alexander out from the group portrait of the boisterous Ekdahl family, following him through his widowed mother's disastrous remarriage to the stern Bishop Vergerus—the colors lose their luster and the dramatic tone turns sharp and thin. This isn't *Diva*, after all. When Bergman returns to the opening tone—with Alexander's rescue from the monstrous churchman and the birth of two new Ekdahl daughters—Vergerus's dark presence remains, a shadow latent in the sunshine.

Bergman is quoted in the press kit as saying, "*Fanny and Alexander* is the sum total of my life as a filmmaker," and the film does have an arbitrary, unintegrated, "best of" quality. Within the first few minutes, Bergman invokes his familiar symbols of artifice (a puppet theater), identity (a hallway mirror that splits young Alexander in two), time (a mantel clock that ticks like a countdown to the grave), and sexuality (a marble statue of a nude woman that, rather awkwardly, comes to life under Alexander's gaze); all that's missing is a black-robed figure packing a chessboard (though there will, later, be an eight-foot marionette of a rickety God). It's as if Bergman were editing his own AFI tribute. This sense of crowding and of hurry—the rush to recap as many motifs as possible—persists through the film (though it should be said in fairness that, "last theatrical film" or no, *Fanny and Alexander* is, like *Scenes from a Marriage*, the condensed version of a much longer TV series, and perhaps the pacing is superior in the complete edition). The symbols file by as if on parade; none of them stops long enough to be examined or explored.

If the surface of the film seems to be a series of disassociated fragments, its deepest structure—the opposition of the Ekdahl and Vergerus families— seems equally artificial. Bergman has simply drawn a line between life-loving and death-embracing qualities, giving the Ekdahls ownership of the local theater, the Vergeruses the stewardship of the local church. Where the Ekdahls are round, highly sexed, and predominantly female (the family is full of strong widows who have buried their ineffectual husbands), the Vergeruses are drawn, repressed, and dominated by a man (in the Vergerus household, it's the women who die—the bishop's first wife and two daughters were drowned). As if the opposition needed further underlining, Bergman has introduced harshly contrasting color schemes (a Christmassy red-and-green that gives way to softly radiant pastels for the Ekdahls; unadorned black, white, and moldering gray for the Vergeruses), decors (overstuffed versus stick), and acting styles (the fluttering naturalistic versus the fiercely oratorical). There is one nice touch in all this: the Ekdahls, who live on and for the earth, inhabit the horizontal space of a single-story apartment and summer home, while the Vergeruses, straining toward the heavens, have a multistory, dizzyingly vertical home, dominated by a heavy staircase.

It would be easy to stop here with *Fanny and Alexander*. The flat symbolism and the crude contrasts seem typical of Bergman at his worst, and the filming does nothing to bring them alive. The mise-en-scène is distant and inexpressive, almost perversely indifferent to the deeper movements of the scenario (it's this, I think, that the French critic Michel Chion had in mind when he wrote that Bergman "will always remain in some degree the 'adapter' of his own ideas"), and this is the only Bergman film I can remember without a single impressive performance (there are, in fact, two shockingly bad ones—Erland Josephson as the Ekdahls' Jewish ally Isak, and Jarl Kulle as Alexander's lusty uncle). Yet there is a new element in *Fanny and Alexander*—something that comes from far outside the usual system of Bergman's work—that transforms this museum of old motifs into a haunting, suggestive experience.

After the sudden loss of her husband, a young woman turns for spiritual support (and perhaps also out of a sense of guilt and shame) to a fundamentalist minister, but her two children, a boy and his younger sister, dislike and distrust their new stepfather. The man of God persecutes them mercilessly, beating them and holding them prisoner; eventually, the children attempt to escape. This isn't just the plot of the Charles Laughton–James Agee classic *The Night of the Hunter*. Bergman may not have had the Laughton film specifically in mind (though there are some other parallels between the two films), but he has recaptured its rich and complex point of view. Like *Night of the Hunter*, *Fanny and Alexander* is a psychological drama filmed as a fairy tale, its realistic detailing of a child's experience shaded into the abstraction of myth and legend by the imposition of a child's perspective. Though Alexander is seldom an active participant in the film that has been named after him (Fanny, who barely appears, seems to have been included in the title as a courtesy) and though the film frequently leaves his limited knowledge of the events around him, the child remains the focal point. The drama takes place almost entirely among the adults, but it finds its deepest resonance in relation to him. Bergman's camera doesn't often rise to the adult level, to look the grown-up characters in the face; for the most part it stays low, at a child's level, giving the grown-ups an extra dimension of power and presence, making them a race apart. The harsh thematic oppositions, and the frequently simplistic characterizations that they give rise to, begin to make sense. These aren't real people, but a child's simplified perception of real people—or better, they are people known in childhood reconstructed through the coloring memory of an adult. In a sense, the child has created his own parents.

Bergman is notorious for his elaborate dream sequences, and *Fanny and Alexander* has its fair share of them. Yet where Bergman before has been interested in the content of his dreams, here he seems fascinated by the act of dreaming itself. The film is full of images of sleep, from the opening sequence of a daydreaming Alexander through the lovingly portrayed rituals of putting the children to bed. But the imagery isn't all idyllic: beds are, quite naturally, the sites of the sexual escapades of Alexander's uncle (he seduces Maj, the children's nursemaid, away from Alexander's bed into his own); more ominously, Alexander's father dies in bed as Alexander watches in horror, and Alexander's stepfather, the evil Bishop Vergerus, will be burned to death in his bedclothes (drugged with a sleeping potion by Alexander's mother, he doesn't awake in time to hear the fire sweeping his house). With his obsessive conjunction of death, sexuality, and sleep, Bergman is suggesting a connection: it is in dreams where life and death, Ekdahl and Vergerus, meet.

Dreams are one kind of alternative to reality in *Fanny and Alexander*; the theater is another kind—perhaps a mediating state between the everyday world and the world of dreams. The Ekdahls are a family of actors (even the nonprofessionals—Alexander's uncle successfully poses as a family man in spite of his affairs), and Alexander has both a *toy* theater and a magic lantern, which he uses (while he's supposed to be asleep) to spin tales for his sister. Bishop Vergerus, who stages the funeral of Alexander's father as an immense spectacle, has his own kind of theater in the form of his church, yet this is a theater of truth—of pain and deprivation—as opposed to the Ekdahls' theater of fantasy and comfort. The stories that Alexander invents to entertain his family and friends become, in the Vergerus house, lies to be punished—to be beaten out of the boy.

Fanny and Alexander moves from dreams to fairy tales to theater— and ultimately to the film we are watching. Bergman is tracing the path of creation—the route by which stories enter the world, and by which the ten-year-old Alexander Ekdahl becomes the adult artist Ingmar Bergman. *Fanny and Alexander* falls into three neat acts: one for the Ekdahls, one for Vergerus, and a return to the Ekdahls at the climax. It appears at first to be a facile alternation of life and death, with life predictably triumphant (the two Ekdahl daughters who are christened at the end of the film are clearly replacements for the two Vergerus daughters lost in the flood). Yet the force that drives the film—that provides the transitions between the acts—is death. Two fathers die to move the movie (and the process of creation) forward, and the son believes that he has killed them both (first by recoiling in horror at his father's deathbed, second by wishing for Vergerus's death in a dream). Creation is a murderous process in *Fanny and Alexander*, and perhaps a darkly sexual one as well (the Ekdahls are seen in a performance of *Hamlet*, which underlines the Oedipal theme). Once Alexander has eliminated his two fathers, they become part of his personality, and it is not too much to see in the opposition of Ekdahl and Vergerus the warring sides of Bergman's own contradictory aesthetic: the Ekdahls suggesting the simple, primitive pleasures of making fictions and building spectacles, and Vergerus as the fierce truth-telling side of Bergman—the sermons and philosophical discourses that periodically burst through his films, destroying both the fiction and the pleasure we take in it.

In the end, *Fanny and Alexander* seems less the summation of a career than an evocation of its very earliest beginnings—its beginnings in dreams and primal impulses. The film is the story of Alexander's coming into consciousness as a storyteller, his discovery of the awesome power of art. Over the course of the film, Alexander evolves from witness to participant, audience to author. He learns the power of art to create and to kill, to transform his dream-wishes into reality. In the final sequence of the film, Alexander's grandmother (herself a former actress) settles down to read August Strindberg's newly published *A Dream Play*; the decision to set the film in 1907 seems to have been made solely so that this moment would be possible. It's as if Alexander's experiences had somehow contributed to the composition of Strindberg's masterpiece—the publication of the play makes the perfect climax to Alexander's childhood, the ultimate unification of dreams and reality through the medium of the theater. As his grandmother reads, Alexander falls asleep in her lap. Happy birthday, Mr. Bergman.

The Legend of Tianyun Mountain

Directed by XIE JIN {April 19, 1985}

Xie Jin's 1980 *The Legend of Tianyun Mountain* was one of the early entries in a new wave of Chinese films allowed to criticize the excesses of the Cultural Revolution and the crimes of the Gang of Four. Yet what is commanding and beautiful about this film is due, in a strange but direct sense, to the events it is meant to denounce. Without the Cultural Revolution and the period of isolation it brought to China, *The Legend of Tianyun Mountain* would not be what it is, which is to say a ravishing survival of the Hollywood studio style of the 1950s, presented without a trace of self-consciousness or condescension. The Cultural Revolution meant that China missed the '60s and, with them, the most concentrated period of upheaval in film aesthetics since the coming of sound. Modernism—the new realism of Rossellini, the formal explosion of Godard, the materialism of Straub and Huillet—came (and largely went) in the cinema without China taking much notice. Where even the most cravenly commercial of American films are now marked at some level by the assumptions of modernism (location shooting, asymmetric plotting, a resistance of the "symbolic"), Chinese films display an unruffled classicism, serene in its convictions. And in the hands of a master like Xie Jin, this classicism has lost none of its force: it is still capable of sublime effects, magisterial narratives, dazzling structures.

At least to this distant and imperfectly informed observer, the Chinese cinema seems to have preserved a remarkable continuity since its beginnings at the turn of the century (China's first fiction film was released in 1908), despite the almost constant barrage of invasion, war, revolution, and ideological conflict. The Chinese films I have seen from the '30s are of a piece with the Chinese films I have seen of the '80s: even the addition of wide-screen and color seems not to have changed the basic ways in which scenes are edited and stories constructed. The models for those '30s films were, of course, the Hollywood movies that had achieved a worldwide domination with the coming of sound. The American studio style set the standards everywhere—the Chinese were only following the same examples as the French, the Japanese, and even (by the mid-'30s) the Russians. By the late '40s, the Hollywood studio style was beginning to lose sway, chiefly because, under the double attack of antitrust rulings and competition from television, the studios themselves were breaking up. But thanks to a trick of history, it was precisely at this moment that China chose to institutionalize the studio style. The People's Republic was proclaimed in 1949, and among the new government's earliest acts was the nationalization of the film industry. Louis B. Mayer found his spiritual heir in the unlikely figure of Chairman Mao: under the economic protection of the state, the studio system that was dying in America was given a new lease on life in Red China. Only with a large concentration of capital is a studio system, with its massive physical plant and legions of contract employees, a viable method of production: what had once been possible in the United States (because of the steady income guaranteed by the studio's control of both production and exhibition) continued to be possible in China, thanks to the state's intervention.

The studio system is based on a division of labor, and certain stylistic qualities result from that division: the screenplay must be tightly construct-ed and complete, in order to allow the studio craftspeople (the costumers, set designers, makeup artists, etc.) to know precisely what will be required of them. The filming must also be rigorously planned, in order to make the most efficient use of the soundstages and standing sets and to allow the contract personnel (actors and technicians) to pass on schedule from one project to another. The studio style demands a progression from the abstract and general (the idea of a director or screenwriter) to the particu-lar and physical (the realization of the idea, with actors chosen for the roles performing in a décor constructed for the screenplay). The contribution of Rossellini and the other pioneering modernists of the 1950s was to reverse this process, to move from the particular (a given cast assembled at a given location) to the abstract (the discovery of characters, conflicts, themes— the elucidation of the unique "truth" contained in a given reality) through a process of on-the-spot improvisation. The modernist method leaves an impression of intractable material presence, of discontinuity, cacophony, and irresolution—of the whole range of discomfiting intimations we have come in the 20th century to identify as "realism." The studio style, on the other hand, is immaterial, almost transcendent; it creates a reality in the image of the ideal, with an emphasis on symmetry, completeness, containment—the elements we now associate with a lost classical past.

As the title of his best-known film, the 1964 *Two Stage Sisters*, suggests, Xie Jin is a demon for symmetry: he doubles his heroes, he doubles his villains, he doubles his plots, he doubles his time frames (through his use of flashbacks), and he even doubles his images (a gifted wide-screen stylist, he likes to balance his compositions by placing his actors in opposition at the extreme edges of his frames, and he slips in mirrors whenever he has a halfway reasonable excuse). This kind of structural game playing can seem arbitrary or merely decorative, but for Xie Jin, it is the cement that holds his work together—that gives it a center in the absence of a deeply developed character psychology or a completely plausible, naturalistic plot. The formal design imposes a logic and an elegance that transcend the immediate situations: every shot and every sequence in a Xie Jin film points back to the moment of its conception, to the purely intellectual play of forms in the mind of the writer-director. The result is a kind of double discourse: even as Xie Jin's films narrow in on the most extreme emotions and the wildest melodramatic situations (Chinese audiences are said to sob all the way through his movies), the formal elements introduce an intellectual recoil, a return to the original serenity of the artist as he sits in contemplation of his material. Despite the plot upheavals and the spectacular sufferings of the characters, the form exudes a sense of order and wholeness so powerful that there is never any doubt that balance will ultimately be reattained, that the pattern will be followed through to its completion as a happy (and symmetrical) ending. It's the studio style's constant implication of an ultimate order, of the ultimate "rightness" of the world, that makes it such a formidable ideological tool. In Hollywood melodramas, the sense of order points back to the image of a beaming, benevolent God, pouring down his blessings on the American middle-class family. In Xie Jin's Chinese melodramas, the sense of order points back to the ultimate wisdom and goodness of the state, attending to the welfare of each and every citizen.

The Legend of Tianyun Mountain is set in 1978, during the first political thaw following the fall of the Gang of Four. Song Wei (Wang Fuli) is a party functionary in a provincial capital, charged with reviewing the cases of "rightists" condemned to social ostracism under the Cultural Revolution. She hears of the case of a former party official now living as a cart driver in a remote mountain region, and recognizes him as Luo Qun (Shi Weiji-an), to whom she had been engaged 20 years earlier, when they both were eager young comrades working together on a rural development project. In flashback, we see how Luo Qun's liberal attitudes got him into trouble with the local commissar, Wu Yao (Zhong Xinghuo), and how Song Wei was forced to break with him in order to preserve her standing with the party. But Feng Qinglan (Shi Jianlan), Song Wei's best friend, resolved to stand by Luo Qun and followed him into exile. After their marriage, Feng Qinglan was severely beaten by a band of Red Guards (when she refused to turn over her husband's manuscripts), and as the film returns to the present, she is on the verge of death. Obviously, a clear-cut case for rehabilitation, but Song Wei has one problem to face—she is now married to Wu Yao, who started all the trouble in the first place.

The formal problem for Xie Jin is to reduce all these pairs of contrasting doubles—the two women, the two men, the two marriages, the two time periods—to a final unity, which must represent the freshly rewon unity of the state, at long last cleansed of the perfidy of the Gang of Four. He proceeds by taking another pair—the archetypal thematic opposition of the political and the personal—and blurring the distinction until it becomes meaningless. The political drama is inextricable from the characters' emotional trials: Song Wei's decision to break with Luo Qun seemed to be the correct political choice; Feng Qinglan's decision to stand by him appeared to be a suspiciously personal, emotional choice. But as the plot works through its symmetries and reversals, we find that Song Wei's political choice was actually selfish (she did it to preserve her status with the party) and politically destructive (it promoted the divisiveness of the Cultural Revolution), while Feng Qinglan's personal gesture was actually perfectly selfless (she devoted her life to a hero of the people) and politically just (she stood up to the Gang of Four). Solving the personal problem (Song Wei atones for the betrayal of her lover) solves the political problem (China is made whole again) and vice versa. The emotional and the ideological are put through so many commutations that they end by becoming identical, and it is with the death of Feng Qinglan that final unity is achieved. Luo Qun (now a widower) and Song Wei (who has left her husband) both visit the grave; though they do not speak, their reunion in the same frame reestablishes the original couple of 20 years ago, and balance and harmony return to the land.

It would be easy to take *The Legend of Tianyun Mountain* as a naïve or bluntly propagandistic film, but even the slightest peek beneath the surface reveals the intelligence and artistry that Xie Jin has brought to it. His symbols may seem heavy by our postmodernist standards, yet they are woven into the film's grand design with such skill that their very bluntness comes to seem beautiful: a great storm causes the collapse of a dam, which leads to Luo Qun's definitive condemnation (he had gone against the party officials in proclaiming the construction substandard); it is raining again when Feng Qinglan visits Song Wei on her wedding night to beg for help, only to be turned away by the evil Wu Yao. Near the end of the film, a character throws open a pair of heavy bedroom curtains, proclaiming, "A new historical period is beginning for China!" The effect of the radiant sunshine pouring into the room is astonishingly, almost miraculously moving, not because of the trite sentiment it expresses, but because it is the culmination of a pattern that has run across the entire body of the film. This is studio filmmaking at its finest—somewhere up there, Louis B. Mayer is slapping Chairman Mao on the back.

Pale Rider

Directed by CLINT EASTWOOD {July 5, 1985}

Clint Eastwood's appeal as an actor lies in the contrast between the violent acts he is called upon to perform and the studied restraint of his demeanor—the soft, even voice, the famous quizzical squint. Where most actors work to make their gestures an extension of their characters, Eastwood does the opposite: his movements often seem to contradict the message written on his face. When, at the beginning of *Dirty Harry*, he surveys the wreckage he has just caused by blowing out the tires of a getaway car with his monstrous handgun and walks calmly across the street, continuing to munch on a mouthful of hot dog, it's impossible to make any connection between the mayhem we have just witnessed and the man who has made it. The action genres that Eastwood works in—the Western and the cop movie—depend on the assumption that a man is what he does. But Eastwood's films destroy that assumption: though we see what he does, the man remains a mystery—withdrawn, unreadable, the workings of his soul a secret.

As a director, Eastwood has continued the trajectory of his performances. The films he has made—now 11 in number—play a stylistic extravagance against a hidden emotional core. A surface violence—not simply of action but of exaggerated camera angles, harsh cutting, expressionistic lighting, abrupt contrasts in scale and acting styles—swirls around a center of a strange solidity and calm. As an actor, Eastwood is a master of the art of holding back, of keeping some portion of his character inaccessible to the audience and thus awakening our interest in him. As a director, he does the same thing, establishing a zone of mystery at the center of his movie and building barriers—through conflicting levels of story, style, and theme—around it. Reading an Eastwood movie is often the process of peeling away, and never more so than in his newest film, *Pale Rider*.

The first layer is one of genre. *Pale Rider* is Eastwood's first Western since *The Outlaw Josey Wales* in 1976, and the first major studio Western since the debacle of *Heaven's Gate* in 1980. It is clearly a form that means a great deal to Eastwood—it was with the Western that his career began, first in the television series *Rawhide* and then in the celebrated Italian Westerns of Sergio Leone—and much of the immediate pleasure of *Pale Rider* results from the obvious relish with which Eastwood invokes the sounds and images that have been effectively banned from the big screen since the genre entered its commercial decline. Rendered in Dolby stereo, the clatter of horses' hooves with which the film opens is almost unbearably beautiful, both because it heralds the return of the noblest and richest genre in the

American cinema and because, in this summer of 1985, it is a *forbidden* sound. In it you can hear a shout of defiance against the money men who have decreed that Westerns are dead. It is a supremely natural, physical sound—the sound of contact with the earth—come to drown out the artificial whoosh of spaceships and the electronic beeps of computer keyboards.

The plot of *Pale Rider* is furnished with familiar imagery: a mysterious stranger (Eastwood) appears to protect a ragged community of prospectors against the threats of a big mining company; there is a climactic showdown on Main Street, and even a scene in which a minor character is forced by the heavies to "Dance, mister!" The final shot—a lone horseman riding off into the wilderness—is a reference to the most self-consciously mythical of all Westerns, George Stevens's 1953 *Shane*. Yet Eastwood doesn't follow Stevens's mythologizing techniques: instead of pumping up the conventions with rhetorical bombast, Eastwood simply lets them play, as naturally and naïvely as possible, betting that the sense of transgression that accompanies the production of each cliché will be enough to transform it into something fresh and alive. Where Stevens enshrines his conventions (and thus helps to kill them), Eastwood brandishes his, with a thrilling sense of deliberate provocation.

The broad outline of *Pale Rider* conforms to the conventions of the classic Western as practiced in Hollywood through the early '60s. But as the film progresses, enough details crop up to suggest that Eastwood is skewing the classic plot toward something much more specific and personal. Like the hero of a certain series of spaghetti Westerns, Eastwood's character has no name (the prospectors call him "the preacher," because he wears a clerical collar and seems to have a working knowledge of the Bible). The prospectors, a scrabbly, low-minded lot, are drawn with a taste for broad caricature and burlesque that has more than a touch of the Italian about it, and the villains—monsters of rapacious capitalism—spring from a Euro-Marxist sensibility that isn't exactly Eastwood's own. By the time a gang of hired killers appears, dressed in the dusters made famous by *Once Upon a Time in the West*, we have been subtly led into Leone territory, where Eastwood is preparing a showdown with his old mentor (perhaps in the form of the leader of the hired guns, an older, oddly fatherly man, who recognizes the Eastwood character with a shocked exclamation of "You!").

This movement from the classical and generic into the autobiographical is one of the defining elements of Eastwood's work, and it's repeated on two other levels in the film. *Pale Rider* comes equipped with a social theme—a plea for protecting the environment from the greedy rampages of big business—that seems unusually liberal for an Eastwood film, but the position it occupies in the work is much the same as that of the anti-Miranda invective of the Dirty Harry films. The politics matter much less than the images Eastwood derives from them; again, he uses impersonal, conventional material as a way of entering more subjective terrain. Where the prospectors are content to pan the stream that winds through their camp, the mining company has managed to rig up an elaborate hydraulic system that sends a torrent of water smashing against the mountainside. The dirt and rock are blasted away, exposing the seams of gold. Eastwood lingers over this horrifying sight far more than a simple statement of the ecological theme would warrant. The image acquires a life of its own, and it is a psychological image. As the layers of rock are torn away to reveal a hidden core, it becomes impossible not to identify the craggy mountainside with Eastwood's own stony exterior, erected to protect a similar secret. This violent attempt to tear to the core is played in contrast to the methods of the prospectors, which are also Eastwood's methods as a filmmaker. The natural barriers are respected, and the mountain is allowed to deliver its own treasure in the form of a grain of gold here, a nugget there. A boulder sits in the middle of the stream that runs through the camp: though one of the prospectors (Michael Moriarty) is convinced that there's gold beneath it, he refuses to blast the boulder away. Using dynamite would forever alter the course of the stream and perhaps cause it to dry up. He'll chip away at the rock with a hammer (and Eastwood's character helps him out), but more extreme, more direct methods are out of the question. A violent penetration of character does not reveal the secret—it destroys it.

The most awkward aspect of *Pale Rider* is its metaphysical theme: as a 15-year-old girl (Sydney Penny), a prospector's daughter, prays for protection against the raiding parties sent into the camp by the mining company, the Preacher materializes out of the darkness of the forest—the "pale rider" of the Book of Revelation. Although Eastwood handles this element with a measure of grace (the Preacher enters the camp just as the appropriate words are being read from the Bible, and it's a chillingly effective moment) and considerable ambiguity (the Preacher may be an avenging angel or even Jesus Christ himself; on the other hand, his skill in violence suggests that he may be Death or the Devil), it never connects organically with the narration (as does, for example, the mining imagery). It feels like something stuck on—a bid for a kind of "significance" the film doesn't need. And yet Eastwood is able to repeat his usual process, turning this borrowed, external element to his own ends. More important than who the Preacher "really is" is who he is not—he is not human, not a member of the community and not able to participate in its emotional life. On one level, this is simply an underlining of the traditional role of the Western hero: the gunman kills to protect the community from killers like himself; he can never belong to the civilization he has helped to establish. But Eastwood alters the emphasis: separation is no longer the tragic theme it was in the classical Western but rather something to be accepted, perhaps wished for. Barriers separate, but they also protect, and the visual plan of *Pale Rider* emphasizes just such protective barriers: doors and windows, mountain walls, impenetrable shadows.

It is the necessity of separation that fascinates Eastwood, not its tragedy. Twice in *Pale Rider*, the Preacher refuses a romantic involvement: first with the teenage girl, whose openly sexual advances are motivated by a childish hero worship and a need to replace her missing father; then with her mother (Carrie Snodgress), a tough, mature woman who appears to need no one at all. The second refusal is the most difficult—Eastwood and Snodgress seem to share a sense of isolation, and there's a haunting physical resemblance between the two performers—but the Preacher has no real choice. He must remain alone.

So what is the secret that Eastwood is protecting with so many barriers, so many levels? The beauty of *Pale Rider* is that we never find out—the film follows its logic to the end. A few suggestions do slip out, just as the mountain distributes a sliver of gold here and there—though it is gold of another kind, in the form of the strong, blond-haired woman who has haunted Eastwood's work for so long. Stamped by an inexorable sadness, often in the grip of a troubled past, she made her initial appearance in the first film Eastwood produced for his own company (Inger Stevens in the 1968 *Hang 'Em High*), became Sondra Locke in a whole series of films, and survives in *Pale Rider* as Carrie Snodgress. A figure of both attraction and fear, she is the one irreducible constant of Eastwood's work—its most arbitrary aspect and its most mysterious. Eastwood will probably never tell us who she is, but one thing is clear: the secret is in her hands.

PART 3

Favorites
(Reader)

Twilight's Last Gleaming

Directed by ROBERT ALDRICH {February 11, 1977}

Twilight's Last Gleaming, Robert Aldrich's belated bicentennial gift to the nation, opens with Billy Preston's agonized rendition of "My Country 'tis of Thee" as the main credits roll out in John Hancock's script. Behind the titles, four escapees from an army prison begin an attack on a top-security missile base, passing through fences, gates, a web of closed-circuit TV cameras, and a maze of guards and passwords to get down to the subterranean control room. Once in command, the group's leader (Burt Lancaster) issues his ultimatum: send one million dollars in cash, guarantee safe passage out of the country on Air Force One, and provide the president of the United States as a hostage, or else the nine nuclear missiles under his control will be released.

It sounds like a recap of the doomsday movies of the '60s (*Fail Safe, Seven Days in May, Dr. Strangelove*), but this post-Vietnam, post-Watergate political thriller deals in a subtler kind of cynicism. From the prophetically titled *World for Ransom* (1954) to last year's *Hustle*, Robert Aldrich has held his place as one of the masters of film noir, the dark cinema of defeat, betrayal, and death. For *Twilight's Last Gleaming*, he's created a world of ultimate sterility: exclusively male, pervaded by violence and moral corruption. Restricting the action to three main sets—the control room where Lancaster sits and waits, the Oval Office where the president (Charles Durning) and his cabinet try to come to grips with the situation, and the command post where an army general (Richard Widmark) plots the recapture of the base—Aldrich builds the pressure of claustrophobia. Long dialogue sequences are broken by brief flurries of action, creating a mounting rhythm of tension and release. Robert Hauser's camera gives every image a hard, razor edge, the impersonal furniture of technology taking on a more immediate reality than the characters themselves—men seem weak, fallible things against the sleek geometry of the missile bodies, whose lines reappear in the layout of the Oval Office and in the banks of television screens in the command post. The colors, too, are cold; glacial blues and whites dominate, washing out the flesh tones. Chrome, a surface that captures reflections instead of enhancing them, is everywhere.

This is the world Lancaster is determined to destroy. For he has another, non-mercenary reason for seizing the missile base: as an air force general in Vietnam, he discovered the real military motives behind the war—not to fight communism, but to prove to the Russians that the United States was more than capable of visiting inhuman actions on its own soldiers and the war's innocent bystanders. To prove, in short, that the United States was the most immoral, most vicious nation on earth and was so entitled to be its leader. Lancaster's fourth demand is the release of the secret documents that proclaim this policy, documents so highly classified that the president is unaware of their existence until Lancaster presents his threat. The cabinet members—the officers of the permanent government that created the policy—try to persuade the president not to make the papers public, but he stands adamant in his outrage. The solution is simple: both he and Lancaster must be eliminated.

The story lends itself to liberal bombast, and, too often, the film descends to the level of simple sloganeering. It's hard to avoid the feeling that Aldrich, for once in his career, has succumbed to self-consciousness, letting his political convictions get the better of his art. *Twilight's Last Gleaming* has an awkward air of preachiness about it—a flaw, but largely a superficial one. A darker, more corrosive pessimism exists beneath the moralizing, a pessimism that questions the ultimate viability of adhering to any morals at all.

Many of Aldrich's films are built around this opposition between a corrupt, amoral system—war, the underworld, Hollywood—and a single man from within the system who rises up against it. The system itself remains largely unchanged from film to film: a world in which selfishness is the prime motive and betrayal the main weapon. But the conception of the hero has undergone a change over the course of Aldrich's career. His earliest protagonists are romantic adventurers—like the hero of *World for Ransom*, who risks everything for the woman he loves only to find, in the last reel, that she was only using him to bring back her husband. Faced with a few sobering denouements on this order, the Aldrich hero becomes more of a pragmatist. The characters played by Jack Palance in *The Big Knife* (1955) and *Attack* (1956) have both learned to function within the system, turning against it only when faced with an overwhelming outrage. By the time of *The Dirty Dozen* (1967), the hero's pragmatism has developed to the point where he freely traffics with the monstrosity of the system, becoming a monster himself in order to realize his private, often perversely idealistic, goals. Aldrich seemed to bottom out with *Emperor of the North Pole* (1973), a film that sacrificed the last vestige of conventional outward-directed heroism, offering a protagonist who resorted to brute violence in order to protect his pride and self-containment.

If anything, the system seems to grow stronger with every film—but here, in *Twilight's Last Gleaming*, Aldrich has permitted a glimmer of hope that hasn't appeared in his films for nearly a decade. *Twilight's* two heroes fall neatly into Aldrich's two categories—Lancaster (in what is surely one of his best performances; his distant, vaguely messianic bearing gives the character an almost Dostoyevskian aura) is the noble romantic; Durning, as the shrewd, carefully compromising president, fits the traditional role of Aldrich's pragmatist. The two men, on opposite sides, work toward the same goal (the ultimate release of the documents), both offering themselves as sacrifices. If, finally, their sacrifices mean nothing—the system triumphs with an almost ridiculous ease—at least they've achieved a small fulfillment: they've let their moral selves breathe, however briefly and ineffectually. Which, in the world of Robert Aldrich, is an act of heroism above and beyond the call of sanity and survival.

Movie Movie

Directed by STANLEY DONEN {February 2, 1979}

As the title suggests, *Movie Movie* is vaguely redundant. The last thing the world needs right now is one more parody of old genre films. Me, I'm still recovering from *High Anxiety*—the last straw in a tumbling haystack that included *The Cheap Detective*, *The World's Greatest Lover*, *Blazing Saddles*, *The Last Remake of Beau Geste*, and *Murder by Death*. The list could go on, but my hands are beginning to tremble.

Still, *Movie Movie* has something that the films of the Brooks-Simon-Wilder school lack, something that could be described as wit, intelligence, and integrity if those qualities were not generally considered inimical to the spirit of comedy in the '70s. Against the prevailing winds of comic anarchism (which blow, more often than not, toward sloppiness and the self-defeating spirit of anything for a laugh), director Stanley Donen has erected a firm structure of character and narrative detail. Which is to say that *Movie Movie* has people in it and tells a story.

Actually, it tells two stories. During production, the film was titled "Double Feature," and that's what it is: a seedy black-and-white boxing picture called *Dynamite Hands*, followed by a color musical entitled *Baxter's Beauties of 1933*. The subject of Donen's parody is not so much the internal conventions of the fight film and the musical as it is the eerie, echoing effect of Old Hollywood's assembly-line production policy. Thus, both films begin with the same establishing shot, leading into the same scene in the same doctor's office, with the doctor in both played by Art Carney, one of the few performers of the '70s who offers a professional parallel to the omnipresent character actors of the '30s. Similarly, both films inhabit the same sets (a gangster's penthouse in one becoming a star's dressing room in the next) and draw on the same basic cast (George C. Scott, Trish Van Devere, Barry Bostwick, Red Buttons, and Eli Wallach). And in the last analysis, the two stories are really one: the story of a scrubbed, earnest young man (Harry Hamlin in the first, Barry Bostwick in the second) who discovers his true vocation (fighting, writing musicals) and rises to the top of his profession with the help of a kindly elder who dies, poignantly, at the moment of triumph (Scott in both). But real happiness can come only after the young man's earnestness has conquered the temptations of a femme fatale (Ann Reinking in A, Van Devere in B), leading him back to the arms of his true love, a young woman every bit as scrubbed and earnest as he (Van Devere in A, Rebecca York in B).

The script, by Larry Gelbart (of the television series *M*A*S*H*) and Sheldon Keller, is mainly devoted to twisting dimly remembered dialogue clichés into bizarre non sequiturs—"My guts took a slap in the face"; "I can see with one eye tied behind my back." The formula becomes obvious fairly quickly, and the obvious fades into the tiresome by the film's end. But beneath the facile, flip conceits of the screenplay lies a legitimate and often-overlooked point: plots really don't matter much in the movies, particularly in genre films. The details, of performance and mise-en-scène, make all the difference. When Donen transforms a fight film into a musical, he isn't doing anything that hadn't occurred to the old studio heads. In fact, the fight film that *Dynamite Hands* is most obviously based on, Warner Brothers' 1937 *Kid Galahad*, was casually remade as a circus movie—*The Wagons Roll at Night*—in 1941. No doubt, in some dark and grimy grind house of the '40s, the two films shared a double bill just like *Movie Movie*'s. And, no doubt, nobody noticed the strange similarity between them—or if they did, they didn't care.

Gelbart's self-deflating dialogue continually undercuts the emotional thrust of the plot, but Donen—backed by his extremely able ensemble cast—brings a degree of conviction to the material that almost makes it work on its own, original terms. The real wonder of *Movie Movie*—a film designed to be flat, empty, and ridden with cliché—is that it plays anyway. There is a modicum of feeling, and even suspense, as the plots work their ways to their inevitable conclusions; you find yourself caring about the characters and hoping, abstractly, that things will work out for them. Archetype, in its pure, distilled form, always seems to have this sort of effect: the often-told tale still draws sympathy and interest, not in spite of its familiarity, but because of it. Genre films, perhaps, come as close to ritual as anything in American culture; they have an incantatory effect, seductive and compelling against all will, and often against better judgment.

Donen never violates the integrity of his film. There are no asides, no interruptions; things run straight on from frame one. Parody may only be a game, but it's a game with rules, and Donen has the courage to define and stick to them. Where Mel Brooks starts flinging his premises out the window as soon as they show a little strain, Donen prefers to ride out the rough spots, shifting into low and letting his narrative drive pull him through. Dramatically, *Movie Movie* is as carefully sculpted as any serious film this year (if such a thing can be found). It has a classical balance and fullness; very little is skimped in the way of exposition or development; there is no reliance on the faulty premise (generally assumed by Brooks) that this, after all, is a comedy, and dimensionality doesn't matter.

That same integrity carries over to the performance. Only George C. Scott, alone among the large cast, takes occasional advantage of the many opportunities to lean out of character and address a surreptitious wink or two to the audience—his performance, otherwise, is so blissfully self-involved that he may have thought it necessary to let the audience know, from time to time, that he was in on the joke. No self-consciousness is visible in the supporting parts: Hamlin and Bostwick throw themselves into their callow youths with the dedication and intensity of Olivier's Hamlet. Trish Van Devere, not previously noted for her facility with a punch line, wraps her deep radio voice around Gelbart's dialogue with the loving sobriety of a mother swaddling a child. Her sincerity bounces back from the empty dialogue, a comic echo. But the most spectacular display in *Movie Movie* belongs to Barbara Harris, who enters into her character, a chorus floozy in the second feature, as if it were a Zen trance. Harris, an endlessly fascinating actress who has received far too little exposure in films (and receives far too little exposure in *Movie Movie*), has a way with caricature that transcends simple satire and enters the realm of Being and Becoming: it's as if Stanislavsky had suddenly taken over the direction of Second City. Here, she uses the ritual gestures of classical film acting as if they belonged to an Eastern dance. Every stance and movement is invested with a gravity and dignity that borders on the profound; with her heavily made-up face, she resembles a Kabuki player going through the paces of some obscure and unknowable drama.

Apart from one or two notable exceptions, Donen makes no real attempt to imitate the camera style of the '30s. Charles Rosher Jr., the cinematographer of *Dynamite Hands*, summons some of Sol Polito's harshly contrasted lighting from the Warner Brothers gangster films, and Donen exploits his dime-store expressionism in a well-choreographed fight scene: as soon as the hero tackles the heavy, every light in the room goes crashing to the floor, sending the shadows of Götterdämmerung screaming up the walls. But for the most part, Donen sticks to the tropes of his own style, graceful deep-focus compositions and gliding camera movements. Twenty-five years after he climaxed Gene Kelly's rendition of "Singin' in the Rain" (from, of course, the movie of the same name) with the most expansively exuberant pullback in film history, Donen still flies one of the most elegant camera cranes in Hollywood—as his incidental flourishes in *Movie Movie* demonstrate amply, if often gratuitously.

The Busby Berkeley parody that rounds out *Baxter's Beauties of 1933* carries an extra authority that makes up for its triteness (by now, Berkeley has been parodied so often that he's almost ceased to exist as an artist in his own right). Donen began his apprenticeship at MGM as Berkeley's assistant dance director on a largely forgettable 1949 Gene Kelly–Esther Williams musical, *Take Me Out to the Ballgame*. The experience, apparently, affected him so profoundly that he dedicated the rest of his Young Turk years to overthrowing the Berkeley tradition. In *Singin' in the Rain*, *On the Town*, *It's Always Fair Weather*, *Funny Face*, and *The Pajama Game*, Donen created an alternative to Berkeley's massive, impersonal production numbers, forging a new style out of intimate duets and outdoor ensemble work that breathed in the freedom of fresh air. Still, when Donen recreates one of Berkeley's wheel designs at the end of *Movie Movie*, there is a sudden air of affection and regret, the sense of a son forgiving the sins of his father. The brief Berkeley parody in *Singin' in the Rain* fairly drips with venom—it's small, shrunken, and aggressively vulgar. But the "Baxter's Bicycles" number, conceived in benign remembrance, strains against the limits of satire; you can almost see the director fighting to break free, to do it right—as broadly and grandly as possible.

But, of course, it isn't possible at all. Musicals, of both the Donen and Berkeley schools, are deader than proverbial doornails—in 1979, Hollywood can sell them only as parodies or, evidently, as starring vehicles for John Travolta (which may amount to the same thing). Donen clearly wishes otherwise, and thus his film ends on a strange note of subtextual despair: inside this *Movie Movie*, there's a real movie struggling to get out.

Saint Jack

Directed by PETER BOGDANOVICH {June 8, 1979}

Two weeks ago, Roger Corman's New World Pictures coincidentally swept the *Reader*'s film section with a review of *Last Embrace*, directed by Corman graduate Jonathan Demme, and a piece on New World's current exploitation release, *Rock 'n' Roll High School*. This week, Corman's scrappy independent company has *Saint Jack* at the Biograph, but it's a different kind of film for New World, aimed at the prestige, first-run market rather than the drive-ins that have been the company's traditional target. Corman has been upgrading his productions ever since the exploitation business petered out a few years ago, but his "class" projects, like *I Never Promised You a Rose Garden* and *Avalanche*, haven't been particularly satisfying. Somehow, they've lacked both the energy of his exploitation films and the polish of genuine big-league productions. But with *Saint Jack*, New World has struck an effective compromise between the personal, expressive qualities of its drive-in features and the relative dignity and restraint required for the first-run trade. That compromise is the work of a director who's labored on both levels of the film business, Peter Bogdanovich.

Bogdanovich began his moviemaking career as an assistant to Corman in the middle '6os, working on Corman's seminal motorcycle movie *The Wild Angels*, among other equally scurrilous projects. But with the critical success of *The Last Picture Show*, Bogdanovich was promoted to the big time and worked thereafter only for the major studios. Still, no one in Hollywood survives three consecutive flops of the magnitude of *Daisy Miller*, *At Long Last Love*, and *Nickelodeon* without some loss of prestige and bankability, and, consequently, Bogdanovich's return to Corman has been seen by some as a tail-between-the-legs affair. A number of fine directors, including Martin Scorsese and Francis Ford Coppola, have graduated from the Roger Corman School of Filmmaking, but Bogdanovich, it seems, is the first to flunk.

Or so goes the joke. More generously, *Saint Jack* might be seen as a refresher course, a little brushing up on the basics. And there are few things in this world more basic than a Roger Corman budget. According to industry gossip, Bogdanovich attempted to up the ante while he was on location with the film in Singapore—well beyond the reach of Corman's notoriously tight fist, or so he thought. When the production ran over schedule, Corman allegedly sent a team of private detectives after part of *Saint Jack*'s negative, which he then held in ransom for the shooting company's return. Whether or not it's true, the story makes a wonderfully appropriate addition to the Corman myth. But it's hard to verify it from the evidence on the screen: if the production was curtailed, Bogdanovich has done a remarkable job of covering up. Apart from one or two repeated master shots (a sure sign of last-minute patchwork), the film, though modest, isn't noticeably cramped, and what gaps there are in the story line seem slight and forgivable. All in all, Corman's austerity program seems to have been good for Bogdanovich's soul. Taken away from the expensive distractions of the period films he's been given to lately, the director once again seems able to focus his attention on pacing and character—his two main strengths in his earlier films, and his two main weaknesses more recently.

Saint Jack does have a few awkward breaks in its rhythm, but as a whole the film is controlled and well modulated, working through its episodic structure with a measure of grace and consistency. Consistency, ever since he embarked on the mixed-tone experiments of *Daisy Miller* and *At Long Last Love*, hasn't been Bogdanovich's strong suit. Attempting a Fordian blend of tragedy and comedy, Bogdanovich has more often achieved a sort of emotional collision: the moods are not mixed as much as they are simply jammed together. The problem was compounded by the increasingly unmanageable ensemble casts that Bogdanovich put together: in *Nickelodeon*, everyone seemed to be playing in his or her own movie, and the clash of styles and tempers that resulted further clouded the director's already obscure intentions. *Saint Jack*, on the other hand, centers on only two main characters. And while the actors Bogdanovich has chosen to play the leads employ two very different styles, the clash in manner generates much of the film's meaning. *Saint Jack* achieves a synthesis where most of his recent movies have hung themselves in contradiction. Ben Gazzara, as Jack, plays his part in the high heroic manner of classical Hollywood. The character comes from Bogart by way of a Paul Theroux novel: a hard guy with a heart of gold (hence the "saint" of the title), Jack Flowers is an American operator stranded, willingly, in Singapore, where his job as a contact man for a shady ship's supply company provides him with a thin cover of legitimacy for his real business—by night, he's the port city's leading Anglo pimp. Gazzara draws his consummate self-possession, his boxer's stance, and his sly smiles in the face of adversity from a long-lost film tradition: the performance is assured and seamless and dead-ahead in a way that seems all but anachronistic in the self-doubting cinema of the '70s. From Gazzara, it comes as a virtuoso display, not least because it forces him to abandon the method mannerisms that he exploited—for so long and so well—in the films of John Cassavetes and elsewhere. For one of the few times in his career, Gazzara has allowed himself to be a movie star of the old school—and, surprise, he's good at it.

Saint Jack leaves the more contemporary techniques of the Actors Studio—the shakes and quivers and hesitations—to Denholm Elliott, a fine British actor who is herein allowed (again, for one of the few times in his career) to stretch beyond the farce comedy that he generally plays. At first, his character—a mousy bureaucrat in perpetual flutter—looks suspiciously like the Denholm Elliott stock part, but the cartoonish outlines are filled in with intimations of deep hopes and deeper resignations. Elliott's William is a bureaucrat who still knows how to dream, and his dreams, butted against the knowledge that they will never be realized, give him a tattered nobility in the midst of his middle-aged defeat. An accountant, stranded unwillingly in Hong Kong, William commutes to Singapore once a year to balance the books (fraudulent, of course) of Jack's employers. His annual visits, spent in Jack's raucous company, space the film: William is the constant, of middle-class virtue and stability, against which Jack's exploits are measured. As his visits coincide with key points in the action, Jack's heroic rise and fall is neatly and unobtrusively charted, providing exactly the sort of precise structuring device that Bogdanovich's work has often needed and seldom found.

The audience comes to see Jack largely through William's admiring and astonished eyes: as a grand, colorful, romantic figure, above the petty limitations imposed on us poor mortals. In using William to guide the audience's reaction, Bogdanovich is employing a time-honored literary trick: William falls into the broad category of the Watson figure, providing access to an otherwise unapproachable hero and coloring our impressions with the appropriate tones of worship and wonder. But Watson figures appear too frequently and too compulsively in Bogdanovich's films to be dismissed as simple narrative devices. As Steve Fagin noted in the 1975 issue of Northwestern's *Film Reader*, Bogdanovich's films are rife with viewer surrogates, from the teenagers listening to Sam the Lion's heroic tales in *The Last Picture Show*, to Bogdanovich himself sitting at the knee of his mentor in the interview-documentary *Directed by John Ford*, to Barry Brown's passive contemplation of Cybill Shepherd in *Daisy Miller*. More recently and most suggestively, there was Ryan O'Neal as the film director in *Nickelodeon*, absorbing everything around him through the eye of his camera.

It's easy to read Bogdanovich's personal history into this recurring trope; as a film critic turned director, he projects himself, as a viewer, into all of his movies. But there's something more than autobiography at work here, I think, something that comes out in the relative positions—moral and temporal—of the viewer and the viewee.

To date, Bogdanovich has made eight films, but only two of them, *Targets* and *What's Up, Doc?*, take place in the present. (And even there, it could be argued that these two films take place in the "movie past" of, respectively, the two directors who inspired them, Hitchcock and Hawks.) For Bogdanovich, it seems that the past is the only reliable source of the large-scale drama and romance that his films aspire to; things, somehow, were different then—people were bigger and actions were broader. It matters little where or when "then" was: it can be the art-deco New

York of *At Long Last Love*, the pastoral Los Angeles of *Nickelodeon*, or the dust bowl of *Paper Moon*, as long as it is unmistakably different from the decidedly unheroic times in which we live. And even within that mythical past, Bogdanovich's viewer surrogates remain out of touch with its heroic dimension. They can only look on, as representatives of a debilitated and demoralized present, while the giants who inhabit that legendary landscape parade by them.

Saint Jack has been backdated only to 1971, but the mythical past still hangs over the film in the ghostly presence of the fallen British Empire, as it continues to haunt Singapore. Bogdanovich lingers over the decaying facilities of Singapore's British officer's club, filled with decaying British officers who have turned drunk and despondent at being cast out of their time and place. The grand, golden days of colonialism are behind them, as they are behind William's presence in Hong Kong—they're the caretakers, the accountants and managers, who have been left behind to clean up the mess created by their swashbuckling forebears. Such is the shrunken present that William inhabits, and that Jack transcends.

Exactly how he transcends it isn't quite clear—unless we're to understand Jack's triumph as a matter of force of character and personal integrity. He does have a mission, as sweepingly imperialistic in its way as the search for King Solomon's mines: Jack wants to exploit Singapore's leading natural resource—its prostitutes—to set himself up in business, using his good old American know-how to establish the finest cathouse in town. In putting his plan into operation, Jack stands as a towering symbol of independence and free enterprise over the petty corporate functionaries who surround him. Most of those functionaries are employed by the rival Chinese vice lords, who hope to keep Jack out of their monopoly marketplace. Jack literally towers over them in a climactic confrontation scene, as Bogdanovich uses the only low-angle shot in the film to frame Jack's heroic gestures of defiance: the camera looks up from his feet, and Jack becomes a Wellesian giant. (The point, perhaps, is overmade—Bogdanovich has gone so far as to cast a midget as the spokesman for the gang, a bit of gratuitous exaggeration that very nearly pushes the sequence into parody.) Jack's second heroic gesture, which comes at the end of the film, is less commercially motivated; a quiet, personal moment of moral regeneration, it irresistibly evokes Bogart, in any of a dozen films.

Bogdanovich knows which camera angles to use and which films to quote, but there's something missing in his heroic vision. Nowhere does he discover the genuine nobility of the films that are his obvious sources, those of Ford and Hawks. (Although *Saint Jack* certainly owes something to Sam Fuller as well.) He evokes the forms and outward appearances, the gestures and the moments, but he misses the substance—the inner conviction and sense of purpose that give Ford's heroes their stature. He can't seem to get inside his heroes, and his vision remains that of an outsider—that, in fact, of the spectators, like William, who populate his films. Ultimately, whether by default or intent, Bogdanovich's films seem less concerned with the essence of heroism than its impossibility in the present moment. All value resides in the past, just as Bogdanovich's studiously classical style—which works without zooms or pans or close-ups—is a deliberate anachronism. We can see the past, in memory and on film, but we can never touch it, and we can certainly never bring those mythic times back to life. It is a vision that seems both naïvely nostalgic and profoundly, movingly melancholic.

Nosferatu

Directed by WERNER HERZOG {October 19, 1979}

Werner Herzog's *Nosferatu* is the medieval, apocalyptic version of the Dracula myth, as opposed to the Victorian, romantic version offered by John Badham this summer. It may be the first vampire film since F. W. Murnau's original *Nosferatu* in 1922 to present a wholly unsympathetic Dracula. As played by Klaus Kinski (the mad conquistador of Herzog's *Aguirre, the Wrath of God*), the count is a moldering corpse, with ratlike fangs instead of the more discreet incisors of the Lugosi-Lee-Langella school. The makeup, like the script, depends heavily on Murnau's expressionist classic: Kinski, like the pseudonymous "Max Schreck" of the original, becomes a tall, stiff, black-robed figure, topped by a decaying skull that holds two dull, deep-set eyes. As in the Murnau, Kinski's Dracula seems corporeally incomplete, his physical dimension lost in the layers of his wardrobe. Herzog's camera registers only the fleshy extensions that are his hunting tools—the clawed hands, the searching mouth. When this Dracula complains in a climactic sequence that the worst thing about his existence is the lack of love he has suffered through the centuries, our hearts don't go out to him, as they automatically would in any other horror film that pushes the empathy button. Our reflex identification with the social outsider represented by the misunderstood monster (a response that horror films have exploited since their inception) is short-circuited here by Herzog's unflinching focus on his Dracula's low animality. This is a Dracula who strikes not because he is tragically doomed to do so, but because killing is his essence, his reason for being. He is a predator, pure and simple, and his appeal for understanding only makes him more repulsive. He has no right to claim human feeling.

As a sexual myth, Dracula has been embodied as a male fantasy in the drooling, lustful count played by Christopher Lee in the Hammer films, and as a female-dream lover in the Transylvanian poster boy incarnated by Frank Langella. As another alternative, gay critic Robin Wood has constructed a reading of Murnau's original version in terms of the director's repressed homosexuality. According to Wood's suggestive account, the vampire represents the return of the repressed, in the form of a homosexual lover who threatens the false security of the film's central romantic couple and hence (to follow Wood's argument to its ideological conclusion) the stability of the nuclear family and the bourgeois values it encapsulates. There is a hint of homophobic horror in the Herzog film as the count rushes forward to embrace his terrified houseguest, Jonathan Harker (Bruno Ganz). Later, he appears in Jonathan's bedroom, an overtly gay variation on Dracula's traditional seduction scene. But overall, the most strikingly original aspect of Herzog's interpretation is its lack of sexuality. There is not a single heaving bosom to be glimpsed in the film, no evidence of physical passion or consummation. I was amazed when I read Jack Kroll's account of *Nosferatu* in *Newsweek*, in which he theorizes that Jonathan's wife Lucy (Isabelle Adjani) is somehow sexually fulfilled by her ritual sacrifice in the last reel, the film's sole remotely erotic encounter. Admittedly, a smile does play on Lucy's lips as she lies in the dawn of light, but in the terms Herzog has set out, it is only the self-satisfied smile of chastity in triumph over depravity, a triumph, moreover, that turns out to be ambiguous. I can understand how someone not familiar with Herzog's films could leap to such a spectacularly wrongheaded conclusion, but for anyone who has experienced the asceticism of *Fata Morgana*, *The Great Ecstasy of the Sculptor Steiner*, and *Heart of Glass*, the idea of Herzog trading in sexual ecstasies can only seem ridiculous. Of the two great subjects of Western literature, Herzog is less interested in sex than death—death, that is, as contained in a transcendent visionary experience. Perhaps that is why Lucy smiles.

The closest reference point to *Nosferatu* in Herzog's past work is *La Soufrière*, his eerie documentary on the empty island city of Guadeloupe, abandoned in expectation of a volcanic eruption. Herzog and his camera crew roam the deserted streets, taking in the sights and sounds of utter desolation, themselves standing in immediate physical danger. At last they discover two old men who have refused to leave their home. For Herzog they are heroes, pilgrims at the shrine of the apocalypse. Never mind that their own expressed reasons for staying behind are much less mystical (more a matter of enervation than inspiration): Herzog identifies his morbid yearnings with theirs, and the film ends on a bizarre note of disappointment when the disaster fails to take place. In *Nosferatu*, thankfully a work of fiction, the apocalypse does come off, as the vampire's army of 500,000 rats spreads plague through the streets of Delft. Herzog's camera assumes an exalted overhead position to observe the serpentine parade of coffins through the town square, and descends for rapturous close-ups of the waves of rats spreading across the pavement. A danse macabre takes place around the edges, completing the iconographic transfer to the Middle Ages, where Herzog's morbid mysticism finds its spiritual home.

Herzog, in a way, could be considered a John Ford in reverse: he is interested not in the formation of communities but in their dissolution, the inevitable fall of the social organism in the face of brute nature. Where Ford celebrated the birth of civilization in the wilderness, Herzog, in *Aguirre*, *Heart of Glass*, and *Nosferatu*, rhapsodizes over the revenge of the wilderness as entropy enters and destroys the system. The monkeys scurry across Aguirre's pathetic raft, the rats scamper through the sewers of Delft. This is not a time for despair but, for Herzog's visionary heroes, a moment of individual epiphany. The vain pretenses of society have been shattered, and the world stands revealed in its proper horror and beauty. Herzog's world, conceived in medieval terms, is an animistic, prescientific one: behind every natural object stands an unnameable but irresistible force. Hence his protracted, static shots of water rushing down riverbanks, and clouds streaming over mountaintops—images that become more exotic and threatening the longer they are held, like words on a page that lose their familiarity and meaning when the reader stops to study them. *Fata Morgana*, Herzog's finest film, is built entirely on this principle from estrangement. From its opening sequence—a shot of a plane landing at a desert airstrip, taken through a space-distorting telephoto lens and repeated over and over and over—the viewer is either caught up in Herzog's hypnotic, alienating vision or, if the hypnosis fails to take, bored to distraction. That's the danger built into Herzog's technique: if he can't communicate his intensity, can't cast his spell, his films degenerate into cold, inert formal exercises (as did, for me, *Heart of Glass*). Herzog's medieval mindset precludes any hint of humanism: his films have little or no character interest, no inherent emotion to fall back on between epiphanies.

If Herzog's documentaries are his most successful films, and I think they are, it must be in part because the documentary form excuses his lack of interest in narrative character development. The people and the situations are given, and Herzog can proceed directly to what really concerns him: namely, the spiritual emanations of his images. When Herzog deals in fiction, he tends to shirk his responsibilities, and, without the objective underpinnings of truth that attach themselves to documentaries, we sense something missing—the redolent images are spaced out by a sort of shadow play, a thin drama that never rises to independently engage our attention or interest but remains a mere pretext. For Herzog, plot is mainly a support structure: it holds the images, it doesn't generate or advance them. There are long stretches in all of Herzog's fictions that play out perfunctorily—times when he's just going through the motions of the story, in order to move his film from epiphany A to epiphany B. *Aguirre* is Herzog's best fiction, not because the characters are unusually sharp or commanding (only Kinski comes across with any force), but because the images are constantly surprising and suggestive. When—in a *Stroszek* or *Heart of Glass*—the image flow is interrupted, the film stagnates.

Clearly, Herzog was attracted to *Nosferatu* because the material, with its riot of death images, plugs into his preoccupations. But there might have been another reason. Perhaps Herzog thought that the ritual quality of the plot, made familiar by its endless repetitions over the years, might free him from the distractions of storytelling. If we all know what's going to happen, there's no point in belaboring it; we can skip right on to the good stuff. To a degree, that's true: the aesthetic interest of genre films generally lies in the personal variations that the director works on traditional material. But our interest in genre films is seldom, if ever, purely aesthetic. *The Search-*

ers is a profound meditation on American culture, but it is also a superior Western. If a director is going to depend on generic conventions, he'll have to reckon with generic expectations as well. Herzog has failed to do that in *Nosferatu*: whatever the film's value as a personal testament or as a mood piece, it's a dismal failure as a horror movie. Which is to say, *Nosferatu* is never very frightening. Suggestive, yes, and even eerie. But nowhere does Herzog deliver on the genre's promise of brute physical stimulation.

Herzog has never been a scrupulous technician, and part of the film's failure can be laid to his general ineptitude when it comes to executing a very routine flourish of narrative filmmaking. For example, there is the sequence in which Jonathan and Dracula race from Transylvania to Delft, Jonathan by land and Dracula by sea. The sequence calls for an elementary application of parallel montage, but Herzog fumbles the rhythm of his crosscutting. His shots are poorly timed and badly matched. There is no sense of simultaneous action, and hence no suspense.

But beyond the technical shortcomings, there is Herzog's refusal to reimagine the material or even to adjust it to contemporary standards of plausibility. Part of me admires his iconoclasm, another part regrets the lack of surprise and seductiveness. Herzog flings himself head-on into the hoariest clichés of the story: Jonathan announces his intention to visit Dracula's castle to an innkeeper, and suddenly plates crash, jaws drop, and a hundred peasant faces turn to gape in amazement. The dialogue and characters have been reduced to their barest, ritual essentials, but the effect is often less incantatory and compelling than mechanical and alienating. As Lucy, Isabelle Adjani affects a silent-film acting style, all mime and poses, which makes an appropriate iconographic identification between her character and the unnatural purity of early movie heroines. Still, an unnatural Lucy doesn't work at the film's climax; her sacrifice seems remote and academic rather than immediate and meaningful.

Nosferatu, finally, is no less ambiguous than Herzog's total career. There's no doubt about the uniqueness and power of his sensibility, but he's hardly a natural filmmaker. With its petulance over matters of form and development, *Nosferatu* sometimes made me wonder why Herzog was attracted to narrative filmmaking at all—why he hadn't invested his talents in a more accommodating medium like photography or poetry. But then, at the end of his film, Herzog executed one of his very few variations on Murnau's original design. Superficially, the film's finale is only an obvious reversal of a well-worn cliché, but it carries a deeper charge. In Herzog's terms, his ending is a happy one, and his film is redeemed by the weird exhilaration of its last shot—an expression of ghoulish joy and mystical awe that chillingly justifies everything that has come before.

Knife in the Head

Directed by REINHARD HAUFF {October 24, 1980}

Reinhard Hauff's *Knife in the Head* has the brooding, doom-laden spirit of a film noir, though it isn't fate that's waiting to trip the characters; it's the equally powerful, equally abstract late '70s equivalent: ideology. Where Anthony Mann, Edgar Ulmer, and the other grubby tragedians of the '40s presented a dark, skewed world ruled by unseen, unknowable forces, Hauff's film is set in a bleached and sterile Miesian environment, gleaming linoleum and polished chrome taking the place of film noir's commanding quicksand shadows. The forces that rally against Hauff's protagonist likewise lack the scale and mystery of the ruthless, crushing Destiny that ruled the '40s, but they're just as strong, just as cold, and just as remote.

Hauff's hero is Berthold Hoffman (Bruno Ganz), a molecular biologist who appears to have no personal politics. He does, however, have a wife (Angela Winkler), who has left him for an abrasive, punkish leftist (Heinz Hoenig). The film begins in a highly noir-ish mood, with Hoffmann alone in his office, looking down at the night city below. In voice-over, he declaims, "An American in my place would start shooting out the windows," crystallizing both his romantic predicament and the film's larger theme of impotence. Hoffmann takes to the street, Hauff's camera moving with him in tight, traveling close-up. When he rounds the corner of the youth center where his wife and her lover work, the camera pulls back from Hoffmann's face to reveal a police raid taking place in eerie silence behind plate-glass windows. Hoffmann rushes in, hoping to save his wife from the escalating riot, but she's already outside, straining to call him through the din. Hoffmann races through the building, searching; he enters a small room that houses a printing press, and, just as he turns to face an oncoming policeman, the screen goes black.

Hoffman has been bludgeoned and shot, left a cripple who must learn again to think, to eat, to speak. The newspapers call him a victim of terrorism; to the authorities, he's a knife-wielding radical; the leftists see him as a martyr to police brutality. Hoffmann's battered mind is a blank; each institution sees in him what it most can use: an exploitable story of personal tragedy, a way of shifting guilt, a cause to rally round. And Hoffman's mind, for quite a while, remains a blank: sealed up in a modern hospital, he is only dimly aware of what is happening outside. His physical recuperation parallels his mental rebirth: starting from virtual scratch, he must rebuild both his body and his character, and the only models available to him are the images reflected back by the press, the police, and his wife's political friends. Hoffmann has his choice of identities, but whichever role he picks, something pulls him in another direction. Though no knife was found, there is always the possibility that, in his blind panic, he did attack the cop. He can't dismiss the idea: the unfound knife stays with him, inside his head.

The concept of the "fatal flaw" is a central one in film noir. If the hero displays the slightest weakness in character (having one drink too many, looking too hard at the blond in the typing pool) or relaxes his moral guard for a fraction of a second (helping himself to a few bucks from the cash register), it is enough to unleash the most frightful forces of his fiercely punitive universe. The knife in the head, the sense that he may be capable of murder, is Hoffmann's flaw: Did he come to the youth center to attack his wife and her lover? Did he pull a knife on the cop? Hauff isn't telling, and by keeping Hoffmann's motives cloudy, he makes us share the character's uncertainty, his desperate search to know himself.

But Hauff is after something more than a moral point. Beyond the question of Hoffmann's capacity for killing, there's the problem of his restlessness, his frustration, his thwarted urge to action. Whatever his reasons for coming to the youth center, his attempt to rescue his wife seems noble, heroic—a positive release of the pent-up energy we saw when we first set eyes on him, alone and tense at his window. The subject of *Knife in the Head* isn't politics or the problem of terrorism, but something more personal and philosophical: it's about what happens to private individual acts when they bleed over into the public sphere. It's Hauff's observation that no gesture, in the polarized, politicized atmosphere of Germany, is innocent of ideology—that every act, by virtue of its time and place, is a political act. In itself, that isn't an original observation: Godard has been arguing it for years, most recently (and brilliantly) in his *Every Man for Himself*. What gives *Knife in the Head* its twist is Hauff's sympathy for the unfashionable position—that the individual has a right to his actions, that society shouldn't be allowed to co-opt them.

There's an old axiom of moviemaking that holds "Comedy is in long shot, tragedy is in close-up." A possible corollary might be "Politics is in long shot, psychology is in close-up"—that's the implication of Hauff's pullback from Hoffmann's face, to reveal the raid behind the window. The narration shifts levels at that point: where before we've been placed, through close-ups and subjective camera movement, in Hoffmann's mind, we suddenly find ourselves in a wider context, a political world beyond Hoffmann's consciousness. Hoffmann is still separate from it—as the riot goes on in silence behind the glass, it seems dreamlike, unreal—but the camera movement has noted the intersection of Hoffmann's private feelings and the political forces; it's held them, tenuously, in the same frame. This early shot is probably the only moment of intersection in the film: though the camera movements continue, they remain subjective, moving with Hoffmann, and though the long shots continue to intrude on Hoffmann's private struggle, they no longer have the depth of focus of the early one. Hauff closes down to a very narrow field, holding only one figure—foreground of background—in sharp focus against slightly blurred surroundings. When he pulls focus, from one character to another within the shot, he's emphasizing the limits of objectivity—the sense of harmony, the "big picture," that the long shot creates. Hauff's frames are made up of a myriad of points of view, each limited: when he pulls focus, he pulls the character out of his social, political context and makes him an individual, often against his will. Hoffmann has acted on an impulse—an impulse not, perhaps, to become a hero (the act, in any case, is absurd, because his wife is already safe), but to assert himself, to do *something*. The remark about the American, as bizarre as it may sound to us, is suggestive: Hoffmann's crisis is emotional, but it is also, to dig up a musty word, existential. He has lost his wife to this strange new force afoot in the land; he's been rendered neutral, impotent. His march to the youth center is his last stand—his attempt to step out of his isolation and passivity and fling himself at the world. But the world brushes him off: he's denied the personal confronta-tion with his wife and is thrown, instead, straight into the impersonality that threatens him most, this abstract collision of cops and kids. (Though the film displays a slight leftward slant, perhaps out of sheer underdog sympathy for the kids, it really doesn't take sides; Hauff never raises the issues that led to the confrontation, and he dresses both cops and kids in the same paramilitary uniforms—leather jackets and scowls.) And what Hoffman gains from this confrontation is a literal, physical incapacity to go with his emotional paralysis: he may have felt like a lump before, but now he is one.

Perhaps Hoffmann clings to the idea of the knife during his recovery because it is some proof of his personal power, his effectuality. It's not a flaw but a strength: that he could pull a knife on a cop, much less on his wife's lover, is evidence of his willingness to fight, to put himself forward. As the leftists and rightists struggle for Hoffmann's slowly returning identity—the left wants a saint, the right wants an assassin—Hoffmann holds on to the knife as an image of who he is, an emblem of his private rage.

The knife is the film's central image, though it never appears. Hoffmann pulls another knife on his wife's lover, as proof that he isn't the helpless, pure-hearted victim the left wants him to be, but he can't use it—perhaps because the issues, in Hoffmann's mind, have grown beyond personal revenge. At one point he may have wanted to kill a man, but now his anger is larger. Fully recovered, Hoffmann goes in search of the cop who shot him. He wants to recreate the circumstances of the shooting, hoping to discover the truth about the knife at last—whether he held it or simply wished that he had.

The film ends with another suddenly darkened screen, again cutting off Hoffmann in mid-act. But the ambiguity at the end is less fruitful than that of the start: it's less a suggestive omission than a blank, glaring absence, and it throws off our reading of Hoffmann. Some important information—about the strength of his will, the depth of his anger, his ultimate moral standing—has been withheld. *Knife in the Head* is a film of ideas, and by throwing away the emotional climax, Hauff makes his priorities clear: the ideas are over, even if the story isn't. It could be the creeping sentimentalist in me, but I felt cheated: it's as if, by reducing Hoffmann to the status of an idea, an element in an abstract discourse, Hauff has done exactly what his villainous ideologues wanted. He's stamped out the last embers of Hoffmann's individuality, left him drained and empty—the symbol everyone wanted all along. But for most of its length, *Knife in the Head* is a rigorous, gripping film, a movie that attends, with insight and compassion, to the cry of lonely voices.

Macbeth

Directed by ORSON WELLES {January 30, 1981}

The Orson Welles *Macbeth* and the Laurence Olivier *Hamlet* were both released in 1948. Ironically, there is more of *Citizen Kane* in the cavernous deep-focus interiors and gliding crane movements of *Hamlet* than there is in the sweaty close-ups and sketchy stage settings of *Macbeth*. Welles must have been stunned when Olivier walked off with the Oscar, leaving Welles unhonored and underfinanced, to wander the backroads of independent, international coproduction for the next ten years.

Macbeth, of course, would never have won an Oscar, even without Olivier's competition. It was made, on a 23-day schedule and a miniscule budget, for Republic Pictures, a studio best known at the time for its Roy Rogers Westerns. (The process shots used for *Macbeth*'s craggy landscapes are clearly on loan from Roy; Scotland has never looked so much like Texas.) After a few disastrous previews, 21 minutes were cut from the film and Welles's original Scottish-accented soundtrack was replaced by an American dub job. What must have begun as a prestige project for Republic president Herbert J. Yates ended as an embarrassment, and the film received only a limited release. Oscar doesn't like failures, particularly B-budgeted ones.

Welles did take a kind of revenge on Olivier with his subsequent *Othello*, which begins with a funeral procession that seems a direct challenge to *Hamlet*'s death-march finale. Welles uses the same dramatic backlighting and similar compositions around the bier, and out-Gothics Olivier at every turn. But Welles's real vindication is the newly restored version of *Macbeth*, cut footage reinserted, Scottish soundtrack replaced, that has been assembled by the UCLA Film Archives (it plays this Saturday, January 31, at the Midwest Film Center). The new *Macbeth* still isn't among Welles's major work, but it is much more coherent now, better rounded and better paced. *Hamlet*, mangled by Olivier's own injudicious cuts in the text, now seems the crippled film.

Welles has been haunted by a reputation for profligacy—for spending too much, shooting too much, and aiming for too much—but his later films have always struck me as imaginative and honorable jobs of fitting the vision to the budget. (Even *Citizen Kane*, despite its apparent excesses, was not an unusually expensive film.) Faced with a Republic budget, Welles conceived a minimalist *Macbeth*, shot largely on a single sound stage with an unadorned set, simple costumes, and even some doubling among the cast. The castle set is an ingeniously platformed scaffold affair, given life by a few untidy pools of standing water and billows of offscreen fog. There is no background landscape, only a vast white screen on which Welles projects his night sky and occasional flashes of Klieg-lightning. The space, typically for Welles, is the space of the stage: large, deep, yet surrealistically enclosed.

· 136 ·

Macbeth, in fact, is the most forthrightly theatrical of all of Welles's films. The stage stylization extends beyond the set to the film's few evident exteriors, which are made unreal by vast quantities of swirling fog and—as Birnam wood advances upon Dunsinane—a striking, discreet use of slow motion. More than ever, the up angles of Welles's famous "heroic" shots begin to look like the view from the orchestra seats. Long shots abound, defining the exact dimensions of the castle set, though (suggestively) there is no attempt to place the film's handful of interiors (a banquet hall, a bedchamber) within it. It's as if the transition from castle to hall requires a physical shifting of scenery: each scene occupies a separate "stage" of its own, and there is no spatial continuity between them. (I'm reminded here of the famous opening shot of *Touch of Evil*, an overhead crane that follows a car from the center of a border town to its outskirts. As in *Macbeth*, Welles is using the camera movement not to describe a continuous, "realistic" space, but to lay out the physical limits of the action; the crane shot turns the entire town into a single, self-contained stage set.) There's nothing in *Macbeth* with quite the pure theatricality of the celebrated kitchen scene in *The Magnificent Ambersons*, in which Welles parks his camera in front of his actors (again, at that slight, orchestra-seat incline) and plays out the scene in a single, uninflected take. There is, however, a slightly more elaborate, more abstract variation on the same idea: the return of Macduff (Dan O'Herlihy) and Malcolm (Roddy McDowall) to Scotland, where they are met by a synthetic figure—a Holy Father (Alan Napier)—of Welles's own devising, is shot in an extended single take. Blocked with fiendish complexity, the actors move toward and away from the camera as the camera moves toward and away from them; crossing and recrossing each other's paths, they trace out a small arabesque. As in *Ambersons*, the shot preserves the spatial continuity, the theatrical integrity, of the scene, though there is an extra element here, one that has less to do with dramatic art than with choreography. The camera becomes an unseen partner in a cinematic dance.

What's curious about *Macbeth* is that, for all of the film's insistence on its theatricality, it isn't really concerned with the play as a play. Shakespeare's words aren't showcased, brought forward: unlike the Olivier *Hamlet*, in which several of the monologues are read over blank, neutral images, the better to emphasize the independent imagery of the language, the Welles *Macbeth* sucks the speeches into the mise-en-scène. Like the fog that slinks into almost every frame, Welles's dark, oppressive compositions envelop the text, shading it, twisting it, sometimes obliterating it. The images come first, not merely illustrating the text, but determining it, shaping our understanding. Most of the readings, Welles's included, do little to develop the poetry: accents are ignored or deliberately misplaced, and Shakespeare's verse comes out with a continuous, prosy sound. (Welles's readings do have a strange, interior rhythm, but it's an inflection that often seems weirdly divorced from the sense of the text—again, something abstract. I'd expect no less from the man who can read "We will sell no wine/before its time" and make it sound like Ezra Pound.) *Macbeth* isn't a mounting of Shakespeare's play, but something more rare: a reinvention of it in the terms of another medium, using Shakespeare's themes but not his methods. Verdi's *Otello* is not Shakespeare's, and neither is Welles's *Macbeth*. The reinvention may not be wholly successful in this early attempt, but by the time of *Chimes at Midnight* (1967), Welles's transformational approach will produce a masterpiece.

Chimes at Midnight is a synthesis, assembled from bits and pieces of five plays; *Macbeth* is a stripping down, a streamlining that preserves the essential action and themes but gives the piece a modern, highly cinematic suppleness—a sense of speed and headlong dash. Shakespeare's inimitable digressions, with their echoes, parodies, and inversions of the main action, are gone (though I do wish that some *Macbeth* somewhere would preserve the "Hecate" scene, in which the witches are upbraided by their superior for overstepping their bounds—for demonstrating the same kind of eager ambitiousness with which they have cursed Macbeth). But what the script loses in structural complexity it gains in momentum: the opening passage, from the meeting with the witches to the murder of Duncan, plays out with a breathlessness worthy of Raoul Walsh. Still, there is no loss of sense: the hero's dizzying, helpless sense of forward propulsion is conveyed no longer by the speeches but by the pure, formal rhythms of editing and whip pans. (I don't mean to use Olivier as a whipping boy, but the editing of the text is yet another area where Welles's instincts are far superior: Welles cuts the text to get at its elemental drive, while Olivier—by cutting, for example, much of Hamlet's dark, disturbing wit—edits for the sake of simplifying, sometimes trivializing, the underlying ideas.)

Macbeth is a highly theatrical film, made from a streamlined, movie-ized play. That conflict, between film and theater, lies at the center of much of Welles's work, and it gives his films much of their tension, variety, and constant inventiveness—the way, for example, he can change the style of *Citizen Kane* completely, from theatrical long take to cinematic montage, from sequence to sequence. (There's not so much of that leaping mutability in *Macbeth*, which may be why it lacks some of the excitement we expect from Welles.) But there is a deeper conflict in Welles's work, one that gives a personal, emotional significance to the stylistic division. Like many actor-directors—Chaplin, Lewis, and more recently Clint Eastwood— Welles uses his movies as a mirror, a way of examining, criticizing, and sometimes glorifying his image of himself. Theatrical space, for Welles, is psychological space: in film after film, he imagines himself as a tiny figure lost in cavernous, threatening interiors, a little boy lost in a hostile world. But yet, as an actor, Welles is bombastic, dominating, spectacular: he casts himself as characters of vast, mysterious power, and he holds his close-ups imperiously, commanding our attention to his face, his voice, and (in the later films) his sheer size. Self-aggrandizement alternates with self-hatred: the actor expands, the director diminishes. What the theatrical style sets up, the cinematic style tears down: the primacy of Welles the actor is constantly threatened by the offscreen authority of Welles the director.

Macbeth, in Welles's hands, becomes the story of a little man made big by forces beyond his control, against his better judgment and his best understanding of himself. There's something of the psychobiography here—the wunderkind who has profound doubts about himself—but at his best, Welles strikes a resonance much deeper than the tinny sound of private neuroses. His films are sounded from a crash of perceptions: the interior against the exterior, the subjective against the objective, film against theater. It's not too much to suggest that *Macbeth*'s witches, drawing their voodoo image of the thane of Cawdor from their boiling pot, taunting the doll with toy crowns and "daggers of the mind," are the representatives of Welles the director within the film. They elevate the actor, act on him, and finally bring him down.

The Woman Next Door

Directed by FRANÇOIS TRUFFAUT {November 20, 1981}

I can't really argue with Pat Aufderheide's film-festival review of François Truffaut's *The Woman Next Door*, but now that the film has settled into the Biograph for its regular commercial run, an afterthought or two might be in order. The picture is rigid, cold, and unsatisfying in the late Truffaut manner, yet—once its failure as an emotional experience has been accepted—it strikes me as Truffaut's most intelligent, most imaginative film since *Jules and Jim*. For the first time in a decade, Truffaut is giving hard thought to the formal properties of his medium: he is rethinking his visual style, looking critically at his choice of camera setups, and dealing self-consciously with the implications of his design. Truffaut has been moving uneasily toward modernism in his last several films. With *The Woman Next Door*, he finally embraces it—and if the results aren't what we once expected (and treasured) from Truffaut, they're hardly without interest. Truffaut has moved from Gallic humanism to Gallic abstraction: now he belongs not with Renoir, Pagnol, and Carne, but with Duras, Godard, and Bresson.

In retrospect, it seems clear that Truffaut's flirtation with modernist self-consciousness began with 1973's *Day for Night*, the first of his films to take moviemaking as its explicit subject. Following on the heels of *Such a Gorgeous Kid like Me*, the unquestioned low point of Truffaut's career, *Day for Night* couldn't help but look like a desperation move—a retreat into formalism. When an artist has nothing left to say about life, he starts making art about art, or so the saying goes. But what no one noticed at the time was how decisively the emotional center of Truffaut's work had shifted. There was a genuine affection in *Day for Night*, though it wasn't an affection for anything human—it was a love for camera and lights, for laying tracks and cutting film. (The picture's most sensual moment was set in the cutting room: a swoony, delirious close-up of a stream of celluloid pouring out of an editing machine.) *Day for Night* treated movies as a love object (an attitude that I found chilling, perhaps because it hit too close to home). For Truffaut, movies had ceased to be the means to an end—a "medium" in the true sense—but had become an end in themselves, a self-contained value.

Day for Night also marked the emergence of the obsessive drive of late Truffaut (though it had appeared earlier in *Fahrenheit 451* and the Hitchcock homage *The Bride Wore Black*). Leaving aside obvious divertissements like *Small Change*, Truffaut's films from this point on are concerned with overweening emotions, irreversibly fixated: on a particular man (*The Story of Adele H.*), on women in general (*The Man Who Loved Women*), on the

· 140 ·

dead (*The Green Room*), and on the past (*Love on the Run, The Last Metro*). The object of obsession grows larger and more abstract with every film until it apparently collapses back into its original dimensions with the man-woman dynamics of *The Woman Next Door*. But only apparently, I think. The love of Bernard (Gérard Depardieu) for Mathilde (Fanny Ardant) is of a more general and metaphoric nature than Adele's love for her soldier. *Adele H.* is still, more or less, a story of human passion; *The Woman Next Door* is a story of cinematic passion, of the love of the spectator for the image on the screen. It's a dangerous, unnatural love, one that can't, shouldn't be consummated. When Bernard is led to try, the outcome is fatal.

In *The Woman Next Door*, Truffaut mixes a modernist examination of his medium with obsession, intellectual investigation with morbid passion. It's a tone unlike any I've encountered before: undeniably sterile and schematic, yet with a vague, compelling darkness, an undercurrent of madness that seeps into the most rational and studied of formal contexts. Truffaut begins the film like a scientist setting up an experiment, laying down the two kinds of shots he intends to deal with. Under the opening credits, we see a helicopter shot of an ambulance rushing through a suburban village: this is the continuous, embracing overview favored by Renoir's camera, the camera that becomes a "window on the world," able to see everything and admit everything in a rolling, seamless present. Against the flowing long take of the helicopter shot is posited the restricted close-up of the opening dialogue scene, in which Truffaut's Jamesian narrator, Madame Jouve (Véronique Silver), addresses the camera directly, admonishing it at one point to move back from a close-up so the audience can see her crippled leg. This is the camera of Griffith, Eisenstein, and the montage directors, using a relatively fixed frame like the frame around a canvas, a frame that excludes, setting a limit to the image. Madame Jouve's direct instructions to the camera make us aware of what the frame is leaving out; it's a demonstration of the image's boundaries and limitations, in strong distinction to the free-flying camera of the credits. One kind of shot presupposes a unified, coherent world, a reality that exists before the camera. The other, narrower kind can show us only fragments, pieces of a "reality" that we must create for ourselves, mentally assembling the scattered shots into a continuous space that is never actually shown.

Bernard's dealings with his family, his friends, and his coworkers are shown, more or less consistently, in long-take "shot sequences," in which the camera moves in harmony with the blocking of the actors. (The most extraordinary of these is a long scene in which Bernard visits Madame Jouve at her home—the conversation moves through three rooms without a cut.) But when Bernard is reintroduced to Mathilde (they'd had an affair some years before; she's now married to the man who has taken the house next door to Bernard's), Truffaut shifts into fragmented montage, presenting Bernard and Mathilde in a series of alternating close-ups. On the rare occasions when they are allowed to appear together in the same frame, Truffaut is careful to introduce unsettling elements into the compositions: foreground objects that block our direct access to the characters, staircases and other strong lines that divide and add tension to the frame, and, most significantly, added "frames-within-frames" of doorways and windows that keep the two characters apart. After the shock of meeting again has passed, Mathilde phones Bernard in hopes of arranging a rendezvous: the cutting in this sequence follows the traditional plan for telephone conversations, with each character held tightly in his or her own frame and setting, but the crispness and strict division of the characters in this sequence becomes the model for all of their future encounters. Bernard and Mathilde meet in a shabby hotel room to make love, but even in this isolated, extremely private space, they are held apart by the editing, which has a hardness and sharpness that suggests not so much the smooth, invisible flow of standard shot alternation, but something almost surgical, clinically precise and soulless.

Space is a key element in *The Woman Next Door*, as it is a different kind of space. Where *The Last Metro* was obsessed with an idea of "interiority"—it was a film about a man hiding in the basement of a theater located inside a courtyard contained in the Nazi-occupied city of Paris—*The Woman Next Door* is concerned with lateral space, side-by-sideness (the French title, *La femme d'à côté*, translates literally as "the woman on the side"). After establishing the two houses as distinct entities through isolating, still shots, Truffaut lays down the relationship between them by tracking along with Bernard's son as he runs from his front yard to greet his new neighbors. This lateral movement is repeated throughout the film, not only between the two houses, but in the general tendency of Truffaut's blocking to move his characters from one side of the set to the other, rather than toward or away from the camera. This stylistic figure is condensed in an image associated with Madame Jouve: she is the proprietor of a tennis camp, and in the background of many of her shots we see side views of the courts, the players facing each other over the line of the net.

In his alternation of long takes and crosscutting, and in the tension he creates between lateral movements of camera and actors and static close-ups, Truffaut is laying down a rhythm of continuity and disruption, unity and fragmentation. It's as if there were two different orders of human life in the film, one belonging to those who can exist together in the same frame, one to those who cannot. What makes the difference, what turns continuity and wholeness into disruption and fragmentation, is an eruption of voyeurism: it's when the characters regard each other erotically or possessively that the continuity breaks down, when they become separate, competing individuals. They cease to live and begin to look. It's too simple to say that Bernard is the voyeur and Mathilde is the exhibitionist (for Truffaut cleverly changes their roles from time to time), but by and large it is Bernard who spies and Mathilde who is exposed (twice literally—once when her husband makes her model a revealing dress, once when her dress is accidentally torn at a garden party). Bernard idealizes Mathilde as an erotic object, yearns to possess her—for him, Mathilde exists on a separate physical plane, apart and away from his wife (who, as someone he can quietly coexist with, is truly "the woman on the side").

The barriers between Bernard and Mathilde—the tightness of the frame, the isolation of the close-up, the relentless confrontational rhythms of the crosscutting—are the same barriers that stand between the spectator and the screen. Mathilde is an image, something abstract and half-real, chimera (just as her character, the femme fatale, is derived wholly from movies, perhaps exists only *in* movies). Bernard is the distant watcher: he looks at her as he would look at a screen. (At one point, Bernard and his wife go to a movie, but later Bernard can't remember seeing it—he's got his own movie playing in his mind.) The spectator looks at the screen straight on, directly confronting the images presented to him—a spatial configuration that is the exact opposite, in fact the perpendicular, of Truffaut's idea of "lateralness." Bernard's fatal mistake lies in his belief that he can, as a spectator, enter the frame, turn the movie-viewing situation on its side and take true possession of his love object, the actress. At the film's climax, Bernard finally seems to break through—but by entering the frame he has created for Mathilde, he leaves life behind. He exists now only in morbid fantasy: the movies have seduced him, and they will do worse.

The Woman Next Door's understanding of the perverse relationship between spectator and star, of the love for something illusory and inhuman that becomes, somehow, more elevated and intense than human love, is a long way from *Day for Night*'s unproblematic idealization of the film for film's sake. Truffaut has matured: though the object of his fascination is the same, he is more self-conscious of his fascination, more willing to look at how it really works, to see its morbidity as well as its romantics, its dangers as well as its glories. It seems to me that Truffaut has come across something profound. *The Woman Next Door* may mark his rebirth as an artist—an artist of a very different kind from the François Truffaut we used to know, but no less valuable.

Lola

Directed by RAINER WERNER FASSBINDER {October 1, 1982}

It's hard to accept the idea that there won't be any more Fassbinder films. When Rainer Werner Fassbinder died this spring at the age of 36, the most prolific career in modern movies came to an end; we had all become accustomed to seeing two or three new Fassbinder films a year, and suddenly the flow had stopped (though not quite, of course—Fassbinder's last two films, *Veronika Voss* and *Querelle*, are still awaiting release, and there are a dozen or two early Fassbinder films that have not yet been shown in this country). An output that consistent and that intense creates its own context: in evaluating Fassbinder, you don't first compare his work to other directors' films, but look instead for where each film fits in the overall Fassbinder canon. Fassbinder, with his ever-evolving style, continually reacted against himself, spinning each film off in a direction subtly different from the one before. Some of his films are shining successes, several are murky failures, but they all make sense in the general sweep of his career: he runs down the blind alley of a *Chinese Roulette* the better to find the startling clarity of an *In a Year of 13 Moons*.

No single Fassbinder film stands alone, though some do stand above others. To make so many films is, in itself, an artistic decision: Fassbinder's aesthetic counts quantity as much as quality, with the suggestion that no one film is complete in itself, but rather that each draws its meanings from the movies around it. The paradox of Fassbinder's career—and also the great sign of his originality—was that he was a master filmmaker who made no masterpieces. Even his best films—*The Bitter Tears of Petra von Kant, Ali: Fear Eats the Soul, In a Year of 13 Moons*—don't have the wholeness and weight of great works of art; there is something missing from every one of them. It's as if Fassbinder, by committing himself to his hectic schedule, had consciously decided against making masterworks. His films are a repudiation of the idea of the final, the definitive, the all-embracing; he thrives instead on the provisional, the exploratory, the disposable. Fassbinder's output, of course, isn't all that extraordinary when compared to the studio directors of 30 or 40 years ago, for whom two or three films a year was the rule. Fassbinder drew on those American directors for many of the stylistic ideas in his films, though he was hardly unique in doing so—Godard, Truffaut, and dozens of others had raided Hollywood before him. But he was unique in trying to duplicate the pace of a Hollywood career—unique, in this age of the Grand Auteur who issues one perfect film every five years— in setting a schedule and sticking to it, in taking on projects that weren't quite perfect, in issuing his work with a regularity that became routine and expected. A new Fassbinder film was no big deal—they weren't big events but simple occurrences, part of the life of the regular filmgoer in the same way a new Curtiz would have been in the '40s. Perhaps, by turning out so many films, Fassbinder was trying to make himself ordinary. He was no genius who thundered from above, but an acquaintance you encountered at regular intervals. Through his high output, Fassbinder became part of the everyday life his films depicted with such crushing force. Sometimes he was boring, sometimes he was brilliant, but always he was there.

Suddenly he isn't there anymore, and his absence affects the films that he left. *Lola* is no longer The Latest Fassbinder, but, more ominously, a Late Fassbinder, and we can't see it the same way we might have a year or two ago. It's part of a finite series now, rather than just another episode in Fassbinder's ongoing serial, but the film has no sense of finality, no autumnal quality to it. Instead, it is a treading-water film, as befits its position as the middle episode of the trilogy that began with *The Marriage of Maria Braun* and will conclude with the forthcoming *Veronika Voss*. But more than that, it is a film that deliberately resists climax—it exists in a state of dramatic suspension, muted emotions, and thematic ambiguity. *Lola* is not the grand finale that we may have hoped for, and neither is it the new beginning that may have made Fassbinder's death seem even more tragic; rather, it's a perfect second-act movie, a film about the middle states between outrage and resignation, hope and despair, beginnings and ends. If *Lola* has a single subject, it isn't the corrupting power of capitalism or the state of the German soul, but the simple act of going on—of finding the compromises necessary to survive, the means to continue. *Lola* doesn't conclude with the crashing chords of the ironically overstated tragedy Fassbinder was so fond of, but with a soft note of genuine pathos, a tone I have never heard in his work before.

The plot line has been lifted from Sternberg's *Blue Angel*, but it has been bent to different ends, different emphases. Like Sternberg's Lola, Fassbinder's heroine (Barbara Sukowa) is a professional seductress; she works as a singer in a plush bordello, where she has become the "private whore" of the plump, happily corrupt building contractor Schuckert (Mario Adorf). But Fassbinder's Lola is a more self-conscious, more practical creature than Sternberg's: she seduces not for the pleasure of it but for the profit. Corresponding to Sternberg's upright professor is upright building commissioner von Bohm (Armin Mueller-Stahl), but his morality is less a matter of fierce sexual repression than a gently glowing idealism. When Lola sets upon him, she has her Sternbergian motives—she wants to lower him a notch or two, prove he's no better than she is—but they quickly broaden. She enjoys being the demure young lady she is in von Bohm's eyes, partly because an alliance with him may be the path to respectability she's been seeking, partly because she is genuinely fond of the man, and partly because that demure young lady lives on in some part of her soul. Von Bohm, for her, is a remembrance of another time, another possibility.

As in *The Blue Angel*, the psychological drama is centered on the male; the woman drifts out of focus, her figure becoming more abstract and her motives more blurred, until she enters the mythical. Fassbinder has always had problems with the plausibility of his female characters; he allegorizes his heroines, pushing them to the limits of lust (*Jail Bait*), greed (*Maria Braun*), or victimization (*Mother Küsters Goes to Heaven*), while denying them the dramatic life he gives to his men. Lola, ultimately, is no more full a figure than Maria Braun, but the lack of dimension is less of a drawback here—the narrative, and not just the director, places her at arm's length, and if in the end she is nothing more fleshy than the spirit of capitalist corruption ("I am corrupt," she announces to von Bohm, with a finality that amounts to a dictionary definition), it's because von Bohm has come to see her—and accept her—that way, too. When von Bohm discovers who she really is, his first reaction is blind rage: he launches an investigation meant to smash her mentor Schuckert, as if Schuckert were solely responsible for her fall from virtue. Von Bohm is enough of a romantic to believe that once he has identified evil it will flee before him, but when evil not only stays put but lights a cigar, von Bohm is enough of a realist to know when to quit. Ironically, the fury of his attack has impressed Lola with how much he loves her: she is finally ready to accept him, and he, now a broken man, can accept her—along with her continuing relationship with Schuckert. Von Bohm has been taken down a notch and Lola has been raised: in this microscopic moral trade-off, Fassbinder finds stability, and with it a species of happiness.

Fassbinder's visual style also draws on Sternberg: this is a crowded, cluttered movie, with baroque compositions and a dozen different textures in every frame. And from his old master Douglas Sirk, Fassbinder has taken a bold, abstract color scheme: the crowd of objects in the images is matched by a jangle of bright, unnatural colors, pushing the images toward sensory overload. Sensory, but not sensual: there is a lot to intrigue the eye but little to please it; these pictures are too pretty to be beautiful, too rich to be digested. Flirting with cliché, Fassbinder assigns different colors of light to his protagonists—a clear, celestial blue for von Bohm, an overheated mauve for Lola—but he avoids cliché (and here is his technique in a nutshell) by pushing the device to its limits. The contrasting colors are used so frequently and so insistently that they cease to have a simple metaphorical function. The colors don't "express" the characters as much as they come to entrap them. The actors are isolated in separate color spheres—separate moralities, separate worlds. The colors glow from them like a deathly efflorescence; they could almost be the symptoms of a disease.

Unsupported dramatically, this kind of extreme stylization can lead to an exercise as empty as *Chinese Roulette*—a 1976 Fassbinder in which the lead character seemed to be a glass and metal bookcase. But Fassbinder has altered his direction of actors since *Chinese Roulette*, and in *Lola* he has found a style that can effectively play off the visual stylization—which

turns out to be, surprisingly, a quiet, contained naturalism. Though the Fassbinder stock company is out in force for the minor parts, the foreground of *Lola* is occupied by new faces: Barbara Sukowa, who starred in Margarethe von Trotta's *Marianne and Juliane* (a.k.a. *The German Sisters*); Armin Mueller-Stahl, an East German émigré making his Western debut; and Mario Adorf, a veteran character actor. There are problems with Sukowa's performance—her looks and manner seem too sharp to attract a rumpled, bearish man like von Bohm—but she is still the least affected of Fassbinder's leading ladies, the least given to signposting her emotions. And Adorf delivers a tight, professional character turn—perhaps a little slick, but slick in the ways the character is slick. But it is Mueller-Stahl, with his large, open face and crystal-blue eyes, who really brings the film home; his easy integrity, honesty, and slow grace are immensely appealing. He is the least neurotic character in Fassbinder, and also the warmest.

All of this is a far cry from the theatrical posturings that have been (often effectively) the hallmark of a Fassbinder performance. The cast of *Lola* doesn't merge, as Fassbinder's players frequently do, with the artificiality of the mise-en-scène; they are still human enough to struggle against it. It's this easiness, this naturalness, that I like most about *Lola*: for me, the technical highlight of the film lies not in the elaborate, multiplanar shots of the bordello, but in the two very elementary over-the-shoulder shots Fassbinder applies, in gentle alternation, to the street-corner conversation of Lola and von Bohm in the dead of the night, just before they kiss. There is intimacy here, and grace and spirit too—all expressed with sublime economy. Speaking through the simple things, giving the basic techniques their full expressive power, is a talent most directors don't acquire until late in their careers. Fassbinder seems to have found it in *Lola*, surprisingly early and regrettably late.

Valley Girl

Directed by MARTHA COOLIDGE {April 29, 1983}

Traditionally, some of the best American films have been studio assign-
ments that the director has managed to penetrate with his own personality
and artistic interests—they aren't personal films but films that have been
made personal. But in the '70s, this whole range of achievement was somehow lost; at the moment, Hollywood directors seem to be divided into two
fiercely exclusive camps: those who generate their own material, and those
who blindly mount what they're given. You must be either an auteur (a
misapplication of a term originally coined to describe the studio filmmaker
with a personality) or a hack. One of the strongest pleasures of *Valley Girl*—
and it has many—is the sense that the middle ground has been discovered
again. It's an assignment with a lot extra, a frankly commercial film that
acquires a warm, personal glow because the director, Martha Coolidge,
has taken a personal interest in it. Coolidge has followed the conventions
of the genre she's been given to work with—down to the flashes of female
nudity, without which no exploitation film would be complete—but she's
connected with those conventions in ways that freshen and humanize
them. *Valley Girl* probably isn't a project that Martha Coolidge would have
generated on her own, but in the end it's a Martha Coolidge film.

Is there anything more exploitative than a teen movie based on last
year's fad? A few years ago, there was a ragged Canadian film titled *Pinball
Summer* that didn't even make it to the theaters before the pinball craze
collapsed in the face of video games; it was hastily and grotesquely retitled *Pick-up Summer*. If all *Valley Girl* did was recycle the catchphrases
made popular by Frank Zappa's novelty hit (Zappa, by the way, has no
involvement with the film), it wouldn't be worth much more than a secondhand Hula-Hoop. The producers, Wayne Crawford and Andrew Lane,
also wrote the screenplay, and they've wisely put the Val-talk up front (in
an opening sequence set in one of those hermetically sealed, world-apart
shopping malls), both to hook the audience and to get it out of the way. The
catchphrases—"gag me with a spoon" and so on—keep up for the rest of
the picture, but it's a tribute to Coolidge's skill with actors that they cease
to have quotation marks around them. The catchphrases aren't laugh cues
but components of (more or less) normal speech, and through their repetition they acquire different shades of meaning; they become expressive. It
was said, I think, of Ralph Richardson that he could read the phone book
and make you cry, which is nothing compared with finding the dense emotional subtext in a line like "barf me out." I'd like to see Richardson try that.

For Coolidge, the Val-talk isn't just a laugh cue, used simply to get a rise from the audience, but also something that functions within the film. Coolidge is very sensitive to the ways in which social groups define themselves. The film is full of insights on the subtle differences in dress, manner, and morality that separate the classes, sexes, and generations. The chief of these differences is language—language used not to communicate but to set the limits of a subculture, to constantly assert who belongs and who does not. When Julie (Deborah Foreman) settles down in the neighborhood Du-par's for a cheeseburger with her friends, it isn't only an occasion for gossipy conversation, but also the convocation of a complex ritual. The repetition of key phrases and intonations has a mystic, incantatory quality; it is the social magic by which identities are created and sworn to.

It's through these insights that Coolidge turns yesterday's joke into a surprisingly moving romantic comedy. The language gimmick, considered as a social ritual, becomes the basis of a solid drama: the conflict between two language groups, two different teenage cultures. Jean Renoir intended to follow *The Rules of the Game* with a modern-dress version of *Romeo and Juliet*, but after writing several treatments—with the conflict transposed to squatters versus homeowners in the Paris suburbs, and then to farmers versus truckers in Algeria—he abandoned the project: there didn't seem to be a single modern setting that could plausibly support the rivalry of the Montagues and the Capulets. *Valley Girl* finds that setting, without stretching the point a bit, in metropolitan Los Angeles, where the middle-class credit-card culture of the San Fernando Valley is divided from the urban sleaze of Hollywood Boulevard by the imposing natural symbol of the Hollywood Hills. The conflict is much more meaningful than it is in the academic adaptation of *West Side Story*: it isn't just rival gangs but rival classes, rival environments, rival musics, and rival values.

Randy, the boy from Hollywood, is played with loping New Wave anomie by Nicolas Cage; with his hooded eyes and hound-dog delivery, he's like a lobotomized Robert Mitchum. When he shares the screen with Deborah Foreman, who has big, clear eyes and a chipmunk smile, it's a perfect montage effect: the opposites collide and produce a new meaning. Coolidge has a background in documentary (her best-known film is the feature *Not a Pretty Picture*, about a teenage rape victim), so her sharp eye for the expressiveness of physical detail—of clothing or environment—shouldn't be surprising. What is surprising is her confident, intimate rapport with actors, which again suggests Renoir. Casting is almost always the most serious practical problem in making a low-budget film: it isn't easy to find good performers willing to work for cheap, and when a film is a nonunion production, it's practically impossible. Yet it's the actors—in the absence of money for production design or elaborate cinematography—who must first establish a film's authority. If they're cheesy, no amount of good direction will prevent the film from striking the audience as cheesy too. Coolidge has found strong leads, but she's also been able to fill out the supporting parts with unusually sharp presences; Julie's circle of friends (Elizabeth Daily, Heidi Holicker, and Michelle Meyrink) has a degree of definition that would seem striking in a much more lushly financed production. The secondary cast (which includes guest appearances by Colleen Camp and Frederic Forrest as Julie's aging hippie parents) is a very diverse collection of types; the performing styles range from acidic parody (Michael Bowen as Julie's loathsome Valley boyfriend) to muted naturalism (Meyrink). Yet, just as Renoir was able to integrate the theatrical hamminess of performers like Jules Berry and Erich von Stroheim with the sensitive understatement that his casts are most famous for, so does Coolidge manage to find a harmony between broadly satiric and warmly naturalistic playing. It's the crux of her style as a filmmaker.

The screenplay of *Valley Girl* could easily lend itself to low-grade social satire; what makes the film special is Coolidge's decision to draw an emotional validity out of it too—to flesh out the cartoon characters and cartoon conflicts. The tone is pitched in the seldom-explored realm between satire and romance; Coolidge's control of that tone is remarkable accurate, and her medium of control is the acting. Coolidge doesn't alternate satire and romance but finds a way to play both at once: her lead performers must simultaneously create broad social types (for the comedy) and detailed, feeling individuals (to validate the emotional themes). The seams are never visible: there's a beautiful moment when Randy, having lost Julie to her old peer group, stands high in the hills and looks down on the valley. "She's out there somewhere," he sighs, like a knight steeling himself to search for his kidnapped lady, and the juxtaposition of the chivalric sentiments and the prosaic landscape is very funny. But at the same time, there's an earnestness in Nicolas Cage's delivery of the line that leaves, for all his ironic self-awareness, no doubt of the depth of his emotion.

Coolidge doesn't condescend to teenage emotions and teenage conflict; she never trivializes her material. But neither does she project an overblown adult romanticism on her teenage heroes, as Francis Ford Coppola does in *The Outsiders*. The issues of *Valley Girl* aren't Coppola's operatic oppositions of love and death, but more modest, concrete ones: conformism versus individuality, social status versus personal satisfaction. I don't think peer-group pressure has ever been so strongly portrayed in a film: Coolidge's portrait of the pleasure and security to be derived from belonging to a clique is so strong that when Julie is forced to choose between her old friends and her new beau, the decision is an extremely difficult, dramatically active one. The choice isn't clear, which makes Julie's final decision seem that much more significant and liberating; Coolidge has put something real at stake.

Sometimes, the stakes are a little too real. A subplot centered on the competition between a (divorced) mother and her daughter for the same teenage boy raises issues of a more intense, primal nature than the film's light framework can contain. But when the subplot turns out to be an elaborate premise for a joke on the audience, we can't help but feel betrayed; some bond of trust, as well as a standard of seriousness, has been violated. The sequence does suggest Coolidge's willingness to grant adults a degree of credibility rare in teen pix; though the film in outline seems to follow the genre tradition of portraying grown-ups as ridiculous clods, Coolidge is able to insinuate occasional hints of human depth. Only a jittery driver's ed instructor (Richard Sanders) remains entirely unredeemed. An obnoxious English teacher reveals a surprising vulnerability in the course of her windy prom-night speech; Julie's parents, who begin as barely breathing caricatures of southern California's '60s hangover, eventually give her the nonconformist courage she needs.

Perhaps the deepest pleasure we take in entertainment films comes from the skill with which the director suggests a gradual, plausible, logical movement toward the unification of contradictory elements, the making of a symmetrical, satisfying whole out of apparent division and chaos. It's a secret that was well known in the old studio Hollywood, where it was called a happy ending—the elegant fulfillment of expectations. *Valley Girl* moves toward the unification of its opposites—boys and girls, Hollywood and the Valley, friends and lovers, parents and children—with a pleasant, teasing grace; it makes the inevitable look fresh and surprising, miraculous. Shakespeare knew about that technique, too. Randy and Julie are a long way from Romeo and Juliet, but they do inhabit a corner of the Shakespearean terrain—midsummer's night in the San Fernando Valley.

Gremlins

Directed by JOE DANTE {June 29, 1984}

As a rule, movies are either the reflection of a single strong personality or pure committee products, bordering on anonymity. It's rare to find a film like *Gremlins* that has two distinct authorial voices—that of the producer, Steven Spielberg, and that of the director, Joe Dante. Spielberg doesn't totally dominate the film, as he did in his production of Tobe Hooper's *Poltergeist*, and neither does he distance himself, as he did in his godfathering of Robert Zemeckis's *Used Cars*. On *Gremlins*, he seems genuinely to have shared creative responsibility with his employee, yet the Spielberg-Dante conjunction doesn't feel like a partnership—there are too many tensions in the end product, too many contradictions. My guess is that Spielberg worked mainly on the concept and scriptwriting stages, and left Dante alone during the actual shooting. The Spielberg elements in *Gremlins* are more literary than cinematic: to him belong the themes, the structure (a positive influence here—the story is much more cleanly and effectively told than is usual for Dante), the characterizations, and the setting. But, because movies are movies and not screenplays, it is always the man who points the camera who has the last word. Dante's direction undercuts much of Spielberg's planning, pushing the themes to unforeseen extremes, setting the story to sounds and images that establish a sense of their own. *Gremlins* isn't a wholly successful film—it couldn't be under these conflicted circumstances—but it is a fascinating one. It's a vivid illustration of that still-mysterious something extra, something unique, that the act of filming imposes on a narration.

Let's trace the Spielberg strain first. All of his films (apart from the Lucas-dominated Indiana Jones saga) stand on a simple, ingenious formula: a family melodrama is invaded by the fantastic. In film after film, a family that has somehow strayed from the Eisenhower-era model (generally it is the fault of the father, who—either too feminine or too childlike—has let his disciplinary responsibilities drop) is regenerated through contact with a larger-than-life force. In some of the movies, the supernatural element is evil: in fighting it, the father rediscovers his lost masculinity, and the family is saved (*Duel, Jaws, Poltergeist*). In others, the supernatural element is benign and loving; it introduces a new emotional center to the imbalanced family and causes a redistribution of parent-child roles (the childish father of *Close Encounters* is allowed to become a child again when he is adopted by the aliens; in *E.T.*, the extraterrestrial is both parent and child—a substitute for the boy's missing father, at the same time he's a baby the boy must protect and care for). Depending on which set of symbols you care to subscribe to, Spielberg's outside forces can either be bluntly Freudian (the shark as *vagina dentata*; E.T., in Veronica Geng's insightful analysis, as a cuddly phallus) or grandly religiose (the sacred-mountain imagery of *Close Encounters*, the resurrection business of *E.T.*). Spielberg's vagueness on this point may well be the secret of his vast popularity; his films play on our century's confusion of the sacred and the subconscious, the priest and the psychiatrist. Whomever we pray to, our supplications are answered in Spielberg's films: he tells us that there's something big and beautiful out there watching over us, ready to settle our problems, ready to set us on the right path.

The opening scenes of *Gremlins* quickly sketch in the Spielberg universe. Dad (Hoyt Axton) is a big, burly, boyish man with a perpetual grin; his childishness is suggested by the toylike gadgets he surrounds himself with (he's an inventor of madly complicated household appliances) and his lack of control by the fact that his gadgets consistently backfire (always in the messiest, most scatological way imaginable). To make up for Dad's failures, Mom (Frances Lee McCain) has become one of Spielberg's suburban matriarchs—tough, independent, infinitely understanding. It's difficult to assign an age to Billy (Zach Galligan). He could be anywhere from 16 to 21, and Spielberg's lack of definition on this point seems to be part of his strategy. Though Billy lives in an attic room filled with children's toys (and his best friend appears to be about 12), he has a sexpot girlfriend, Kate (Phoebe Cates), who works in a bar, as well as a job as a bank clerk that makes him the real breadwinner in his family. Billy isn't an adult and he isn't a child; he's suspended between two states, waiting to be told where to jump.

Looking for a Christmas present for his son, Dad goes into a Chinese antique store and comes out with a "mogwai," a furry little long-eared creature with big, moist eyes and a lovable disposition (it sings when it's happy). For Dad, the creature is just another toy (he nicknames it "Gizmo," as if it were one of his inventions), but, as the old Chinese man tells him, "with mogwai come responsibilities." He must never expose the creature to bright light, never get it wet, and never feed it after midnight. Dad happily turns the responsibilities over to his son, who raises the creature for what it clearly is—a human baby.

As in *E.T.*, Spielberg surrounds his huggable totem with a maze of identifications. Engendered by an irresponsible parent and then abandoned, Gizmo is plainly a stand-in for Billy in his relationship with his father. Billy assumes the parental role his father declined (a quick shot of Oedipus here) and treats his new pet with all the care and affection he has. But, inevitably, Billy makes mistakes: he lets the creature watch television (shades of *Poltergeist*), and while he's showing his new pet off to his buddy, he lets a few drops of water splash on the creature's back. Abruptly, Gizmo is transformed from child to parent: hairy spores pop from its body and rapidly develop into half a dozen new mogwais (mogwaii?). But these new creatures aren't as round and cute as the original; their snouts are sharper, their teeth more pointed, and one has a shock of stiff, yellowish hair that suggests a punker's Mohawk. They soon trick Billy into feeding them after midnight, an action that immediately induces puberty (here, gooily envisioned as "the larval state"). Emerging from their sticky cocoons, they've become leaner, meaner, more reptilian, covered in black scales that glisten with the shine of a biker's leather jacket. They're angry, rebellious, uncontrollable teenagers now—teenagers hopped up with the kind of resentment Billy himself must have once felt. The gremlins multiply by diving into the YMCA swimming pool: with their ranks now numbering in the hundreds, they open a guerrilla war on the town's authority figures—teachers, cops, the flinty old maid who holds everyone's mortgage. It takes the combined power of all three of the film's father figures—Billy, Gizmo, and Billy's newly virile dad—to restore social order and family tranquility.

Steven Spielberg's *Gremlins* is a finger-wagging moral fable, a stern warning to parents who have children for the wrong reason (because they're cute and cuddly—little living toys) and then aren't ready to raise them up in the father-dominated nuclear family that Spielberg (and his public) sees as the American ideal. Joe Dante's *Gremlins* is something else again, and the something else enters almost entirely through the style. Spielberg is always careful to give his fantasies a firm naturalistic grounding: his films are set in sprawling suburbs just like the ones that surround the shopping centers his work is designed to be shown in. He grants his characters a modicum of psychological depth, and he links the episodes of his narration into straight, sturdy lines, with no disconcerting loops or discontinuities. He favors a wide-screen integrity with long, lateral tracking shots that imply a wider though equally continuous world beyond the edges of the frame. A Spielberg image presents a stable, ordered, coherent world, in which the characters are held in a tight, trusting relationship to the objects and people around them.

Spielberg's long-take style finds its exact contradiction in Dante's montage technique. Dante, who learned his craft cutting trailers for Roger Corman's New World Pictures, favors an onslaught of often-disconnected images. Where a Spielberg edit always preserves the spatial continuity of the scene, Dante cuts on instinct and impulse, shattering the sequence into dozens of different fragments that can't always be mentally reassembled into a coherent whole. Dante shoots much closer to his subjects than Spielberg, eliminating the spatial reference points—horizon lines or elements of décor—that create the illusion of depth and stability. Dante's world is flat, flimsy, insecure, and highly unreliable—an explosion of anxiety that contradicts Spielberg's smooth assurances from frame one.

Dante and Spielberg differ not only on the arrangement of images but also on the nature of the image. For Spielberg, the frame contains a pure photographic reality; the frisson of his special effects comes from the fact that, when they enter this stable field, they become "real" too. For Dante, the image is something made—something fabricated and arbitrary, not so much photographic as painterly. He is perhaps the first filmmaker since Frank Tashlin (*The Girl Can't Help It*) to draw his style primarily from animated cartoons, feasting on the notion that there is no preordained reality to be reckoned with—no laws of physics or narrative continuity—and that the frame consists solely of what the artist chooses to sketch there. Dante's frame *is* a special effect—it's the actors who are the intruders, and when they enter Dante's cartoon frame, they lose some of their reality, turning into cartoon figures themselves. Hoyt Axton gave an appealingly naturalistic performance as the father in Jonathan Kaplan's *Heart like a Wheel*, but from his first appearance as Dad in *Gremlins*, his plump figure seems to fill out into caricature: he's a rolling collection of rounded masses, bouncing along like the Michelin tire man. Dante has filled out the supporting cast with veteran performers like Keye Luke, Scott Brady, Edward Andrews, Harry Carey Jr., and Kenneth Tobey—actors whose faces have become so familiar from thousands of movie and TV appearances that they seem pure creatures of celluloid. Even the setting—Spielberg's beloved suburbia—has been caricatured: the main street has been rendered as a one-sided, backlot construction (there can't be anything behind those flimsy storefronts), a parody of the small-town paradise of Frank Capra's *It's a Wonderful Life*. Nothing in the film has a real-world heft: Dante's universe is one of recycled images, remembered clichés, and junk culture—the false imitating the false.

Though it's legendary Warner animator Chuck Jones who gets the walk-on homage in *Gremlins*, the film seems more directly under the spiritual patronage of Jones's old colleague, Bob Clampett (who died a few weeks ago). Clampett was the most violent, surreal, and dynamic of the Warner animators—and, ultimately, the most childlike, drawing much of his primal, almost precognitive humor from explosions of sound, color, and movement that defy written description. Dante's tiny monsters are the direct descendants of the ferociously, zestfully destructive little critters that Clampett designed for his World War II propaganda cartoon *Russian Rhapsody*. Though its topical value has long since faded (when things went wrong in the fighter planes, the pilots attributed the glitches to "gremlins"—in Clampett's short, they eat through the wings of Hitler's personal bomber), the cartoon still plays on Saturday morning television, where two generations of children have had no trouble identifying the gremlins' joyful rampages with their own barely checked impulses. In the film's longest and funniest sequence—the monsters take over the bar where Billy's girlfriend works— Dante handles the action exactly as Clampett would, tossing all narrative considerations out the window and going for a succession of quick-cut, unrelated gags. The sequence becomes a kindergarten remake of *The Wild One*, an anthology of aggressively antisocial behavior enacted by snarling toddlers. The film is no longer Spielberg's stern warning, but a celebration of childish enthusiasm, evoked through the mediums—old movies and old cartoons—of childhood. The pat meanings become ambiguous, clouded: we begin to identify with the gremlins as a liberating, rejuvenating force a lot more fun than square old Billy.

Live-action films, of course, can never reach the cartoon's level of pure abstraction. No matter how stylized Dante's universe is, it still comes to us through the lens of a camera, and photography can't help but impose an impression of reality. The real force of Dante's direction comes from this tension of the abstract and the real, the cartoonish and the photographic. Dante's segment in *Twilight Zone: The Movie* was spun from a similar tension: a little boy has the power to make cartoons come real, and what was cute and funny in the context of animation becomes hideous and terrifying when brought to life. But where the *Twilight Zone* segment merely crossed the line, *Gremlins*—more disturbingly—dances along it, sometimes leaning toward one side of the fence and sometimes toward the other. Dante's stylization makes the gremlins much more sympathetic than Spielberg's naturalism would have (even when the special effects fail, as they sometimes do, the gremlins are still lovable—they look like the hand puppets or stuffed toys they will doubtless soon become), but Dante can't stylize the violence—the camera, bound by the laws of physics, won't let him. In a cartoon, movements are automatically stripped of their physical force (one of the hardest illusions to create in animation is that of weight—it's a world without gravity). But in live action, the movement is real even if the mover is not. Gestures necessarily have weight and consequences, have impact. Though Dante tries to confer a cartoonlike elasticity on his characters (one figure, plainly squashed flat by gremlins behind the wheel of a bulldozer, is later reported to be recovering nicely in the hospital), Dante cannot lighten the sting of a blow or the crunch of a bite. The film sets up a curious rhythm of attraction and repulsion, or humor and horror, a rhythm Dante doesn't seem able (or willing) to control. He pushes every scene to its furthest extreme; whether it ends in a laugh or a shudder seems purely a matter of chance.

When Billy's Mom mashes one gremlin in a food processor and explodes another in her microwave oven, we don't know how to take it—is it funny in a horrible way, or horrible in a funny way? It's a sequence that would never pass the cutting room in a Spielberg film, where every audience reaction is perfectly programmed and perfectly clear. Dante, though, doesn't try to determine our response; he just lets the scene play out according to its own logic, without trying to force a reading. Dante's approach is more honorable, but it's also more dangerous: in the moment of ambiguity it opens up, all kinds of disturbing associations rush in. Are we watching a woman defend herself, or (because the gremlins are so consistently and winningly associated with the imagery of childhood) are we watching an unspeakably awful act of child abuse? The film's most distressing moment comes later, when Billy sets fire to a theater full of several hundred gremlins. These cartoon creatures are sitting enthralled in front of a cartoon—not a Warner cartoon, but Disney's much more socialized *Snow White*. It's now impossible to avoid the fact that the gremlins are children, and that Billy's act is one of pure monstrosity—the revenge of an embittered adult against the natural exuberance of youth. And yet the act is rationally motivated, perfectly understandable—the little buggers can sure be a pain sometimes. By pushing the material to this extreme, by allowing its contradictions and darkest implications to escape, Dante destroys Spielberg's pat fable, and a complacent film comes unsettlingly alive.

Forty years from now, Spielberg will probably be classed with Disney, Capra, and DeMille as a great entertainer in the classical tradition. But Dante, even if he continues to work in the commercial cinema, will more likely be ranked with the modernists—with the filmmakers who have worked to open up the medium, to explore questions posed by its form and nature. Consciously or not, there is more than a little of Godard in Dante's open-ended montage technique. Instead of simply executing a screenplay, Dante packs his film with as many crazily diverse elements as possible and lets them rub against each other. Like Godard, he doesn't impose a program but waits for happy accidents. In *Gremlins*, they come.

PART 4

Autopsies/ Minority Reports

The Last Tycoon

Directed by ELIA KAZAN {Reader, February 4, 1977}

There are at least five distinguishable strains of authorship in *The Last Tycoon*: the movie's confusion is one of the inherent drawbacks of the "package deal" system of production that now dominates the American film industry. Producer Sam Spiegel put together a package guaranteed to send little orgasmic squirms up the spine of every money man in Hollywood: a novel by F. Scott Fitzgerald, a screenplay by Harold Pinter, direction by Elia Kazan, and a cast headed by Robert De Niro and featuring Jack Nicholson, Jeanne Moreau, Robert Mitchum, Tony Curtis, Dana Andrews, and Ray Milland. The name-heavy cast (with most of the actors appearing in brief cameos) makes the project sound like an intellectual *Poseidon Adventure*: the combined credits of the creative staff would yield enough Oscars, Tonys, and assorted critical citations to line a *Citizen Kane*–sized mantelpiece. Before its release, in fact, *The Last Tycoon* was considered a heavy contender for this year's Academy Awards; Spiegel, it was widely believed, had another *Lawrence of Arabia* or *Bridge on the River Kwai* on his hands. But something went wrong—the film has been neither a critical nor a financial success, but instead an unfortunately expensive way of demonstrating what the proverbial too many cooks are still capable of.

Spiegel's contributions—the overproduction, the distracting and unnecessary star cameos—are easy to assess, but those of Elia Kazan, the film's nominal auteur, are more obscure. Kazan's reputation is that of a realist: emigrating from Broadway in the middle '40s, he brought the New York schools of strident social consciousness and method acting to a Hollywood that still preserved its privileged isolation from brute naturalism. From *A Streetcar Named Desire* and *On the Waterfront* in the '50s to *Splendor in the Grass* and *America, America* in the '60s, Kazan's career has centered on torn T-shirts and the use of actual locations (weather permitting). But his emphasis on psychological realism, authentic settings, and left-liberal themes has never disguised his essential lack of a personal point of view, and his films therefore seem more valuable for the isolated moments of interpersonal drama they offer than for any overall coherence or insight. *On the Waterfront*, Kazan's finest film, amounts to little more than a shrewd apology to the liberal establishment for informing on his friends at the HUAC hearings, but mixed in with the endless self-justification are some of the most gripping performances the American film has to offer.

One looks long and hard at *The Last Tycoon* for any evidence of the Kazan of old. Fitzgerald's novel, with its main character, the studio head Monroe Stahr, carefully modeled on MGM's Irving Thalberg, is (in one sense) a paean to the kind of moviemaking that Kazan has always resisted. A studio film about studio filmmaking, *The Last Tycoon* couldn't seem further removed from the mainstream of Kazan's career—only the sex scenes, with their sweaty passion, evoke the feel of his past work. Where Kazan has always given the emotions of his screenplays a broad, theatrical dimension, everything here is marked by a careful restraint; no one is bellowing "Stella!" from the street, the acting is quiet, dignified, discreet.

Robert De Niro's interpretation of Monroe Stahr sets much of the film's tone. Fitting himself into the character of a Jewish intellectual with as much technical precision as he's ever shown, De Niro has conquered the considerable problems of portraying an introvert on the screen. Life, apparently, goes on behind the dead calm of Stahr's face, but what outward manifestation it receives comes in the form of clues politely offered to the onlookers, expressions passed out like little gifts. In playing a man defined by his monumental loneliness, De Niro calls on the odd sense of impenetrability that always accompanies his performances—the sense that the actor's own personality is locked up somewhere behind the character's, so carefully repressed that he seems to be carrying a ghost around with him, an unknowable, unreachable alter ego.

Superficially, Fitzgerald's novel would seem to offer little to Harold Pinter's postmodernist, post-cynical sensibilities. If Fitzgerald was the Last Romantic, his *Last Tycoon* is the last romance, and a sad, sordid story it is. Stahr, brilliant, powerful, and completely alone, meets a woman who reminds him of his late wife. He throws himself at her, and she of course turns out to be the one woman in the world who isn't impressed by who he is and doesn't want to be a movie star. She doesn't even go to the movies that much. Stahr's self-destructiveness comes to the surface; he loses his grip on his business, starts to drink, and finally, inevitably, she leaves him.

The film has its immediately obvious Pinter touches: in the opening scene, for example, a studio tour guide (John Carradine) tells his group how the special effects department creates cinematic earthquakes. Naturally, an earthquake occurs in the next scene. Small epistemological games like this turn up from time to time throughout the film, deconstructing the narrative and exposing the fiction at just those moments when the viewer feels most comfortable with the characters.

A more elaborate version of the same device, in fact, is at the center of Pinter's conception. Midway through the film, De Niro acts out what amounts to a Pinter playlet. In trying to explain the essence of movies to a contemptuous British novelist (Donald Pleasence), De Niro improvises an enigmatic scene in which a mysterious woman nervously enters the writer's office and, not seeing that he's there, carefully burns her gloves in the stove, empties her purse out on the desk, and takes a nickel out of her change purse, while another man, whom neither she nor the writer can see, watches from the doorway. "What's the nickel for?" Pleasence asks.

A seasoned screenwriter who is looking on responds, "For the movies, of course." In the last scene of *The Last Tycoon*, De Niro, alone, reenacts his play, which now seems, filtered through flashbacks, to be his own story: the mysterious woman is the girl he has lost, the man at the door is his unknown rival, and the "nickel for the movies"—his right to dream—is for all that remains to him. It's a brilliant conceit, a nearly perfect way of bringing Fitzgerald's unfinished novel to a smooth, logical conclusion—but somehow, it doesn't fit; the ending's baroque construct of fact, memory, and imagination isn't supported by the woozy romantics that have come before.

The film's ultimate failure centers on the character of the woman, Kathleen Moore, and Kazan's inadequate direction of the actress in the part, Ingrid Boulting. Along with Lady Brett of Hemingway's *The Sun Also Rises*, Fitzgerald's Kathleen is one of the most convincing arguments in favor of the long-standing theory that American novelists are unable to create convincing female characters—she exists in a romantic haze, a blurry figure who serves mainly as the object on which the hero projects his fantasies. Kazan has done little to flesh her out. Kathleen remains an ambulatory hallucination of obscure motives, given to ponderously dramatic statements like "I want to live a quiet life" emitted in a low sigh and accompanied by much rolling of the eyeballs in a celestial direction. Kathleen should rightly be something more or less than a full, concrete character, since the point of the film lies in Stahr's subjective vision of her, not in the woman herself. But Kazan hasn't found the subjective Kathleen either, leaving his film about loss with nothing to be lost.

The one positive result of this conglomeration of talent—Spiegel, Kazan, De Niro, Pinter, and Fitzgerald—is that, out of the gaggle of voices, at least one authorial cry seems to make itself heard above the din of every scene, which gives the film a consistent interest even though it's clearly running out of control. There's little you could point to, apart from Boulting, and label plain bad. But the chaos takes its toll, and *The Last Tycoon* is finally as unsatisfying as it is ambitious.

A Wedding

Directed by ROBERT ALTMAN {Reader, September 29, 1978}

It would be much simpler for everyone concerned (myself, particularly) if *A Wedding* could be quietly written off as a complete disaster. The temptation is overwhelming: much of Robert Altman's new film is immediately and obviously bad. Reportedly, Altman had promised 20th Century-Fox that *A Wedding* would be funnier (read, more profitable) than *MASH*, but as a comedy, it fails on the brute physiological scale, prompting more derisive chuckles than liberating belly laughs. It may be that *MASH*'s strangely confrontational slapstick has now been subsumed by the greater excesses of *Animal House,* and that Altman is right to turn his attention to more pointed social comedy. But as satire, *A Wedding* lacks something in breathtaking originality. In all earnestness, it sets out to demonstrate the shattering proposition that money can't buy happiness, and when it succeeds, it's hardly surprising. In the quality of its observation, *A Wedding* isn't much more profound than Joseph Bologna and Renee Taylor's unambitious farce of a few years back, *Lovers and Other Strangers,* and it never approaches the wit and understanding of Vincente Minnelli's 1950 *Father of the Bride.*

But all of that, somehow, is beside the point. I have never had much trouble thinking of Jerry Lewis as an important filmmaker, even though I no longer find him very funny. Altman, certainly, is entitled to the same consideration. *A Wedding* is clearly intended as something more than funny ha-ha; the film is so eccentric in the way it plays—it's impossible, for one thing, to figure out who is married to whom until it's almost over—that it nearly screams with formal ambition. Altman, as perverse as ever, seems to have settled on the most inconsequential script of his career as the basis of his one big shot for all the marbles. *A Wedding* seems designed as Robert Altman's answer to *Rules of the Game*; it is to be a major breakthrough in the way movies are put together and in the ways in which we understand them. It's still, I think, a failure, but on that vaunted level, the failure is a much more novel one.

A Wedding resembles Jean Renoir's 1939 masterpiece in its particulars as well as its ambitions. As in *The Rules of the Game,* a brief introductory sequence (the wedding itself) leads into the main body of the film, set in and around a country house. In the Renoir, a wealthy aristocrat has gathered some friends together for a weekend house party, friends that include his mistress and his wife's lover. In *A Wedding,* 48 separate and distinct characters (according to the press kit's count) converge on a Lake Bluff mansion to celebrate the union of two families—one old money and one nouveau riche—with a reception that lasts into the wee hours of the night. At both parties, secrets are revealed, long-suppressed emotions are stirred, and true characters emerge as the traditional values of order and propriety crumble into dust. Both Renoir and Altman make use of the polarity between the house and the garden that surrounds it—the house as the repository of civilized repression, public faces; the garden as a private spot, closer to nature and natural feelings. A similar contrast is explored between the masters and the servants: Renoir parallels his Marquis's highly "civilized" acknowledgment of his wife's affair with the brutal jealousy shown by his cuckolded gamekeeper; Altman draws a more facile contrast between the innate emotional honesty of the household staff (a butler, a gardener, a nurse, a visiting musician) and the endless duplicity of the wedding guests. And both films end with sudden death—the final violation of the rules of the game.

Renoir's great advance in the '30s consisted of his discovery that the story need have little or nothing to do with the shape and texture of the final film. Renoir's camera is constantly distracted by details that add nothing to the linear plot. When he digresses—to examine a character, a relationship, or, as he does in *Boudu Saved from Drowning*, to simply let his camera linger over the landscape—he steps back from the traditional ways of telling a story on film. We expect the action to advance in a coherent and "meaningful" way, through the steps of exposition, development, and climax. In a sense, the way the story is told shapes our response to it: the organization of the plot determines what information we will be given and when, tells us what themes, actions, and parallels are important, and gives us a sense of artistic resolution when the physical action is completed. But for Renoir, nothing is ever truly resolved, in art or in life. There are no conclusions to be drawn, only observations to be made. He refuses to lead the audience through his films: we have to decide for ourselves what is important and what is not—whether, for example, the problems facing the characters are more significant than the sound of rustling leaves that fights the dialogue for our attention. In *The Rules of the Game*, it could easily be the leaves. The film concerns a society on the brink of war, and the fact that it is fall, that there is a wind of death in the air, is a valuable point.

Renoir's films can be incomprehensible on first viewings: you're not sure where they're going, or why, or even if they're going anywhere at all. That's particularly true of *The Rules of the Game*, which seems to consist entirely of digressions, scenes that follow one another for no discernible dramatic reason. But at the end of the film, a single image is enough to snap the apparent chaos into perfect artistic harmony. A character is accidentally shot, and the way in which he jerks his body in pain irresistibly evokes an image of death that comes earlier in the film, when a rabbit is killed by a hunting party. The link between the two scenes suddenly makes the structure stunningly clear, and you are ready to see the film again.

Altman's approach to *A Wedding* is no less audacious than Renoir's, but whether it works as well is another question. Again, there is no story, only a series of incidents strung together in temporal progression from morning to midnight. Altman, though, has some more tampering to do. From the start, he purposefully denies us the most basic information about his characters—such as, as I mentioned above, who is married to whom, and further, where the characters come from, what they do, and how they know each other. Not until half an hour into the film do we learn who the mother of the bride is, and not until the end do we get a line on her husband's job and background. By saving the exposition until the end of the film—in the space of a few minutes, we do learn most of the important information that has been withheld—Altman turns his movie on its head. For the viewer, the effect at first is mere annoyance and distraction, accompanied by a creeping suspicion that Altman has finally fallen completely off his rocker, unable to handle even the simplest of narrative devices. But the attack is too consistent to be written off as simple incompetence. Something is happening, but what?

There are at least two possible interpretations. The first, and most obvious, is that Altman has discovered a new tool of realism: since we don't have the benefit of a screenwriter to fill in the blanks when we meet someone in "real life," why should we expect that information to be served up on a silver platter in a movie? The answer, I think, is because it *is* a movie. Altman feels no compunction about stylizing other elements in his film, and I think he is much too sophisticated a director to be misled by the realist impulse at this late date. *A Wedding*, whatever its faults, never descends to the naïve mimesis of Claudia Weill's *Girl Friends*—a prime example of just how banal and meaningless the search for realism in a film can be.

The second explanation strikes me as a little more seaworthy. As elaborated by Stuart Byron in the October issue of *Harper's*, this reading links Altman's repressed exposition to a newly acquired formal self-consciousness. Because Altman's fractured story construction forces us to reconsider the way we look at a movie, forces us to be aware of the narrative devices that intrude on our understanding, *A Wedding* belongs to the burgeoning modernist movement in film, alongside such self-reflexive works as Jacques Rivette's *L'amour fou*, Jean-Marie Straub's *Not Reconciled*, and Jean-Luc Godard's *Numéro deux*. I think there is some truth in that, particularly since *A Wedding* follows on the heels of one of the maddest formal experiments in American film, *3 Women*. But the narrative experiments in *A Wedding*, granting that they exist, seem to me ultimately empty, neither as insightful nor enlightening as the similar gambits in Straub, nor as subversive as Alfred Hitchcock's manipulation of the narrative line in the aptly titled *Family Plot*. Altman, no doubt, has made a tremendous advance in his mastery of form, but that form remains in the service of a severely limited artistic personality.

For all of its resemblance to *The Rules of the Game*, *A Wedding* is not genuinely "open" in the sense that Renoir's film is. There may be no plot to guide us through the film, but there are other structures at work that limit and determine its meaning. The basic narrative unit of *A Wedding* is the "revelation" scene. Again and again, the same situation is played out: a character who appears at first to be in perfect control is suddenly exposed as the victim of a crippling flaw or possessed of a devastating secret. A bishop turns out to be senile, a doctor turns out to be an alcoholic, a teen-age girl turns out to be a nymphomaniac, two characters are closet gays, another is an epileptic, another is a drug addict. Few of these issues are examined with any care or depth. Altman simply throws them in our faces, gloats a bit, and then moves on to the next one, displaying all of the tact and sympathy of a reporter for the *National Enquirer*. The characters are tossed away like used Kleenex as soon as they have yielded up their souls. Altman shows no interest in how they have managed to survive, and little respect for whatever courage they may have mustered in dealing with what, after all, are fairly normal human frailties. His involvement begins and ends with their humiliation. Through their sheer numbers, the characters become depersonalized, reduced to functional variables in a structural equation that adds up to little more than a flat observation. To wit, that behind this facade of gentility lurks despair, corruption, and death.

In *A Wedding*, death is the biggest secret of them all. Lillian Gish, the family matriarch, dies before the reception begins, but, in some sense, she still determines the course of the action, through the need to keep the news from the guests. Otherwise, the wedding would become a funeral—but in a way, Altman implies, it already is. As Robin Wood noted in his seminal anti-Altman piece in *Movie*, the ultimate subject of Altman's films is breakdown, decay. He begins with images of order and security (such as the authoritarian structure of the old-age home in *3 Women*, or the formal ritual of the wedding here) and watches as those images crumble into moral chaos. In *McCabe & Mrs. Miller*, the order belongs to the capitalist system; in *Nashville*, it belongs to something vaguer, an undefined sense of "America." *A Wedding* gains something in conciseness by restricting the breakdown to the manageable metaphorical level of a wedding reception, as all of the best-laid plans of the "wedding coordinator" (Geraldine Chaplin) collapse under assorted contingencies. But beyond that, the actual subject of *A Wedding* is the death of the American family. As the various secrets emerge—for example, that the bride's sister (Mia Farrow) is pregnant by the groom (Desi Arnaz Jr.)—the family structure is subverted, contorted, and finally destroyed. It's a worthy and valid subject, but Altman's obser-vation is strictly limited to the spectacle of decay. Granted the decline of the family, Altman is unable to suggest any alternatives that might exist. The few that do arise are hastily denied or subtly evaded.

Death is not so much a tragedy in Altman's films as it is the inevitable end point of their thematic drift. *That Cold Day in the Park*, *Brewster McCloud*,

McCabe & Mrs. Miller, Images, The Long Goodbye, Thieves like Us, Nashville,
and *3 Women* all end with the deaths of important, if not always primary,
characters. Curiously, there is seldom a sense of grief to mark their passing.
More often, the films end on a note of emotional debilitation, of emptiness,
as if an inevitable process had run its course, leaving only stillness, a void.
Altman's pessimism is total, unyielding: human aspiration means nothing
in the fact of its ultimate end, so the best we can do is try to deaden the
pain while we wait for the end to arrive. The characters he seems to admire
most are those who have developed an almost surreal degree of emotional detachment (Shelley Duvall in *Thieves like Us* and *3 Women*), while he
comes down hardest on those who cling to their vain ambitions (Warren
Beatty's McCabe, Bud Cort's Brewster McCloud). In *A Wedding*, it seems
to be no accident that the two characters who come closest to forming a
genuine emotional bond—Carol Burnett and Pat McCormick—are also the
most flatly written, grossly caricatured, and poorly acted. Altman's visual
style emphasizes isolation and alienation, the evasion of feelings and commitment. Even though the film is in Panavision—the ideal screen ration
for developing relationships among a large group of characters—few of the
group shots have any cohesiveness. Altman prefers to capture his characters away from the group, their faces held in tight close-up against an out-
of-focus background, as his zoom lens coldly closes in on their individual
angst. A disturbing motif of drinking and drug-taking runs throughout the
film—most of the cast seems to aspire to the sweet nullity of feeling that
grips the crowd at the end of *Nashville*, singing "It Don't Worry Me" as they
drift into mass oblivion. The last reel of *A Wedding* brings two more deaths,
but by then the characters have learned how to cope. They simply shrug
their shoulders and walk back to the party, untouched. Apparently, numb
to the core, they have achieved Altman's peculiar brand of perfect nirvana—
they are not, in the term that Altman used to describe Shelley Duvall at the
end of *Thieves like Us*, "survivors." I found it horrifying.

The formal design of *A Wedding* is intended to bring the audience into
the film, to make us, in a sense, participate in its creation. When Altman
casts off the traditional structure of exposition, development, and climax,
when he withholds important information about his characters, he is asking us to make our own judgments based on the ambiguous and often
contradictory evidence on the screen. But the ambiguity is only skin-deep.
Beneath the rhetorical tricks lies a set of rules—rules that are hard, narrow,
and oppressive, rules that guide our impressions to a single, and singularly
bleak, conclusion. Openness of form means nothing when it is linked to
a structure and sense that remains resolutely closed to all human possibility. There is no real freedom in the world of Robert Altman, formal or
otherwise, unless it is the freedom of blank resignation, of ceasing to care.

Apocalypse Now

Directed by FRANCIS FORD COPPOLA {Chicago, October 1979}

Apocalypse Now has already become a classic example of the creature that Hollywood calls a "runaway production"—a project that has a mad, malignant life of its own. Runaways (the genus includes such films as *Cleopatra*, *Hello, Dolly!*, and, more recently, *New York, New York*) seem to grow larger and costlier by their own accord, generating an irresistible internal momentum that whirls the cast and crew up into a spiral of increasing expenses, swelling ambitions, and, in the end, mounting desperation. *Apocalypse Now* was originally budgeted at a relatively modest $12 million and scheduled for 16 weeks of shooting. Eventually, it devoured some $32 million and sprawled out over 238 days of location work in the Philippine jungle—work complicated by a typhoon that destroyed the early sets, a heart attack that struck star Martin Sheen midway through the filming, and a consistent shortage of crucial equipment. But the problems didn't end with the completion of the principal photography. Director Francis Ford Coppola returned to the United States with more than a million feet of film and then spent two well-publicized years trying to carve his mountain of footage into manageable and meaningful dimensions. Coppola's struggle—to finish the shooting, to impose some dramatic shape on the material, to find an acceptable ending—makes a story at least as spectacular and punishing as the one told by his film. That parallel hasn't escaped Coppola's notice—the program books that accompany the movie offer a careful chronology of every disaster that befell the production, as well as Coppola's own summation of his experience: "I found that many of the ideas and images with which I was working as a film director began to coincide with the realities of my own life, and that I, like Captain Willard, was moving up a river in a faraway jungle, looking for answers and hoping for some kind of catharsis."

Coppola's public confession carries a vaguely offensive subtext of special leading—as if he were asking to be congratulated, not for making a good film, but for making any film at all under those appalling circumstances. But his statement does suggest why *Apocalypse Now* has come to be regarded as something more than a mere movie. With all of the reports and rumors about the production that have been filtering through the press for the past three years (sometimes with Coppola's mediation, sometimes without), it's no longer possible to consider *Apocalypse Now* entirely on its own terms, as a particular vision of the Vietnam War. Seen from a media-propped perspective, the film seems more concerned with another heroic effort, one quite apart from its ostensible subject—Coppola's own dark adventure, his titanic struggle to wrest something, anything, from the wilderness of the Philippines and from the depths of his own troubled artistic soul. Coppola's wife, Eleanor, busied herself during the long weeks on location by shooting a documentary on the making of *Apocalypse Now*, which may someday be released. But that documentary, in some sense, is already contained in Coppola's film: every shot is a record of obsession; every sequence, visual evidence of the director's indestructible ego and implacable will. *Apocalypse Now* is more than a movie: it's a souvenir of a grueling sojourn in the jungle, a monument that one man has built to his heroic vision of himself, the concrete product of *la folie des grandeurs* played out to its limit. And when the film works at all, it works on that level—as an unformed, indirect expression of personal testing and triumph, staggering in its scale, appalling in its vanity, and finally beautiful, in some strange way, in its utter lack of necessity. For *Apocalypse Now*, in and of itself, seems to me a nearly complete artistic failure.

Apocalypse Now is a visionary film without a point of view and, hence, without a true vision. Designed as a succession of fantastic images, a visual stream of consciousness, the film aims for an enveloping experience of descent, darkness, and horror. But it lacks the moral perspective, the dramatic grounding, to make that experience anything more than physical. And even along the route of the emotional roller-coaster ride that is the substance of *Apocalypse Now*, there are more valleys than peaks. Coppola has never demonstrated a strong sense of narrative rhythm—his *Godfather* films alternate between stasis and explosion—but where his previous failures of pacing could be covered by the emotional power of his plots, *Apocalypse Now* has no inherent human interest to fall back on. It's entirely rhythmic, entirely mechanical, and when the rhythms go wrong, or when the technological machinery breaks down, the film dies, turning into a tired, Felliniesque tour of the local depravities. When Coppola puts his most powerful, most devastating sequence in the first third of his film (a helicopter attack on a Vietcong village, conducted as a fiery descent from Olympus), he's making a mistake that any first-year film student could see. The movie never regains the impact of that scene, never recaptures its fierceness and intensity. The horror of *Apocalypse Now* doesn't mount—it meanders. The film moves from genuinely inspired moments, both mad and surreal, to passages that are strikingly overplayed and banal (for example, a USO girlie show that degenerates, with witless inevitability, into an attempted mass rape) to an equally striking obscurity in the final third which, being lumpishly "poetic," is a banality of a different sort.

As everyone must know by now, *Apocalypse Now* is a repotting of Joseph Conrad's short novel *Heart of Darkness*, shifted from the Belgian Congo to Southeast Asia. The irresistible pull of Conrad's narrative structure has made the novel a classic: as critics have noted, the primal psychological power of its journey motif draws on myths as resonant and disparate as the Grail quest and the Stations of the Cross. The novel is seductive, compulsively readable: the journey of Conrad's narrator from white, sepulchral Brussels to the teeming upriver trading camp in the heart of the Congo's darkness is an unyielding process of penetration, a journey that darkens and deepens on several levels. But *Apocalypse Now*, which recasts Conrad's mad trader Kurtz as the leader of a tribal guerrilla band, ultimately has no movement apart from the literal progress upstream. Its point of departure is highly suspect, and its destination extremely hazy. Coppola's narrator, Captain Willard (Martin Sheen), is discovered at the outset to be in a state of mental collapse: banging around a hotel room in Saigon, he suggests a manic version of *Taxi Driver*'s Travis Bickle. Willard already seems destroyed by the war. He has nothing left to lose, and the film finds little for him to gain.

Willard is assigned to travel to the Cambodian border to "terminate, with extreme prejudice," a certain Colonel Kurtz who has apparently turned renegade, seized by the insane idea that America is in Vietnam to win the war. (Does the film endorse his position? It's never quite clear.) The journey begins on a patrol boat populated by an ethnically diverse crew that could be out of a World War II bomber movie, and we see it through Willard's eyes (that is, through endlessly repeated reaction shots of Sheen's wondering face) and hear it in his voice—a past-tense narration written in an obtrusive tough-guy style. Willard is there to root the spectacle in personal terms, but the vagueness of his character makes his perspective play less like a point of view than a simple point of reference. Willard functions purely as an audience-identification figure, and an uncomfortable, unreliable one at that.

But the crucial failure of character, both in Conrad and in Coppola, lies in the figure of Kurtz. Conrad promises a confrontation with the ultimate evil: when he can't deliver, it's not surprising—but it is, inevitably, disappointing. Kurtz remains a gaseous presence in the novel, drawn with none of the precision and nuance that characterize *Nostromo* and *The Secret Agent*, Conrad's genuine masterpieces. *Heart of Darkness* may not be major Conrad, but its failings—of vagueness, of incompletion—might well be the reasons for its powerful grip on the imagination. It's a novel that the reader helps to write, filling in Kurtz's blank space with personal associations, private intuitions.

But movies, with their commanding physical presence, limit our imaginations much more than novels. Conrad is able to lose—and liberate—Kurtz in the dense foliage of his language: a film director, working in concrete images, doesn't have that option. Unfortunately, Coppola takes it anyway, casting a hazy filter over the final passages. Marlon Brando's Kurtz, photographed entirely in sinister half-light, pokes his head in and out of the darkness like a spaceship rounding a planet in *2001*. His shadowy physical presence (we never see him full figure; instead, he comes in close-up bits and pieces) is matched, in the script, by equally elusive dialogue. Explaining the secrets of the universe, Brando speaks . . . very slowly . . . like this . . . so it becomes . . . very difficult . . . to understand what he's . . . saying . . . much less whether . . . it makes any . . . sense. To give Kurtz's pronouncements some authority, Coppola allows him to quote T. S. Eliot ("The Hollow Men") and linger over his cotside nightstand, where the reading material includes *The Golden Bough* and *From Ritual to Romance*, proudly displayed like coffee-table art books. The climax of the film, in which Willard carries out his mission, is a masterpiece of muddy ambiguity. Kurtz's death is filmed in such a way as to suggest (a) licensed, justifiable homicide; (b) a mad act of patricide; (c) a ritual sacrifice to an unknown god; (d) the end of the world; (e) the redemption of the world. None of these interpretations is endorsed. Instead, the movie ends on an abrupt, abstract image of release, which plays uncomfortably close to resignation.

In the end, *Apocalypse Now* suggests that Coppola's greatest talent may lie in hiring talented people: he's a better producer than director. The performances of Robert Duvall (as the helicopter commander, a broad caricature out of *Dr. Strangelove* that is redeemed by the actor's complete self-conviction), Martin Sheen (whose tight, jittery performance suggests a depth to Willard that the film never explores), and Dennis Hopper (perfectly awful and perfectly right as a strung-out photojournalist who acts as Kurtz's official greeter) add immeasurably to the weight of the film, just as Vittorio Storaro's delicate natural-light photography and Walter Murch's evocative sound design add to its texture. But no amount of craft can disguise the film's essential inertness, its lack of moral tension and risk, its substitution of scale and spectacle for solid thought and feeling.

Kramer vs. Kramer

Directed by ROBERT BENTON {Chicago, January 1980}

Despite the cool, New-Wave affectations of its style, *Kramer vs. Kramer* is a broad, ripsnorting melodrama at heart. The plot centers on the attempts of an evil parent to steal a cuddly, towheaded child away from a good, loving parent, and there are sudden firings, threats of poverty, and beady-eyed lawyers with pencil-thin mustaches sneaking around the Victorian edges. The modernizing switch here is that the good, loving parent isn't played by Margaret Sullavan or Irene Dunne, but by Dustin Hoffman. I'm not sure if it's a switch for the better. Feminism has encouraged us to accept women in men's roles—that was one of the critical selling points in *Alien*, for example, where Sigourney Weaver was allowed to face down the monster at the end—but does it really mean anything to put men in old-line women's parts? In *Kramer vs. Kramer*, the switch has a subtle reactionary undertone. Hoffman's wife, played by Meryl Streep, walks out on him to "find herself," and Hoffman immediately sees a conspiracy on the part of her feminist friends to upset his happy home and destroy his male ego. As the movie unfolds, the actual case comes to seem more complicated, more ambiguous. But the implicit point remains: when women renege on their responsibilities, it's time for the men to take over, to show what kind of job they can do. Suddenly, being a good mother becomes a matter of macho pride—a man's *still* gotta do what a man's gotta do, whether it means marching off to war or faithfully attending PTA meetings. Hoffman sets out to beat Streep at her own game; it's a test of prowess.

Americans have long used melodrama to explain social changes. With its large movements, sudden reversals, and bold strokes of character, the form lends itself to symbolic, simplified examinations of cultural conflict. Unburdened by the "realism" affected by most dramas of cultural problems—*The Best Years of Our Lives* and the like—melodramas are able to cut a much wider swath through the ambiguity of modern life. They are less "responsible" and more instinctual, offering emotional solutions to intellectual issues. And when the issues are complicated enough, the emotional solution is often the more satisfying one. In the early twenties, the pastoral melodramas turned out by D. W. Griffith and his contemporaries addressed themselves, obliquely but effectively, to a society undergoing a troublesome shift from rural to urban values. The lush romances of the thirties and forties provided spiritual escapes from real-life relationships crippled by depression and war. By the fifties, attention had turned to the emotional crises engendered by the emerging nuclear family, living in sudden isolation from community and tradition in the rapidly spreading suburbs. It's not surprising, then, that the conflict that currently poses the most serious threat to our cultural tradition—feminism and the adjustment in sex roles that it demands—should be addressed by melodrama. Some of the most popular films of recent years—*Julia, The Turning Point, An Unmarried Woman, Coming Home*—have done just that, employing the time-honored structure of tearjerkers to deal with contemporary quandaries. The methods have remained the same; only the issues have changed. *Kramer vs. Kramer* can be accused of carrying a conservative message (feminism is a threat to social order) at the same time that it makes a liberal observation (men can mother children just as well as women). But this apparent contradiction is really the soul of the melodramatic effect: it supports the old while evoking the new, making an emotional connection between two intellectually incompatible ideas. In *An Unmarried Woman*, Jill Clayburgh, deserted by her husband, seizes the opportunity to build a new life, a separate identity, for herself. But her new life is seen as a way of acquiring a new and infinitely more romantic mate (Alan Bates). In *Coming Home*, the liberation of the Jane Fonda character is also linked to a new lover, but the role he fulfills—as a crippled war vet wholly dependent on her—is that of the child she never had with her absent soldier husband. In both cases, a superficial endorsement of "progress" acts as a cover for conventional romantic impulses.

The best melodramas—those directed by Frank Borzage in the thirties and forties, or by Douglas Sirk in the fifties—use the form as a vehicle for personal perspectives; they explore the conflicts and attempt to resolve them. But the most popular melodramas have always been those that best manage the job of having their cake and eating it too—those that remain open, holding their innate contradictions in perfect balance. The effectiveness of popular melodrama seems to depend on the illusion of seamlessness, on how well the director smooths over the inner tensions of his story. On that count, *Kramer vs. Kramer* should be very popular—the juggling act executed by writer-director Robert Benton is well-nigh impeccable, straight down to the breathtaking ambiguity of the final fade-out. The film is conservative and liberal, comforting and provocative, regressive and aggressive, all at the same time. And thus, the film's chief failing as art—its wavering point of view—becomes its most potent commercial guarantor.

But there's a difficulty built into this modern use of melodrama. The genre depends on broad emotions to make its untenable connections seem tenable—it has to sweep up the audience, get us to stop thinking and start feeling. But the young urban audiences to whom these new melodramas are addressed have long since learned to distrust broad emotions in movies; the corniness-threshold of these people is distressingly low. For the director, this poses a sticky problem—how to treat inherently sentimental material in a with-it, unsentimental style. In *Kramer vs. Kramer*, Benton gets a lot of help from the scrupulous production design: the sets and costumes are unassailably authentic, and their accuracy gives the proceedings the weight of reality even when the screenplay is indulging in some of its wildest distortions. Streep can disappear for 18 months—while she and Hoffman apparently undergo some sort of divorce-by-mail—and then reappear (not having worked in eight years) with a high-salaried job as a fashion designer, and as long as it all looks real, it must be real. But Benton's overriding technique is a more obvious one. He simply turns down the emotional volume, hinting at feelings rather than showing them. Like *An Unmarried Woman* and *Julia*, *Kramer vs. Kramer* is a very timid melodrama, afraid of the same emotions that it attempts to exploit.

The central relationship in *Kramer vs. Kramer* is between the father and his son, played by Justin Henry. At times, the two achieve a convincing rapport. But one has only to look back to other films founded on this relationship—notably, Chaplin's *The Kid*—to realize how much has been left out of Benton's rendition. In the space of two or three reels, Chaplin establishes every detail of his love for his boy—how they work together, how they live together, how they play together—while Benton evades most of this material with a discreet use of fade-outs. The course of Hoffman and Henry's coming together is covered entirely by three contrasting scenes at the breakfast table (the idea may be a direct steal from *The Kid*, which features a similar sequence). Otherwise, we have to take it all on faith—the director asks us to do his most dangerous work for him, to imagine what he's too frightened to show. It is, I think, a criminal neglect of duty, and Benton's reticence takes its toll in a remarkably uninvolving climax. As the lawyers are closing in, you can only sit and wonder why you don't care. *Kramer vs. Kramer* ends, like too many modern melodramas, as a movie without the courage of its convictions. The form is there—professionally constructed and solid—but the feelings are gone. And without them, the form loses its function.

The Shining

Directed by STANLEY KUBRICK {Reader, July 20, 1987}

God is a big, black slab from outer space, and the devil is a bartender named Lloyd. In *The Shining*, Stanley Kubrick completes the cosmologic Divine Comedy he began in *2001*: a science-fiction film was his Paradiso; now a horror movie is his Inferno. (Does that leave *Barry Lyndon*, with its pattern of arbitrary punishment and sudden salvation, as his Purgatorio?) Again, Kubrick selects a specimen (here, Jack Nicholson as a failed writer who blames his wife and son for his unhappiness) and runs him through a one-on-one confrontation with Eternity—not the black, hollow eternity of outer space, but the bright, orderly inner space of an abandoned hotel, where Nicholson is left alone to reckon with his (very literal) demons. Again, the confrontation leads to a rebirth, but the blue-eyed space baby has given way to a glowering, red-faced monster. What's surprising is how little difference the moral orientation makes: whether as absolute inno-cence or evil incarnate, Kubrick still insists that man must be remade; the present, ambiguous mix won't do. Always the chess player, always the geometrician, Kubrick remains a neatener, a straightener. He can't tolerate moral ambiguity, human disorder, any more than he can tolerate a speck of dust on his shiny, sterile sets, or a tracking shot that fails to execute perfect 90-degree turns at every corner. Kubrick has raised his compulsiveness to a conception of the universe—if his movies always shake down into harsh, Manichaean antinomies, surely it is because black-and-white divisions of good and evil please his ordered mind, feed his faith in symmetry. If *The Shining* is about anything at all, it's about right angles—the right angles of the monolith, transposed to the chessboard geometry of his huge hotel set.

Kubrick has leaked word (he still refuses formal interviews) that *The Shining* is to be taken as a potboiler—proof, after the commercial failure of *Barry Lyndon*, that he can still command a box-office take commensurate with his artistic need for big budgets. But the movie itself says exactly the opposite: as an audience picture, *The Shining* is a total failure. It meanders on and on, covering huge chunks of dead time with clumsily constructed exposition, getting down to business only occasionally as Kubrick paus-es to mass up small, anthill mounds of tension, only to blow them away when the payoff fails to measure up to the anticipation. He's stingy with his effects, tossing out vague, underimagined shock scenes according to a rigidly spaced schedule; for the audience, it's like feeding time at the zoo— he throws us a bone now and then, just enough to keep us gnawing and docile. Kubrick's attitude toward the spectator is one of blank indifference. He can't even get up his old *Clockwork Orange* contempt for the audience;

he no longer deigns even to manipulate us, won't even meet us on the level of cheap thrills. *The Shining* stays on the screen, self-contained—which is to say that it stays in Kubrick's head, a private ritual with meanings known only to him.

There's no other way to approach the film's first hour, which ostensibly documents the arrival of Jack Torrance (Nicholson) at the Overlook— the rambling, catacombed resort hotel, perched on a Colorado mountain, where he is to serve as caretaker during the winter months when the hotel is snowbound and deserted. Torrance comes in for an interview with the manager (Barry Nelson), after which he's given a short tour. Torrance returns for his winter stay with his wife (Shelley Duvall) and son (Danny Lloyd), and they're taken on another, longer tour. And once the staff and guests have left, leaving the Torrances alone, the tour continues as Kubrick follows his characters on their rounds, watching Wendy Torrance explore the hotel's sprawling shrubbery maze, mounting his camera on the back of Danny Torrance's tricycle as he pedals down the hotel's endless corridors. The tour continues long after its expository function has been forgotten, long after every room has been etched in our minds (although, oddly, Kubrick never suggests how the main rooms—kitchen, lounge, ballroom— connect up; the movie's sense of space is strictly local). Clearly, Kubrick loves his set, and it is a stunner: a vast, boxy cavern, with polished wood floors, carved oak beams, and towering windows that channel rivers of artificial sunlight. But just as clearly, Kubrick loves his set more than he loves his characters; above all, he loves the tracking shots he can lay through it. For most of the film's first half, the actors serve mainly as anchors—fixed focal points that allow Kubrick to tie down the camera movements.

Kubrick's love affair with camera movement goes back to his earliest films: *The Killing* (1956) already finds him driving his dolly through walls as he lays out long, lateral tracks from one end of a railroad apartment to the other. But Kubrick's love is perverse, idiosyncratic. Traditionally, tracking shots have been expressions of fluidity, describing the flow of time (Ophüls), the swirl of space (Murnau), the extension of the spirit (Borzage, Mizoguchi). Kubrick, in contrast, creates a strange, static quality with his tracks. Whether he moves ahead, behind, or alongside his actors, Kubrick always keeps them nailed in the exact center of the frame and maintains a constant, measured distance between the camera and its object. An actor could walk a mile in a Kubrick tracking shot and still not appear to progress an inch: his position on the screen never varies. Instead, his surroundings seem to move around him, receding into the background along Kubrick's carefully established lines of perspective. The set is alive, changeable and changing; the actor is rooted, stuck in place. Many of the more elaborate tracking shots in *The Shining* suggest the flow of colors from *2001*'s star-gate sequence. Keeping his frame lines at a perfect perpendicular with the walls of rooms and corridors, Kubrick creates an optical illusion: as the camera moves, keeping the actor and the angles that contain him constant, the walls themselves seem to be flowing, proceeding from (or returning to) a central point beyond the field of vision, the vanishing point of Renaissance perspective where Kubrick's beloved parallel lines meet at last.

Kubrick's tracking shots create an illusion of movement without progress, of man held in place while his environment changes around him. It's an easy leap from that image to the notion of evolution put forward in *2001*: man does remain in place, until an outside force comes along to kick him into gear—to teach him how to use a weapon, to build a spaceship. In *The Shining*, it's suggested that Torrance, in the same way, has always lived in the haunted hotel: he complains of déjà vu to his wife; later, one of his demon buddies assures him that he's "always been the caretaker." Torrance comes across the country (he has left his job as a schoolteacher in New England) to get to where he's always been. Once he returns to his spiritual home, it doesn't take much to get him back in the swing of things: sitting down at the empty bar (the liquor has been packed away for the winter), Jack moans, "I'd sell my soul for a glass of beer." Up pops an obliging phantom bartender, and the deal is closed.

It wouldn't take much to turn the supernatural story of *The Shining* into a straight psychological thriller: just trim a few of the wandering visions here and there, the ones that strike the boy and his mother, and restore them to their rightful place in Torrance's fevered imagination—and everything could be tied down, neatly, as the hallucinations of a madman. Much of the frustration of watching *The Shining* lies in trying to make sense out of the ghostly apparitions—trying to tease out a traditional psychological explanation for who sees what, when. Danny, who has a gift of clairvoyance (the "shining"), repeatedly sees a pair of twin girls who invite him to "come and play with us, for ever and ever." We find out later that they're the daughters of another caretaker, who went mad and murdered his family. But why do victims beckon to victims? Is Kubrick suggesting that Danny anticipates his own death, that, subconsciously, he's wishing for it? Clearly not—the Freudian framework just doesn't fit. The visions don't lend themselves to interpretation; if they are meant as metaphors, the meaning is too vague to matter. Kubrick, I think, intends them literally (just as he presents them flatly, without flourish or threat): as intersections with a parallel world, the world of parallel lines. The sisters are significant to the extent that they're twins: they embody Kubrick's fearful symmetry. Perhaps Kubrick has parceled out the visions, dividing them unevenly and inconsistently among his characters, with the single intention of forestalling an analytical interpretation. *The Shining* is antipsychological, which is a new twist for the genre: these aren't the monsters from the id that have been clogging horror movies since Hollywood discovered Freud in the late '40s; instead, they're emissaries from an older tradition, visitors from the vivid tableaux of temptation and damnation of the Middle Ages. They exist like the monoliths of *2001*, apart and above.

But if *The Shining* is antipsychological, it is also, in subtler and more disturbing ways, antihuman. Think back to any of Kubrick's mature, post-*Lolita* films, and what you remember first are lines, shapes, colors—the arc of the overhead lamps of *Dr. Strangelove*'s war room; the circular space station of *2001*; the glaring comic-book colors of *A Clockwork Orange*; the hovering horizon lines of *Barry Lyndon*. Geometry charges his films, giving his images their strength and integrity. The human figures that move through his frames come to seem like intrusions, blots on the color field (*The Shining* is designed in shimmering chromatic waves of yellow, blue, and white), interruptions in the smooth flow of the lines. Kubrick seems able to identify with his protagonists only when they, like himself, are seekers after purity: *Lolita*'s Humbert Humbert (James Mason, in what may be the only great performance in a Kubrick film) pursues the abstract innocence of the child-woman; Malcolm McDowell in *A Clockwork Orange* fights family and government for the right to remain his pure, antisocial self; and there is even *Dr. Strangelove*'s General Jack D. Ripper (Sterling Hayden), who is obsessed with the sanctity of his precious bodily fluids. A Kubrick hero succeeds when he merges with the symmetry: the space baby of *2001* imitates the graceful roll of the space station.

In *The Shining*, we may root for Jack Torrance's defeat, but there's no doubt that he is, in every important way, Kubrick's hero. Torrance goes to the hotel to escape from social life, to write and think in serene isolation; his wife and child are excess baggage. Once the demons have awakened the eternal urge in him, he resents his family's emotional intrusions—their needs and demands—more and more; they're clouding up his clear field. We see the "novel" that Jack has been working on: a ream of type-written pages, all filled with various symmetrical arrangements of the single sentence "All work and no play makes Jack a dull boy." (It's like a parody of Kubrick's own work, with sentences repeated instead of tracking shots.) The demons urge him to get out his ax, and thus the film's most striking vision—the torrents of blood pouring from an elevator that both Wendy and Danny see—comes true, completing the buried pun in Jack's last name. When Jack strikes, he does so with perfect respect to the angled mise-en-scène, leaping from behind a pillar and swinging his ax in an impeccable arc, calculated to meet his victim at an accurate 90 degrees. Through all of this, it is hard to forget the press reports of Kubrick's own monkish style of living: holed up in an English country home, reluctant to venture outside.

On the surface, *The Shining* is plainly a bad film (even a crude New World toss-off like the recent *Humanoids from the Deep* builds to better suspense); on a deeper level, it may also be an objectionable film—cold, hermetic, misanthropic. But it is to Kubrick's credit that he continues to use film as a medium of personal expression, no matter how repellant that personality may be. In the cloud bank of commercial blandness that has settled over this summer's films—*Wholly Moses!*, *The Blues Brothers*, *Brubaker*—*The Shining* really does shine. It's a movie to be reckoned with, argued with, confronted; it sticks in the mind in uncomfortable ways.

Dressed to Kill

Directed by BRIAN DE PALMA {Reader, August 1, 1980}

This, I'm afraid, is going to be a clip-and-save review. I don't know how to handle Brian De Palma's *Dressed to Kill* without tipping a plot element here and there, and it's not possible to talk about the film's deeper implications without blowing the "surprise" ending. If you haven't seen *Dressed to Kill*, this might be a good time to go. I'll be here when you get back.

Not that the ending will be a surprise to anyone familiar with movie conventions. De Palma himself gives the game away early on, by posing the prime suspect in the film's sex killings against a mirror. The double image the shot creates is probably the hoariest symbol of schizophrenia available in the filmic vocabulary. From time immemorial, murderers have stared into mirrors and plate-glass windows, reveling in the reflections of their dual natures. But usually their directors won't let them do it until their villainy has been exposed. By putting this glaring marker in the first part of the film, De Palma is demonstrating his hip familiarity with movie clichés, a familiarity that *Dressed to Kill* makes extensive use of. But, of course, he is also banking on the inability of most of his audience to read the visual signal—and the contempt that that implies, the hipper-than-thou attitude, is also something that *Dressed to Kill* exploits.

Buffs like De Palma's films because they're full of references and in-jokes; watching them is like taking a trivia quiz. The mass, teenage audience likes De Palma's films because they're full of sex, violence, and antiparental sentiments (De Palma is second only to Walt Disney in his instinctive understanding of Freudian family conflicts: all his thrillers contain some kind of Oedipal revenge against a parent figure). This is a potent commercial combination, but there's something in De Palma's dual-pronged appeal that makes me uneasy. When *Sisters*, the first of his pseudo-Hitchcockian films, came out in 1973, I admired the way De Palma balanced parody and genre expectations—the film worked as both put-on and shocker. His style hasn't changed a whit since then, but I've come to distrust it more and more, perhaps because the surface of his work has remained playfully shoddy, rattily satirical, while his subject matter has taken a darker turn. With every picture, De Palma moves deeper into the Catholic complex of sex, death, and guilt, turning out increasingly kinky fantasies of sexual disgust and punishment, while his tone remains as jokey-hokey as before. De Palma still asks the adult audience to take his films as gentle gibes at a now-vanished tradition, but the primal, psychological undercurrents that make his films meaningful to kids are running out of control. It's getting harder to ignore De Palma's misogyny, harder to take it as a gag. With

Dressed to Kill, it becomes impossible. The smirking, facetious tone serves as an alibi for half-baked ideas; thick, ill-considered swabs of "technique"; and a fundamentally sour spirit. The mask is slipping, and the face behind it isn't very friendly.

De Palma's films do have two levels—the laugh and the shock—but we don't experience them separately, purely. The levels get mixed up, bound together—you laugh at the violence, you cringe at the jokes (most of them are based on sexual humiliation). De Palma extends the appearance of sincerity, only to snatch it back at the last moment. It's impossible to tell where he stands at any given time, whether he's trying to establish links of sympathy and identification. And there's never any guarantee that he means what he shows: his favorite trick is the "it's only a dream" shock cut (he does it twice in *Dressed to Kill*), in which action that we've been encouraged to take literally turns out to be a fantasy, a fake. De Palma's defenders would probably call this harmless formal play, a shifting of the "levels of reality." But "reality" as a concept has no place in De Palma's films: there's no fundamental difference between the second dream sequence and the "true" action that has come before it; both are spun from the same collection of movie clichés, willful implausibilities, and logical gaps. If De Palma's films are queasy, unsettling experiences, it's because they lack any groundline of reality, however arbitrarily established. He changes the rules every few minutes, but there's nothing to measure the changes against— and the audience is left adrift, more vulnerable to manipulation. When we don't know the rules, we can't cry foul.

If there's no consistent "literal" level in De Palma's films, neither is there a consistent point of view. De Palma's attitudes are as slippery as his plot lines, running all over the map from casual nihilism to embarrassingly intense adolescent romanticism. Luis Buñuel shifts levels of reality with much more freedom and unsettling impact than De Palma does, but his films are unified by his personality—his humor, his values, and his personal, instantly recognizable fetishes. Buñuel stands behind his films; De Palma, if anything, hides behind his. When he trashes a value that he has carefully established, when he turns on characters that he seems to sympathize with, who's to know what he has in mind? Is he exposing himself, or is he covering himself? In the end, De Palma's personality is defined only by his duplicity; if we can't get a grip on his films, it's because there's nothing to hold on to. There's no basic difference between the laughs and the shocks, the things De Palma finds funny and the things he finds horrible.

Dressed to Kill begins with a set piece, Angie Dickinson's already-famous shower scene. The camera awakes in a well-appointed suburban bedroom and creeps stealthily through an open bathroom door. A man stands at the mirror, shaving with a straight razor; the figure of a woman can be seen refracted through the rippled glass door of the shower stall. The camera movement in this shot is a traditional cinematic code of unseen menace—a subjective shot from the intruder's point of view. The audience feels a twinge of anticipation—is the killer about to strike? Not at all. Suddenly we find ourselves in the shower, as the woman begins to masturbate. The "intruder" is us, as we are coaxed along by De Palma's camera movement to take a ringside seat at this sublime, voyeuristic experience. Dickinson (or rather, her double) fondles her breasts and crotch in abstract, dissociated close-ups; the camera style has switched from subjective/threatening to the distanced, depersonalized compositions of pornography. The sequence is clearly being staged for the erotic benefit of the audience. But again, there is a cut to another level. As the steam rises in the shower, creating the cliché we recognize as "mist of fantasy," a male figure appears behind Dickinson. A hand is clasped roughly over her mouth, and an apparent rape begins. Dickinson glances through the shower door and smiles as she sees her husband, still shaving at the mirror. The shots are again coded "subjective," with the point of view tied firmly to Dickinson—this, it seems, is her erotic fantasy, not ours. Cut again, this time to a high overhead angle, looking down on a bed where we discover Dickinson enduring a perfunctory morning quickie with her husband. This, for the moment, seems to be "reality," although the crudity with which the husband's sexual incompetence is characterized—thrust, thrust, done—places the image more securely in the realm of cartoonish exaggeration. The camera angle is ironic, detached: it invites a laugh, and gets one. End of sequence.

What's really going on here? If we interpret the entire bathroom scene as Dickinson's fantasy, we're left with a hopeless muddle: apparently, she's having a sexual fantasy about having a sexual fantasy, dreaming about a rape (by a man who looks like her husband; it's hard to tell if it's the same actor), while her husband is, in effect, raping her. And if it is her fantasy, then to whom does the first subjective shot belong? There's no point in trying to shake the sequence down into anything rational and readable: De Palma, clearly, isn't concerned with how his shots fit together logically. He's more interested in orchestrating them emotionally, psychologically—in leading the audience through an intensely sexual, voyeuristic experience and then giving us a flat, hard slap in the face, descending abruptly from highly charged sexual fantasy to an excessively brutal, sordid reality. He offers a good strong dose of frank pornography and allows us to enjoy the daydream—and then, with the sudden fury of a nun who has caught someone sleeping in confirmation class, he runs up and gives us a rap on the knuckles. It's a dirty trick, and it smarts: we've been led on, betrayed. It won't be the last time.

A couple of quick expository scenes follow. Dickinson, having packed hubby off to work, stops in her son's room, where she finds that he's been up all night, slaving away on his computer project for the local science fair. De Palma pauses long enough to establish Dickinson's incomprehension, and then cuts to the office of her psychiatrist (Michael Caine), where

Dickinson discusses her sexual frustrations. Both sequences are clumsily, awkwardly staged, in harsh contrast to the gliding lyricism of the opening scene. Dickinson seems strangely stiff and inexpressive, dressed and made up like a fashion dummy and reading her inane lines with an exaggerated false huskiness—a phony seductiveness. I was ready to write the awkwardness off to Dickinson's shortcomings as a performer, but then I realized that De Palma was encouraging and exaggerating those shortcomings. He allows his actress to look foolish, apparently for the purpose of undermining her character. With the right director, Dickinson can be a strong, sexy presence (*Rio Bravo* is more than proof of that), but De Palma doesn't want a strong presence—he wants a joke, a joke in the form of a silly suburban matron whose sex problems are comic evidence of her gaucherie. She makes a clumsy pass at her shrink and is (titter, titter) rebuffed.

Having established Dickinson's comic desperation and ineptitude, De Palma segues into set piece number two, "The Museum." The sequence lasts for an entire reel; apparently it's meant to be a tour de force, since there are no words spoken (a sure indication that we're in the presence of Cinema) and the sequence is inflated far beyond its inherent narrative value. Loitering in what is meant to be the modern wing of the Metropolitan (the sequence was actually shot elsewhere), Dickinson conceives a crush on a fellow art lover—a tall, sinister man (Ken Baker) in sunglasses and turtleneck, who looks as if he's on loan from a Bonjour Action Jeans commercial. Dickinson makes a few flirtatious moves and is ignored; she screws up her courage and follows him through the museum, trotting from gallery to gallery. De Palma's model is the gallery scene from *Vertigo*, one of the most beautiful passages in Alfred Hitchcock's work. Based on a subtle, deft use of subjective tracking shots, the *Vertigo* sequence spins an irresistible aura of romantic obsession, as James Stewart moves toward and away from his quarry, Kim Novak. De Palma picks up those tracking shots, but he employs them with such heavy self-consciousness, and at so exaggerated a length, that they're no longer subjective. They don't take us into the character's consciousness: instead, they foreground De Palma's artistic ambitions and pretensions (as well as highlighting his larcenous attitude toward other people's work).

Of course, De Palma retains the alibi that the scene is heavy and vulgar because it's a parody—a spoof of *Vertigo* rather than a cop from it. It's the old Tennessee Williams theory—"If they laugh, it's a comedy"—and it makes De Palma critic-proof: every ugliness can be explained as a gag, every misstep as a comment on his sources. If you don't like it, it's because you're not hip enough to appreciate it. Still, this sort of thing can only go so far, and in *Dressed to Kill* it stops right about here. The cognoscenti in the audience have long since recognized that the first half of *Dressed to Kill* is an extended, direct lift from *Psycho*: De Palma needs the subjective sequence to complete our identification with his star, who is about to be offed Janet Leigh style. The museum sequence must work if the subsequent shock scene is to have any deep impact at all. It doesn't.

Dickinson completes her pickup, and De Palma milks the encounter for more smutty laughs: the driver looks on, huffing and puffing, while Dickinson and her lover paw at each other in the back seat of a cab. But De Palma has yet to deliver the crushing blow: back at the man's apartment, Dickinson discovers a letter from the health department, warning her partner that he has VD. It gets the biggest laugh in the picture—Dickinson's dreamy, romantic afternoon has degenerated to this, a reality much more sordid than anything her husband has to offer. Dickinson runs from the apartment and straight into the arms of a waiting maniac. Slashed by a straight razor, she is left to bleed to death in an elevator.

The cruelty of the joke and the cruelty of the attack come on top of each other, so close that they seem to be two strokes from the same hand. In a way, they are, and the hand is Brian De Palma's. Dickinson, of course, is simply meeting the fate that always waits for sexually aggressive women in horror movies by Catholic-minded directors. She's being punished for her transgressions, and the sentence for sex is death.

A director like John Carpenter, in *Halloween*, will simply accept that peculiar convention as one of the rules of the game: the sexually active girls are murdered, and only the virgin (Jamie Lee Curtis) escapes. The judgment is part of the genre that Carpenter is working to recreate; it's played as just that, one more weapon in the emotional assault on the audience, and it isn't given any extra weight or attention. A director like Hitchcock, in *Psycho*, uses the convention to explore more general meanings of guilt and punishment, questioning the justice of the judgment, looking for its source. But in *Dressed to Kill*, the sex-death link is an object of fascination, in and of itself; it isn't quietly accepted or openly explored, but set up as an independent value. In some ways, it is the film's raison d'être. It's possible that by exaggerating and emphasizing the sex-death trope, De Palma is making another joke, this time at the expense of the Catholic consciousness. Somehow, I doubt it. De Palma's films are so ill-considered, so full of gaps and contradictions, that it seems clear that he works very close to his instincts—he isn't about to go back over his plotting and try to shape it up in rational, cogent forms; to do that would be to destroy its nightmarish, id-soaked quality. Fear and laughter are both primal defense mechanisms; I said before that there doesn't seem to be any difference between the things De Palma finds funny and the things he finds horrible, and that's literally true, to the extent that fear and laughter in his films are both directed toward the same targets—which are, unmistakably and irreducibly, attractive, seductive women.

We're getting dangerously close to armchair psychoanalysis here, and I don't want to accuse Brian De Palma of being a sex pervert. But it does seem clear that his films are essentially, instinctively, erotophobic—the fear of sex, the disgust and distrust, is the only line that links their disparate elements. Consider the figure of De Palma's murderer, a transvestite and frustrated transsexual who feels compelled to murder women who arouse him sexually. This is nonsense as psychology (and as sexual politics, it seems even more retrograde than *Cruising*), but as an adolescent, misogynist fantasy, it's seamless: the killer of monstrous, seductive women is him/herself a monstrous parody of women. De Palma has found a way to blame the victim: the maniac is a would-be woman who kills women who threaten his womanhood. Still, the thrust of the violence is exclusively male, as the choice of weapon—a straight razor, with its deadly, phallic overtones—more than makes clear. Again, it is possible that De Palma intends an homage here: the straight razor had been the exclusive cinematic property of Luis Buñuel ever since he opened *Un chien Andalou* with the most powerful image of sexual horror on record—a razor slicing a woman's eye. De Palma doesn't attempt anything so bold, but there is another quote from *Chien* in the elevator sequence when the killer slashes at Dickinson's open palm, an image that recalls Bunuel's famous shot of ants marching from a similar wound. Is the razor, then, another joke, another cinematic reference held up for our knowing chuckles? I would like to think that it is as harmless and frivolous as that, but there is something in the deep-seated ferocity of *Dressed to Kill* that won't let me laugh.

Raiders of the Lost Ark

Directed by STEVEN SPIELBERG {Chicago, August 1981}

Pace Allen Ginsberg, I have seen the best movie minds of my generation destroyed by madness. The madness is called *Raiders of the Lost Ark*, and it is playing at a theater near you. The film is a collaboration between Steven Spielberg and George Lucas, two of the most commercially successful directors of the seventies (*Jaws* and *Star Wars*, respectively) and two of the most technically adept. One would have thought that an alliance between two talents as potent as theirs would have produced something special—a big film, grand and entertaining in the high old style. But *Raiders of the Lost Ark*, which is meant to be a "fun" picture ("the ultimate Saturday matinee," as one reviewer put it), turns out to be a remarkably callow, peach-fuzzy piece of work. It's a piece of juvenilia unredeemed by innocence, a catalog of ugly adolescent impulses arranged for maximum commercial appeal.

Lucas and Spielberg wrote the original story line and later brought in director Philip Kaufman (*Invasion of the Body Snatchers*) for additional embellishments; the story was then turned into a screenplay by Lawrence Kasdan. What these four men came up with is this: In 1936, a swashbuckling archaeologist, Indiana Jones (Harrison Ford), is commissioned by army intelligence to find the lost Ark of the Covenant, containing the crumbled remains of the Ten Commandments. His competition is Adolf Hitler, who has dispatched a digging crew, led by a sinister Frenchman, René Belloq (Paul Freeman), to Egypt in the belief that possession of the Ark will make his armies invincible. Helped by his hard-bitten ex-flame Marion Ravenwood (Karen Allen), Jones succeeds in finding the Ark, only to see it snatched away by the Nazis. He snatches it back, they snatch it back from him, he snatches it back from them, etc.

As a framework for an action film, this kind of simple plot structure does very nicely. It's the attitude that Spielberg brings to the material that gums it up, turning that sweet simplicity into something merely simpleminded. Spielberg and Lucas have cited the Republic serials of the thirties and forties as their inspiration—films they must know from television, since they're too young to have seen them firsthand. Surely it was the *idea* of the Republic serials, more than the films themselves, that appealed to Lucas and Spielberg: actually seen, most serials turn out to be little more than studies in low-budget resourcefulness, expressive—when they're expressive at all—only of their directors' determination to make something marginally watchable out of the crushing limitations of time and budget imposed on them. A William Witney at Republic or a James Horne at Columbia could occasionally inject some style and dash into his work, but the opportunities were infrequent. (The talented Horne expressed his frustration by dropping outrageous camp moments into his serials; look closely at the backgrounds of *The Spider's Web* and you can see the hooded villains playing patty-cake.) Making serials, it seems, was mainly a matter of working around gaping deficiencies: when your actors couldn't act, and your writers couldn't write, you had to keep your film full of action—at least, your stuntmen knew how to wreck cars.

Spielberg has taken those limitations and made them into an aesthetic. His movie seems purposefully devoid of characterization, purposefully devoid of shading and nuance. In fact, he makes less of an effort to provide connective material between his chase, fight, and escape scenes than the original directors did; there's just one blowout on top of another. Spielberg knows a lot about action editing—working with his regular cutter Michael Kahn, he's put together some stirring, intricate sequences—but he doesn't know, or care, anything about narrative rhythm. It was a problem for him in 1941, too—this question of knowing when to speed up and when to slow down, when to give the audience a jolt and when to give it a rest. Spielberg may not even see it as a problem: When he recut *Close Encounters* for his "Special Edition," his work seemed to consist of smoothing out the peaks and valleys of the original version. He put everything on a single straight line and set the film going at a constant high velocity. With no rhythmic variation, the film became monotonous; it seemed a much less complex, affecting experience than it did the first time around.

Progress in *Raiders* is, again, perfectly linear; the film is assembled like the second cut of *Close Encounters*, with nothing but the search to give it shape (and the payoff at the end is also very similar: we get to peek inside the Ark, just as we got to follow Richard Dreyfuss into the spaceship). Action set pieces simply segue into other action set pieces, linked only by a chain of cause and effect; it's the events that seem to be propelling the film, not the characters. A West Coast critic has identified Spielberg's personal theme as obsession, which is certainly a subject that turns up in most of his films—from the sheriff's obsession with the shark in *Jaws*, to Richard Dreyfuss's preoccupation with the plateau shapes in *Close Encounters*. But I'm not sure that Spielberg sees obsession as something to investigate, to turn into art, as much as he sees it as the simplest possible motivation behind his ruthlessly straight-line plots. Certainly, Indiana Jones is obsessed with the Ark—what else would keep him moving from one absurd danger to the next? But his obsessiveness isn't commented or expanded on. It's simply a given in Spielberg's world, a natural component of his functional characters, who don't have much else to define them.

Part of the definition of a "movie movie," I suppose, is that it pretends not to have any content—that it's "just fun." We're supposed to understand it as pure form, a collection of empty elements, whose only meaning resides in the elegance of their arrangement. But even if we accept this definition of

Raiders (which I can't), it's still a failure: Spielberg simply doesn't have his formal elements under control. Apart from his failings of pace and narrative design, the film is full of troubling loose ends, elements introduced and never developed or resolved. The chase is initially introduced as a search for a missing archaeologist, Professor Ravenwood (Indiana's mentor and Marion's father), but after a big *misterioso* buildup, the subject is never mentioned again. Professor *who*? And Indiana is given a gigantic bullwhip to tote around, in the tradition of action-film heroes who are characterized by their special skill with a special weapon. The whip comes in handy in one or two of the film's endless escape scenes, but its place in the formal design is never established—in the way, say, that John Boorman establishes the sword in *Excalibur*, or even in the less expressive fashion in which George Lucas employs the laser swords in *Star Wars*. The whip never becomes an index to Indiana's character, never takes on any thematic significance; it just lies there, more of a tool to the marketing people (they've got to give those Indiana Jones dolls some distinctive equipment) than to the storytelling.

But Spielberg's most damning formal flaw is his failure to control his rhetorical distance. He wants us to identify with his characters, but he wants us to laugh at them, too—he's got to let us know that he's too hip to take the clichés he's peddling seriously. Contemporary audiences seem most comfortable somewhere between the two extremes of identification and irony, and often the trick in making an action movie these days lies in striking exactly the right balance. George Lucas did it perfectly in *Star Wars* by giving us our choice of two heroes—one cuddly, naïve, and idealistic for the sake of identification (Mark Hamill's Luke Skywalker) and one sarcastic, cynical, and self-interested (Harrison Ford's Han Solo) for the sake of ironic distance. *Raiders*, of course, has only the ironic presence of Ford, and Spielberg doesn't try for balance: he's relying on the sweep of action, rather than on a sympathetic character, to catch us up. I'm not sure that it works in the way Spielberg intends.

There is, for example, a very funny scene in which Jones faces an Eastern sword fighter dressed in black robes and swinging a scimitar (he belongs to another movie entirely, but no matter). Instead of facing the swordsman in an honest fight, as the generations of action heroes before him have done, Jones grimaces, pulls out a gun, and plugs him. It gets a great laugh, probably the best in the film, and I can't really blame Spielberg for going for it. But the gag, in breaking the conventions for comic effect, also calls attention to them. The conventions suddenly become clichés, and they lose their power over us, a power that the action film depends on. We agree to take the conventions seriously for as long as the film lasts, for the sake of enjoying the exciting situations that the conventions give rise to. When Spielberg breaks that agreement, identifying the conventions as absurd within the context of his film, we may feel cheated. We've suspended our disbelief for his sake, and now he's telling us that we're fools for having done so. Our faith in the film is shaken, its hold over us weakened.

When Spielberg breaks the bond, he knows only one way of establishing it again: he throws in a scene of such grating, graphic violence that he pulls a physical response from us—it's too gory to be a joke, and we flinch automatically. It's here, I think, that *Raiders* is at its most reprehensible. Its body count is somewhere on the far side of *Dawn of the Dead*, but there's none of the fundamental moral seriousness that informed George Romero's blackly comic horror film. Instead, there is only a pervasive sense of human bodies as disposable quantities, a sense not too far removed from the spirit of sadism. Spielberg's willingness to sacrifice plausibility for the sake of a gag finds its dark parallel in his willingness to sacrifice scores of extras for the sake of a shock.

The film is inhuman in its attitudes, and also insidiously dehumanizing in its effect on the audience: the violence is so intense, so relentless, that it's numbing, and Spielberg has to keep upping the ante—going for ever more grotesque and graphic effects—to keep us jumping on cue. We're never asked to take responsibility for our enjoyment of violence, as *Dawn of the Dead* forces us to; instead, the film subtly reinforces its inhuman impulses by letting them bleed into the characters. I can think of no other film in which the hero is twice offered a choice between saving the woman he loves and saving the booty, and chooses the booty both times. *Raiders* doesn't criticize Jones for his decisions. They're of a piece with the spirit of the direction, consistent with its adolescent values.

It's here, of course, that the contents of his supposedly contentless, "fun" movie resides. An aesthetic of instant gratification has been creeping into Spielberg's films, increasingly from *The Sugarland Express* to *1941*, and in *Raiders of the Lost Ark* it finally has taken over completely. Spielberg is ready to sacrifice every higher feeling, and every long-range plan, for the sake of an immediate physical effect, be it a laugh or a grimace. He thinks of movies as stimulation machines, pounding along from moment to moment; it never occurs to him that a payoff delayed may be a payoff doubled. He wants what he wants when he wants it, never mind the cost. A lot of people seem to think his effects are worth the price, but to me the cost seems much too high.

A Passage to India

Directed by DAVID LEAN {Chicago, February 1985}

A Passage to India is the 16th film David Lean has directed since 1942, and his first since *Ryan's Daughter* in 1970. Obviously, he's a slow and patient worker, and each of his films—the best-known ones are *The Bridge on the River Kwai, Lawrence of Arabia,* and *Doctor Zhivago*—reflects his passion for detailed scripting, meticulous design, and painstaking postproduction work in the editing room. There is an elegance, and even a kind of beauty, in Lean's method, and *A Passage to India* shares in it: it's a film of straight, cleanly drawn lines, a sturdy structure in which all of the elements interlock perfectly, a smoothly functioning machine without a single superfluous part. And yet it's a beauty of engineering, not of art. Lean puts his creative energy into not the telling of a story, but rather the taming, controlling, channeling of a story. For him, a narration is something to be licked, and he takes his pleasure not from the tale itself but from the neatness and symmetry of its telling.

Lean has long been attracted to stories of English (or Anglicized American) pragmatism confronted with the emotionalism and apparent irrationality of foreign cultures: schoolmarm tourist Katharine Hepburn erring among the Italian aristocracy of *Summertime,* stiff-upper-lippers Alec Guinness and Jack Hawkins battling the inscrutability of Sessue Hayakawa in *The Bridge on the River Kwai,* blue-eyed Peter O'Toole going native in the darkened desert tents of *Lawrence of Arabia.* It's a theme that Lean shares with two of Britain's best filmmakers, Alfred Hitchcock and Michael Powell, yet while those directors let their heroes be absorbed and undermined by strange environments and strange experiences, Lean's protagonists emerge on top, shaken perhaps by what they have seen, but with their rationalism intact and victorious. Lean is unquestionably a loyal servant of the realm, but he is probably less guilty of chauvinism than of narcissism: his characters' experiences reflect his own satisfaction in ironing out the irrationalities—the ambiguities and snarls of meaning—that every story contains. For Lean, fiction is a foreign land, and, like a good colonialist, he sets out simultaneously to explore and reform it. The films he sends back are his trophies, so many boars' heads ready to be mounted above the mantel.

Published in 1924, E. M. Forster's *A Passage to India* is perfect Lean material. Not only does the novel offer a definitive confrontation of cultures, but it also—awash as it is with the shifting perspectives and streaming consciousnesses of the then-emerging Modernist movement—strongly resists the kind of linear narration that Lean likes to impose. Here, indeed, is a wild beast worthy of the hunt. And because *A Passage to India* is a classic, it allows Lean to renew his ties to the British cinema's tradition of literary transcription, where he first made his reputation as the talented young director of two excellent adaptations of Dickens, *Great Expectations* (1947) and *Oliver Twist* (1949). Explicating Forster's Modernist vagaries is no less impressive an accomplishment than condensing the narrative arabesques of Dickens's sprawling serial fictions. After the glossy international epics of the sixties—*Lawrence, Doctor Zhivago, Ryan's Daughter*—*A Passage to India* seems, on several levels, to be a coming home for Lean: a return to a favorite theme, a favorite style, a favorite genre.

In its way, Forster's novel poses as many problems to movie adaptation as the much more celebrated case of Malcolm Lowry's *Under the Volcano.* Much of the novel's effect depends on a dissolution of physical space in favor of an interior landscape, where the physical merges with the emotional and the characters can find their thoughts intermingling with the places and people around them—a landscape that the movies have found notoriously difficult to penetrate. And yet Forster has provided a fairly sturdy plot. Adela Quested, a young Englishwoman, sails for India on her first voyage abroad, dreaming of exotic sights and spiritual experiences; with her is Mrs. Moore, the thoughtful, elderly mother of Ronny Heaslop, the young colonial functionary Adela is tentatively engaged to marry. Arriving in Chandrapur, Adela is disappointed by the distance that the colonials have put between themselves and the natives, but Mrs. Moore is able to strike up a friendship with Aziz, a young Muslim doctor whose sensitivity is somewhat obscured by his overeagerness to accommodate his English visitors. Crushed by the discovery that Ronny has become a stuffy bureaucrat and haunted by the sensuality of the Indian life she glimpses on the edges of the British compound, Adela breaks off her engagement to Ronny. But on a disastrous day trip to the Caves of Marabar, organized by Aziz, she catches a glimpse of something more frightening embedded in the Indian culture—an overwhelming sense of emptiness and futility— and transforms her horror into an imagined attack by the young doctor. Aziz is put on trial, while Mrs. Moore, his only friendly witness, is put on a steamship back to England.

Lean has made some minor alterations in the characters: he permits Adela (Judy Davis) to be much more sympathetic than she is in the novel; the Brahman scholar, Professor Godbole, has been promoted into a comic-relief part for Alec Guinness; and Fielding (James Fox) has been brought closer to the center of the action, where he is offered as a romantic alternative to Ronny. But for the most part, Lean sticks with the material Forster offers him, sometimes using dialogue (as in the superb first meeting of Aziz and Mrs. Moore in a moonlit mosque) taken directly from Forster's text. Lean, by and large, films the action as Forster describes it, and records the characters' words just as Forster puts them down.

And yet this literal approach results in a total transformation. By staying so faithful to the surface events of the novel, Lean strips the characters of their interior lives: his characters are defined by what they do, while Forster's were defined by what they thought about what they did. And without those interior shadings, the characters freeze into stereotypes. Adela is unshakably the frightened virgin, Mrs. Moore the wise matriarch, Aziz the sweet, ineffectual naïf. In Lean's hands, they are no longer characters, but emblems—no longer slippery, elusive souls, but hard-edged signs, figures ready to be fed into an equation. The characters are set from the moment we first see them, and the actors don't have much to do: they read their lines in the slight daze that comes from overrehearsal, without much concern for the emotions behind them. Rather than the subjects of the story, the characters come to seem its objects. The narration works upon them, moving them from place to place like markers in a board game, producing the lovely, synchronous patterns that are Lean's substitutes for plot dynamics.

"Directed and edited by David Lean" is how the credit that Lean takes for himself on *A Passage to India* reads, and unusual wording suggests how important the cutting room is to Lean's method of filmmaking. An image, by itself, doesn't have much meaning for him; a shot comes to life only when it is joined with another shot, producing a significant contrast. When Lean wants to suggest what his characters are thinking, he does it with a cut: A shot of Adela looking in wonder is followed by a shot of a market stall filled with exotic foodstuffs. A shot of Adela looking in horror is followed by a shot of a corpse being carried through the street. This sequence (it comes early in the film, just as Adela enters the city gates of Chandrapur for the first time) is meant to foreshadow her experience in India—an experience that consists wholly of reaction. As a means of communicating thoughts, the shot/countershot method is woefully inadequate, without nuance or substance: Adela reacts to a blunt abstraction labeled "sensuality" or "death" instead of to a real event, and her feelings are registered just as bluntly, just as monochromatically. Instead of allowing Adela to share her frame with "India"—to enter into real contact with it—Lean always forces her to confront it across the quite substantial barrier of a film splice, a barrier that cuts off all involvement, all connectedness. But as it turns out, these barriers are just what Lean has in mind. They serve to divide the unmanageable, ambiguous entity called "India" into a series of handy, pocket-size fragments, tiny abstractions that can be dealt with more conveniently.

Lean is the most Aristotelian of filmmakers, continually narrowing the categories of his fiction until he can go no further—at which point he believes he has arrived at the truth. But more often than not, it is an overrefined, purely intellectual truth. (Aristotle was a scientist and essayist; it was Plato, the great synthesizer, who was also a great storyteller.) Still, there is a moment in *A Passage to India* when Lean's analytical method works supremely well. While virtually any other filmmaker would have shot the visit to the Marabar Caves as a swirl of mystical imagery, Lean approaches it as a purely tactical problem. He focuses not on the "meaning" of the caves but on the movements of the characters as they approach them. The preparations for the journey, the trip by train to the mountainside, the climb through the foothills, the dropping out first of Mrs. Moore, then of Aziz—all of this is filmed with the geometric clarity of a battle plan, a great march of precisely interrelated events that finally, inexorably, leads up to Adela's moment alone in the darkness. What she finds in the cave is the end point of all of Lean's logic and analysis—it is, precisely, nothing, a strip of blank, black film. It is the ultimate David Lean shot/countershot, and a moment of absolute horror.

Hannah and Her Sisters

Directed by WOODY ALLEN {Chicago, March 1986}

Hannah and Her Sisters clearly represents some kind of turning point in Woody Allen's career, yet to compare the film to a Chekhov play, as some critics have done, is wild hyperbole. The comic personality that Allen created in his early films has proved so enduringly charming that people are willing to forgive him anything, even the string of surly, withdrawn films he's made since *Stardust Memories*. With *Hannah*, Allen returns with open arms to the adoring public that he turned his back on in *Stardust*; he's made himself lovable again, and people have been waiting a long time to love him. It's nice to have this Woody back—he's funny, and he isn't ashamed of it—yet there's something resigned and exhausted in the way the film plays out. *Hannah and Her Sisters* is ultimately a paean to complacency: whatever inner torment has been urging Allen on these past years is over, and I don't know whether to feel relieved (that his work has finally regained a level of relaxed sociability) or disappointed (that he appears to have resigned all ambition).

As a performer, Allen's little-boy vulnerability has earned him an enormous amount of affection that has carried over, unjustly perhaps, to his work as a writer and filmmaker. Film critics coo over him as if he were a child learning to walk, and every tiny step is hailed with a chorus of indulgent hosannas. In fact, Allen has never mastered (or even shown much interest in) the plastic side of his medium. Seventeen years after he directed his first movie, *Take the Money and Run*, Allen's visual style hasn't progressed beyond cramped, TV-style close-ups, with an occasional overcomposed long shot (static figures standing against stark white walls) for dramatic emphasis. When he moves his camera (*Hannah* provides a good example in a three-way restaurant conversation between Mia Farrow, Dianne Wiest, and Barbara Hershey, in which the camera circles the table like a beast of prey looking for an opening), he does it so self-consciously that the intended effect is lost; the heaviness of the form completely absorbs its function.

Hannah does mark a breakthrough for Allen's storytelling abilities, though it's a relatively primitive step, and one that most writers cross long before they begin to publish. Before *Hannah* (and with the partial exception of *Manhattan*), Allen's scripts were composed in a naïvely narcissistic, first-person mode: Allen put most of the moral points he wanted to make (and all of the laugh lines) directly into the mouth of his character; the other figures in the films existed only in relation to him—to set up his jokes, to provide objects for his romantic longings, or (most offensively, I think) to work as moral counterexamples to Woody's own excruciatingly correct behavior. With this new film, Allen has moved on to the next level: instead of identifying himself with a single character, he's learned to divide the components of his personality among a group. Here the Michael Caine character (Elliot, a financial adviser having an affair with his sister-in-law) embodies Allen's guilt and hesitancy; the Max Von Sydow character (Frederick, a self-regarding painter) carries his intellectual pretensions and snobbism; and the Sam Waterston character (David, a smooth young architect) is the recipient of his charm and seductiveness. Of course, Allen is in there himself (as Mickey, the producer of a *Saturday Night Live*-ish comedy show), and he still gives himself all the best lines and the superior moral position. But the effect is much less claustrophobic: for once, Allen has been able to create the illusion of independent, self-contained characterizations, even if they are all ultimately derived from himself. Allen is still a long way from being able to imagine, in depth, human beings who are substantially different from himself (maybe then we can start talking Chekhov). Even in *Hannah*, when he directs other actors he can't help but give them the same stuttering inflections, the same fluttery gestures, that he uses himself; the idea that different people ought to move and speak differently still hasn't penetrated.

Allen's difficulty in creating coherent, independent characters has also crippled the narrative design of his films. The depth isn't there to sustain an extended dramatic development, so Allen has tended to compose in vignettes—short, choppy, unrelated scenes built around a single gag or facet of behavior. Unable to integrate comedy and character exploration, or to express his themes through patterns of action rather than direct verbal statement, Allen finds his films falling into jagged, start-and-stop rhythms, in which gag scenes alternate with speeches. *Hannah* doesn't solve this problem, but it does find an ingenious way around it: rather than try to force a flow on the ill-matched material, Allen has used subtitles ("The Hypochondriac," "The Abyss") to mark off each vignette individually; what might otherwise have seemed a collection of fragments suddenly becomes a series of playlets—a deliberate stylistic choice, rather than a shortcoming. And instead of trying to integrate the gag comedy and the moral drama, Allen has largely ghettoized the jokes to a subplot centered on his character that stands apart from the main narrative line. On one level, the film is a family melodrama (very similar to *Interiors*) about three sisters whose close relationship is threatened by romantic and professional rivalries. On the other level, it's a wry farce (similar to *Take the Money*, though without the overt surrealist touches) about a man who believes he's dying of a brain tumor and tries to prepare himself for the Big Sleep (Woody contemplates converting to Catholicism, in a sequence that could have come straight from one of his early films). The transitions between the two plot strands aren't graceful, and the jumpy effect is exaggerated by the fact that they're shot in two different styles (muted and naturalistic for the sisters, stylized and subjective for Allen). Though the interposed subtitles help, again, to bridge the gaps, the film is still compromised by a sense of channel-flipping: the two levels don't function in counterpoint (there's no thematic echo between them) as much as they simply seem to spell each other. When the drama threatens to become too heavy (though it never really does), Allen sends in the second team to lighten things up. Perhaps he has found a way to have his cake and eat it, too—to be funny Woody and serious Woody in the same film—but the dual structure is only a stopgap measure. It won't work again, and only when Allen finds a way of expressing serious concerns through comedy will he belong in the company of Lubitsch, Sturges, Keaton, and Tati—filmmakers for whom humor was the surest route to the human soul.

Allen first discovered his three-women plot in *Interiors*; with a few refinements and variations, it's served him for *Manhattan*, *Stardust Memories*, *A Midsummer Night's Sex Comedy*, and, now, *Hannah and Her Sisters*. It's the bedrock of his style—the source of whatever narrative propulsion his movies have—yet it's also limiting. For Allen, women come in three categories: the warm and protective (Marie-Christine Barrault in *Stardust*, Mary Steenburgen in *Midsummer*), the ripely sexual (Jessica Harper in *Stardust*, Julie Hagerty in *Midsummer*), and the neurotically scatterbrained (Diane Keaton in everything). In his search for true love, Woody (or one of his alter egos) bounces from one type to another; to the old stereotypes of the Mother and the Whore, Allen has added another—the Other Self, the woman as confused and insecure as he is. In *Hannah and Her Sisters*, the three roles are filled, respectively, by Mia Farrow (mother to a brood of swarming children), Barbara Hershey (ravishing in sweaters and tight jeans), and Dianne Wiest (costumed to look like Diane Keaton of *Annie Hall* and *Manhattan*). This time, it isn't Woody who runs all the bases (he moves only from Farrow to Wiest, while Caine, picking up the play, goes from Farrow to Hershey and back again), but the plot progression is the same: after sampling the stereotypes, the hero returns to self-involvement (though it is a self projected on a female body), and the process remains an annoyingly shallow, narcissistic one.

What's different about *Hannah* is the crushing finality of the resolution: while Allen's films have habitually ended on a tentative note (with Woody finding the courage to go on with the little pleasures of life), this one runs through the standard conclusion (the little pleasure this time is an afternoon show of *Duck Soup*) and then moves into a coda that provides, in a single image, the reconciliation and unification of all three of Allen's female types. Standing before a mirror with Wiest, Allen looks into the glass and sees her reflection (the Other Self); he kisses her and she responds passionately (the Whore) and then tells him that she's pregnant (the Mother). The search for true love, after all those films, is suddenly over; yet the moment, though warmly rendered, feels disturbingly arbitrary. Nothing in Wiest's behavior has prepared us for this abrupt apotheosis (in fact, she seems dangerously unstable); her perfection is simply stated, and Allen asks us to take it on faith. But is the ending an act of faith, or an act of something less noble and outreaching—an act, perhaps, of impatience, frustration, retreat? Allen has put an end to the questing—philosophical and romantic—that has defined his films since *Annie Hall*; that it comes at a time when the members of *Annie Hall*'s baby-boom audience are themselves rounding 30 and getting ready to settle down to marriage and child-rearing will probably help the film's commercial changes—not since *Annie Hall* has Allen so accurately sensed the emotional wavelength of his public. We're tired of all that heavy stuff—the Bergman films, the psychoanalysis, the Kübler-Ross books, and the Jackson Pollock paintings; we want to stay home and chuck the kiddies under the chin. The new Woody may be content, but it isn't a contentment honestly earned. It's something he's backed into, because he hasn't got the energy or will to go forward anymore. Yes, *Hannah and Her Sisters* is a turning point, but around this bend there's only a dead end.

Salvador

Directed by OLIVER STONE {Reader, April 25, 1986}

In the context of all the violent right-wing fantasies Hollywood has been churning out lately, the liberal message movie, once America's most Oscarized genre, is having a hard time cutting it. The quiet pleas for racial understanding, social justice, and peace on earth that filmmakers like Stanley Kramer and Fred Zinnemann once specialized in can no longer be heard above the din of the chattering assault rifles and thundering grenades of the Stallone battalion. The right has stolen all the special effects and heart-pounding rhetoric, leaving the liberals without a single stylistic trope to capture the attention of the easily bored MTV generation. Luckily, Oliver Stone—the screenwriter of *Midnight Express*, De Palma's *Scarface*, and *Year of the Dragon*—has arrived to rescue the disenfranchised forces of liberalism with a wholly new concept: in *Salvador*, which Stone also directed, he has created the first violent *left-wing* fantasy.

Set in the early 1980s in a lightly fictionalized version of the troubled Central American country of the title, *Salvador* follows the random trajectory of a hopped-up American freelance journalist named Richard Boyle (James Woods) as he soaks up the sights and sounds of an impoverished nation beset by a sadistically repressive military on the one hand and an army of faceless Marxist guerrillas on the other. Boyle (a real person, it seems—he shares credit for the script with Stone) arrives in Salvador fresh from a busted-up relationship; with his equally at-liberty buddy, an unemployed DJ who uses the name "Doctor Rock" (Jim Belushi), Boyle seems to be looking to drown his sorrows in the cheap drugs, cheap booze, and cheap women made available by the chaotic local economy, but because the screenplay contrives to make him a witness to every major outrage of the rightist death squads, he does not remain above (or, more accurately, below) the struggle for very long.

The dispassionate journalist whose slow and objective pursuit of the facts leads him to finally embrace the political position espoused at the outset by the filmmakers has long been a staple of propaganda movies. John Wayne used him to justify America's presence in Vietnam in 1968's *The Green Berets*; Roger Spottiswoode used him to endorse the Sandinista cause in 1983's *Under Fire*. His popularity is easy to understand: he makes life so much easier for the screenwriter, who finds in him not only a way of conflating ideological and dramatic ends (the drama, otherwise lacking, becomes the story of the reporter's personal political awakening), but also a way of tying together, through the reporter's dimly plausible presence, a whole collection of topical events that would otherwise be without any nar-

· 198 ·

rative linkage. The danger in this formula lies in the superior attitude the filmmakers invariably adopt toward the character: they know something he doesn't (having long since been convinced of the wisdom of their own positions), and the film becomes a tiresome run through a rat's maze as the lab-coated director, clipboard in hand, administers electric shocks to his hapless creature, prodding him toward the ideological cheese at the end.

In *Salvador*, Stone stakes an advance over the usual formula by refusing to make Boyle a bland audience-identification figure. No see-through representative of middle-American common sense is he: Boyle is a screamingly baroque composition, assembled of equal parts Robert Capa, Hunter Thompson, and Bugs Bunny. Wising off to every available authority figure, from the politician who secretly heads the death squads to the good-old-boy CIA operatives who populate the US embassy, Boyle is a manic blur; he soon abandons chemical stimulants in favor of the greater rush he gets from running mad risks. It's not so much that Boyle is an original character as he's an original character to this genre. We've seen his like a lot lately, specifically in the antiauthoritarian heroes played by Eddie Murphy, Bill Murray, and Tom Hanks in the new American comedies; what Stone has done is taken this stylized figure and put him in a realistic context, in which—unlike, say the protected environment of *Beverly Hills Cop*—an ill-judged wisecrack could easily earn a bullet in the brain. Stone also occasionally allows Boyle to look vain and ridiculous ("While Schanberg was grabbing his Pulitzer, I was still getting my ass shot at in Cambodia" is a remark that loses its charm after three or four repetitions), and his decision to back away from a complete idealization of the character pays off very nicely. If Boyle were more of a hero, he'd be much less persuasive as a mouthpiece (which was one of the problems with the Nick Nolte character in *Under Fire*).

But if Boyle is a successful and at least semicredible mix of positive and negative traits, the figures around him stem from the moral extremes of the most antique melodrama. Major Max (Tony Plana), the murderous *jefe* modeled on Roberto D'Aubuisson, is the oiliest scumsucker in the Banana Belt; Stone mysteriously has omitted the scene in which he picks his teeth with the bones of roasted children. Representing "the people" is Elpedia Carrillo, the doe-eyed actress who was Tony Richardson's Latin Madonna in *The Border*; here, she's the gold-hearted prostitute whose radiant innocence and vulnerability finally force Boyle to take sides. To the role of the well-meaning but ineffectual American ambassador, Michael Murphy brings the vaguely caricatural good looks that Robert Altman exploited so memorably in *Brewster McCloud*—with his Ivy League face creased by an ineffable weakness, Murphy is an icon of American idealism gone soft, a compromised Kennedy.

Stone can't be accused of feeling superior to his characters, though it's less because he genuinely respects them than because, most of the time, he's just as confused about what's going on as they are. Though most of the reviews have treated *Salvador* as if it were Stone's first film as a director, it is, in fact, his third, following two low-budget horror films (*Seizure* in 1974; *The Hand* in 1981); still, Stone directs like a writer, with no sense of space to speak of and a very shaky understanding of how to shape the rhythm of a sequence. Though his scenes are strongly conceived, they're often executed with a jittery uncertainty that diminishes their impact. Any scenarist would give his eyeteeth for a moment as fresh and sharply conceived as the scene in which Boyle, helped out by an American religious lay worker (Cindy Gibb), barges into the dank jail where his buddy Doc is being held, his arms laden with gifts for the menacing guards (bottles, a television) in an attempt to bribe his pal out. The suspense is focused on the delicate process of negotiation: if Boyle puts his proposition too bluntly, his friend will be killed and he'll be thrown in the cell himself. But rather than focus on Boyle's desperate need to bring his panic and fear under control, to speak calmly and conspiratorially to the men who hold his friend's life, Stone chooses to amplify the hysteria—he goes rushing in with a jumpy handheld camera, whip-panning around the room like a ferret in heat. Stone seems to want to communicate Boyle's anxiety as directly and vividly to the audience as possible, but all he's done is upstage his character, interposing his own hyped-up emotions between us and Boyle. It's still a powerful scene, but the execution completely obscures the psychological fine points of Boyle's behavior—fine points that might have brought us closer to the character and refined the suspense into something much more piercing and personal than it is.

It's Stone's horror of the dull speechifying and trite sentimentality that usually marks the liberal message movie that has led him to the hysterical excesses of *Salvador*, and it's certainly a justifiable impulse: for all its chaos and wild overstatement, it's an infinitely more watchable film than Haskell Wexler's similarly themed *Latino*, which was released to general yawns a few months ago. But like every filmmaker who searches for an immediate visceral impact at every moment and at every price, Stone ends by cheapening his effects. The rape and murder of the four American nuns (an incident that occurred in December 1980) is meant to be a turning point in *Salvador*, but given all the violence that surrounds it, it doesn't stand out much more than one of Boyle's frequent bar fights. (And Stone's filming of the scene—that handheld camera again, rushing in for close shots of ripe breasts spilling from ripped bodices—is a little too titillating for comfort.) There are times when the film threatens to turn into a simple sensual assault, leaving all narrative import behind in a hailstorm of bullets and beatings.

Stone isn't staking out a radical position in *Salvador*: the Marxist guerrillas, too, turn out to have an imperfect commitment to human rights, and Stone can envision no political solution to the ongoing agony. Ultimately, the film's focus shifts from the ideological to the emotional, and Stone's epic vision of a country in torment collapses around the isolated figure of Boyle, helpless and seething with impotent rage. This, too, is a classic maneuver of liberal filmmaking—to substitute the romantic angst of the sensitive individual for the historical crisis of an entire people—only this time Stone isn't able to revise and revive it. Rather than recommend action (the formation of a responsible left, for example), *Salvador* concludes with that old, strangely comforting fantasy of hopelessness. For Boyle, scarred forever by what he has seen and heard, there is nothing to be done—except, perhaps, to write a screenplay.

Afterword

In November 2013, I left the world of film journalism to take a curatorial job in the Department of Film of the Museum of Modern Art (MoMA).

In critical jargon, this is what is technically known as a "happy ending."

I love my new job, which consists of programming series for MoMA's theaters, working with MoMA's gifted team of archivists (and its archive of over 25,000 films) on restoration projects, and looking for new opportunities to circulate films through the digital technologies that have so profoundly transformed our perception of cinema.

I'm often asked if I miss writing, and the answer is not so much. After almost forty years in the field, I think I've said pretty much what I had to say, and I'm happy to leave the heavy lifting—the hard work of keeping up with contemporary filmmaking—to younger minds with fresher ideas and different perspectives.

Free of the need to feign an interest in superheroes and mumblecore, I'm largely content to live in the past. As a card-carrying bourgeois formalist, I continue to be fascinated by the classical period in general, and by the American films of that period in particular—not because I believe they are more accomplished than what was coming out in Germany, Japan, or Argentina during the same time frame, but because, as an American, they remain the most accessible to me, both culturally and pragmatically. After a lifetime spent absorbing Hollywood films, I have some dim hope of someday achieving a general sense of the landscape, something that will forever elude me in the no less verdant field of the French cinema, simply because so much of it remains out of my reach.

If I've matured as a critic over the last many years, it's in coming to realize that criticism isn't about a relentless search for individual masterpieces but about seeing the connections between works. Those connections can take the form of genre conventions, stylistic developments, business practices, social mores, authorial personalities, and so on—connections that are lost or obscured by a "great works" approach.

We now know, for example, that sound came to the movies not in the form of an overnight "revolution" touched off by the runaway success of *The Jazz Singer*, but as a gradual transition over a period of years—and we know this because many of those transitional films, mostly in the form of Vitaphone shorts, have been preserved and made available to scholars in the last several years. I'm convinced that our understanding of deep-focus cinematography—the next great stylistic frontier for the movies—will have to be similarly reconfigured away from Wyler and Welles as more discoveries are made in the work of early '30s deep-focus pioneers like Raoul Walsh and William K. Howard. (With all due modesty, I should mention that MoMA has played a role here in restoring key works like Walsh's 70-millimeter *The Big Trail* and Howard's *Transatlantic*, a forgotten masterpiece uncovered in the museum's holdings of nitrate prints from the Fox Film Corporation.)

A deep dive into the oceanic output of classical Hollywood reveals all kinds of fascinating creatures who may not count as major artists on the Hawks-Hitchcock-Ford scale but nonetheless have their discreet charms. It takes time and patience to uncover the dark energy behind the prolific output of a B-director like Lew Landers; his personality does not emerge from a random viewing of three or four of the 175 films credited to him, but once the outlines of his edgy compulsiveness begin to emerge, they are not soon forgotten. There is a special poignancy in the downward career spiral of silent film veterans like Elmer Clifton, Christy Cabanne, and William Beaudine, who directed big stars in big pictures in the '20s but found themselves out of fashion and out of luck in the sound era. All former associates of D. W. Griffith, they found themselves putting their Biograph experience to work on Poverty Row in the '40s, pumping out 65-minute features with the fervor—if not the passion—with which they once produced one-reelers.

At this point, classical Hollywood seems to me inexhaustible. Hardly a week goes by when I don't stumble across a new name to investigate or a new cache of films to explore. I know I will never come to the end of it during my professional life. I doubt that I will ever even finish with 1932.

In the introduction to his 1968 study of Howard Hawks, Robin Wood characterized Hollywood as "a great creative workshop, comparable to Elizabethan London or the Vienna of Mozart, where hundreds of talents have come together to evolve a common language." If anything, I suspect that the comparison underestimates Hollywood. Shakespeares and Mozarts may be rare on the ground in Los Angeles, but the industry supported plenty of Marlowes and Spensers while reaching, of course, an incomparably wider audience than Shakespeare could have ever conceived.

But no creative community lasts forever, and now we are facing the obsolescence of the particular form that was Hollywood's specialty—that of the self-contained, feature-length film projected for a large audience. I have no doubt that moving images will continue to be used to tell stories for generations to come, but I am no less certain that the theatrical experience will exhaust itself within a decade or two, at least in the West. There's nothing surprising about that. Forms come and go all the time, and soon that construct we think of as "the movies" will go the way of five-act tragedies in verse as a viable commercial format.

Driven by digital technology, theatrical film is already approaching a post-narrative era as movies come more and more to resemble the video games that were digital's first and most-apt expression. Characters are little more than avatars introduced by one or two lines of simple backstory; plots do little more than propel characters through successive "levels" as they pursue treasure or magical objects; spatial coherence and continuity of movement are shattered by rapid-fire editing that serves only the shallow goal of "refreshing the screen." If virtual reality—VR, with its immersive, 3-D, 360-degree experience—is indeed the next step in the evolution of moving-image technology, it is difficult to imagine how any but the most primitive form of narrative can survive the sensory onslaught. VR sounds like the ideal format for pornography; it may be less hospitable to more nuanced, cerebral storytelling.

No longer at home in feature films, narrative has—along with much of the adult audience—migrated to television. "Television," of course, no longer refers to an over-the-air, broadcast delivery system—the same content can be delivered on cable, disc, or, the true coming thing, Internet streaming—but to a particular narrative form, in which characters recur in multiple episodes, each of which may have its own narrative arc, through the course of a season, which has an overall narrative arc of its own. Each season then finds its place in the multi-year evolution of a show, which may come to a definite endpoint or simply trail off into an infinity of reruns. Television thus offers a superabundance of storytelling of a sort that hasn't been seen since the 19th-century novel—a parallel that has not been lost on PBS, with its endless adaptations of Dickens and Trollope, Balzac and Zola. The polar opposite of the sensation-centered digital cinema, today's television builds its effects slowly and meticulously, creating a sense of one-on-one intimacy—I would almost say domesticity—with the viewer, as it unfolds over hours, weeks, years on cuddle-up media like TV screens, tablets, and cell phones. In place of the telegraphic visual expressiveness of the classic cinema, television offers duration and expatiation, a sense of chatty companionship. Indeed, the tone of the "episode recaps" that have supplanted movie reviews in many publications is one of gossipy speculation about real people, as if the characters had lives and wills of their own.

Such is the powerful illusion that contemporary television creates. For audiences accustomed to televisual intimacy, the classical cinema can seem remote and mysterious, centered on personalities too large to be contained by the tiny screens of today. Amy Schumer wants to be your bestie; Greta Garbo doesn't know you exist—and doesn't want to. And as the classical cinema slowly becomes more inaccessible—the profusion of classical releases on disc in the '80s and '90s has been replaced by the dearth of black-and-white movies on the streaming services of today—we are producing new generations of viewers who are barely aware of the older form's existence. In New York City, at least, it is rare to see viewers under 60 at archival programs; I can only hope that things are better elsewhere, though from what other archival programmers tell me, the situation is much the same in Munich and Tokyo.

All of this is a natural process, and we shouldn't be tempted into pointless nostalgia and sentimental mythmaking. At the same time, I'm convinced that this eclipse is only temporary—though it may be temporary to the tune of a hundred years or more—and that the classical cinema will certainly be rediscovered and placed back on a platform perhaps even higher than before. That's what happened to Shakespeare, and it can happen to Howard Hawks too (though Lew Landers might take a little longer). In the meantime, to draw on an even mustier parallel, it behooves those of us in the archival world today to take our inspiration from the monks of the Middle Ages, who kept the texts of that first classical period safe while all the world was preoccupied with other matters. I'm sending my tunic out to get pressed. This work will not be forgotten.

Dave Kehr
October 2016

APPENDIX: TOP TEN LISTS, 1974–86

1974

1. *Le petit théâtre de Jean Renoir* (Jean Renoir)
2. *Ali: Fear Eats the Soul* (Rainer Werner Fassbinder)
3. *The Tamarind Seed* (Blake Edwards)
4. *Wedding in Blood* (Claude Chabrol)
5. *The Three Musketeers* (Richard Lester)
6. *Chinatown* (Roman Polanski)
7. *The Phantom of Liberty* (Luis Buñuel)
8. *Lacombe, Lucien* (Louis Malle)
9. *The Godfather, Part II* (Francis Ford Coppola)
10. *Juggernaut* (Richard Lester)

1975

1. *Lancelot du Lac* (Robert Bresson)
2. *The Middle of the World* (Alain Tanner)
3. *A Woman under the Influence* (John Cassavetes)
4. *The Passenger* (Michelangelo Antonioni)
5. *La rupture* (Claude Chabrol)
6. *Love among the Ruins* (George Cukor)
7. *Fist-Fight of Freedom* (Rainer Werner Fassbinder)
8. *The Romantic Englishwoman* (Joseph Losey)
9. *Hard Times* (Walter Hill)
10. *Supervixens* (Russ Meyer)

1976

1. *Family Plot* (Alfred Hitchcock)
2. *The Age of the Medici* and *Blaise Pascal* (Roberto Rossellini)
3. *Robin and Marian* (Richard Lester)
4. *Jonah Who Will Be 25 in the Year 2000* (Alain Tanner)
5. *The Man Who Would Be King* (John Huston)
6. *The Shootist* (Don Siegel)
7. *Just Before Nightfall* (Claude Chabrol)
8. *Mother Küsters Goes to Heaven* (Rainer Werner Fassbinder)
9. *French Provincial* (André Téchiné)
10. *Allegro non troppo* (Bruno Bozzetto)

1977

1. *F for Fake* (Orson Welles)
2. *The Memory of Justice* (Marcel Ophüls)
3. *The Marquise of O* (Éric Rohmer)
4. *A Piece of Pleasure* (Claude Chabrol)
5. *Numéro deux* (Jean-Luc Godard)
6. *Moses and Aaron* (Jean-Marie Straub, Danièle Huillet)
7. *Islands in the Stream* (Franklin Schaffner)
8. *The Gauntlet* (Clint Eastwood)
9. *Padre padrone* (Paolo and Vittorio Taviani)
10. *The Rescuers* (Wolfgang Reitherman, John Lounsbery, Art Stevens)

1978

1. *Days of Heaven* (Terrence Malick)
2. *That Obscure Object of Desire* (Luis Buñuel)
3. *The American Friend* (Wim Wenders)
4. *The Meetings of Anna* (Chantal Akerman)
5. *The Messiah* (Roberto Rossellini)
6. *The Driver* (Walter Hill)
7. *Halloween* (John Carpenter)
8. *Big Wednesday* (John Milius)
9. *Blue Collar* (Paul Schrader)
10. *Filming "Othello"* (Orson Welles)

1979

1. *10* (Blake Edwards)
2. *The Left-Handed Woman* (Peter Handke)
3. *Dawn of the Dead* (George A. Romero)
4. *Perceval* (Éric Rohmer)
5. *The Warriors* (Walter Hill)
6. *Luna* (Bernardo Bertolucci)
7. *Escape from Alcatraz* (Don Siegel)
8. *In a Year with Thirteen Moons* (Rainer Werner Fassbinder)
9. *Fedora* (Billy Wilder)
10. *Angi Vera* (Pál Gábor)

1980

1. *The Devil, Probably* (Robert Bresson)
2. *The Human Factor* (Otto Preminger)
3. *The Contract* (Krzysztof Zanussi)
4. *The Big Red One* (Samuel Fuller)
5. *Used Cars* (Robert Zemeckis)
6. *Quadrophenia* (Franc Roddam)
7. *The Black Stallion* (Carroll Ballard)
8. *Gloria* (John Cassavetes)
9. *Mad Max* (George Miller)
10. *The Long Riders* (Walter Hill)

1981

1. *Melvin and Howard* (Jonathan Demme)
2. *Loulou* (Maurice Pialat)
3. *The Chant of Jimmie Blacksmith* (Fred Schepisi)
4. *Ici et ailleurs* (Jean-Luc Godard)
5. *Every Man for Himself* (Jean-Luc Godard)
6. *Confidence* (István Szabó)
7. *From the Clouds to the Resistance* (Jean-Marie Straub, Danièle Huillet)
8. *Modern Romance* (Albert Brooks)
9. *Atlantic City* (Louis Malle)
10. *Reds* (Warren Beatty)

1982

1. *The Aviator's Wife* (Éric Rohmer)
2. *Barbarosa* (Fred Schepisi)
3. *Coup de torchon* (Bertrand Tavernier)
4. *Eijanaika* (Shôhei Imamura)
5. *Mes petites amoureuses* (Jean Eustache)
6. *Moonlighting* (Jerzy Skolimowski)
7. *Le pont du Nord* (Jacques Rivette)
8. *Smash Palace* (Roger Donaldson)
9. *Too Early/Too Late* (Jean-Marie Straub, Danièle Huillet)
10. *Victor Victoria* (Blake Edwards)

1983

1. *Francisca* (Manoel de Oliveira)
2. *A Room in Town* (Jacques Demy)
3. *Berlin Alexanderplatz* (Rainer Werner Fassbinder)
4. *Ana* (António Reis, Margarida Cordeiro)
5. *Golden Eighties* (Chantal Akerman)
6. *The State of Things* (Wim Wenders)
7. *Exposed* (James Toback)
8. *Risky Business* (Paul Brickman)
9. *Sudden Impact* (Clint Eastwood)
10. *Fanny and Alexander* (Ingmar Bergman)

1984

1. *L'argent* (Robert Bresson)
2. *Love Streams* (John Cassavetes)
3. *Once Upon a Time in America* (Sergio Leone)
4. *Passion* (Jean-Luc Godard)
5. *A Sunday in the Country* (Bertrand Tavernier)
6. *Three Crowns of the Sailor* (Raoul Ruiz)
7. *À nos amours* (Maurice Pialat)
8. *In the White City* (Alain Tanner)
9. *Boy Meets Girl* (Leos Carax)
10. *My Brother's Wedding* (Charles Burnett)

1985

1. *Ran* (Akira Kurosawa)
2. *Lost in America* (Albert Brooks)
3. *Mikey and Nicky* (Elaine May)
4. *After Hours* (Martin Scorsese)
5. *Les enfants* (Marguerite Duras)
6. *Day of the Dead* (George A. Romero)
7. *Pale Rider* (Clint Eastwood)
8. *City of Pirates* (Raoul Ruiz)
9. *Maria's Lovers* (Andrei Konchalovsky)
10. *The Legend of Tianyun Mountain* (Xie Jin)

1986 Ten Best List (*prepared for the Chicago Tribune*)

1. *Shoah* (Claude Lanzmann)
2. *Sacrifice* (Andrei Tarkovsky)
3. *Something Wild* (Jonathan Demme)
4. *Vagabond* (Agnès Varda)
5. *The Fly* (David Cronenberg)
6. *Trouble in Mind* (Alan Rudolph)
7. *Himatsuri* (Mitsuo Yanagimachi)
8. *Heartbreak Ridge* (Clint Eastwood)
9. *Peggy Sue Got Married* (Francis Ford Coppola)
10. *Blue Velvet* (David Lynch)

INDEX